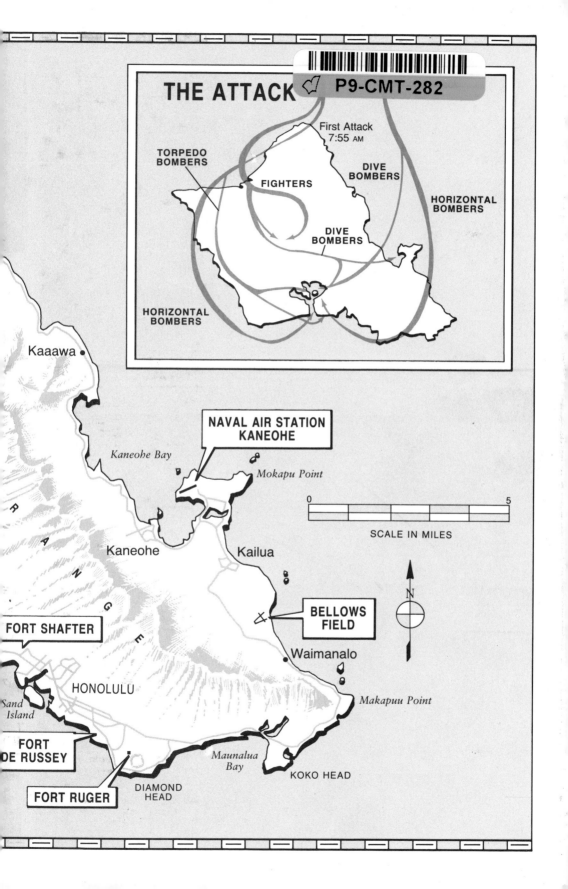

THE ATTACK

P9-CMT-282

First Attack
7:55 AM

TORPEDO
BOMBERS

FIGHTERS

DIVE
BOMBERS

DIVE
BOMBERS

HORIZONTAL
BOMBERS

HORIZONTAL
BOMBERS

Kaaawa

NAVAL AIR STATION
KANEOHE

Kaneohe Bay

Mokapu Point

0   5
SCALE IN MILES

Kaneohe

Kailua

BELLOWS
FIELD

N

FORT SHAFTER

Waimanalo

HONOLULU

Makapuu Point

Sand
Island

FORT
DE RUSSEY

Maunalua
Bay

KOKO HEAD

FORT RUGER

DIAMOND
HEAD

PEARL
HARBOR
GHOSTS

BY THURSTON CLARKE

NONFICTION

Pearl Harbor Ghosts

Equator

Lost Hero

By Blood and Fire

The Last Caravan

Dirty Money

FICTION

Thirteen O'Clock

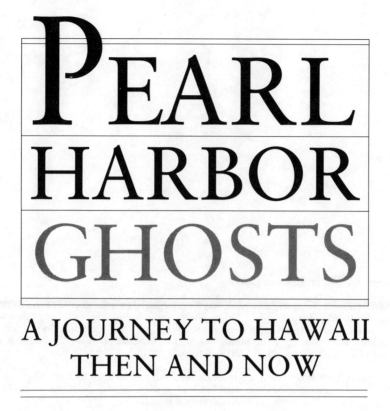

PEARL HARBOR GHOSTS

A JOURNEY TO HAWAII THEN AND NOW

Thurston Clarke

WILLIAM MORROW AND COMPANY, INC.
New York

Library of Congress Cataloging-in-Publication Data

Clarke, Thurston.
    Pearl Harbor ghosts : a journey to Hawaii then and now / by
Thurston Clarke.
        p.   cm.
    ISBN 0-688-04468-9
    1. Pearl Harbor (Hawaii), Attack on, 1941.   2. World War,
1939–1945—Influence.   3. Japanese Americans—Hawaii—Attitudes.
4. Public opinion—Hawaii.   5. Hawaii—Ethnic relations.   I. Title.
D767.92.C558   1991
996.9′004956—dc20   91-382
                                                                  CIP

Printed in the United States of America

First Edition

1 2 3 4 5 6 7 8 9 10

BOOK DESIGN BY BRIAN MOLLOY/CIRCA 86, INC.

ENDPAPER MAPS BY JEFFREY L. WARD GDS

For Sophie

CONTENTS

PART THREE: *December 7, 1941*

PART FOUR: *1990*

PREFACE

April 1990

At the Four Paddle Condominium

Robert Hudson's Japanese dolls fill the shelves of a glass display case, and no matter where you sit in his living room at the Four Paddle condominium in Waikiki, their lifelike eyes seem to follow you. They are expensive dolls, with hand-stitched kimonos and realistic hair. Figurines, swords, and other Japanese curios surround them, and Hudson has more, wrapped in tissue, packed in closets, and none of them cheap, he wants me to know. They are gifts from Japanese "friends" wishing to atone for the torpedo bombers that sank his ship at Pearl Harbor, forcing him to swim to safety through burning oil. His favorite is a carved rosewood box that arrived holding a samurai helmet and a bill of lading showing its value at four hundred dollars. A note said: "Will you kindly accept this appreciation of our friendship?"

Hudson has been making Japanese friends ever since moving back to Honolulu from Minneapolis in 1986. He came to pursue his hobby of historical research into Pearl Harbor, and by luck also found a job with Paradise Cruise, Ltd., as a human historical exhibit on its daily three-hour cruises to Pearl Harbor. During the voyage, he stands at a table displaying a scale

model of the *Arizona* Memorial and his collection of Pearl
Harbor relics: engine parts from a Zero, and yen from a dead
pilot's billfold. His fliers, placed on every chair, say in English
and Japanese, "EXCLUSIVE OPPORTUNITY! You are invited
to . . . ask me any questions you may have about the attack.
Please feel free to take photographs of the display, or with me
if you wish." A photograph shows Hudson, who is tall and
distinguished-looking, wearing naval dress whites and resembling an admiral. When I asked his rank, he blushed. He had
been a torpedoman second class. "Actually it's more of a cos-
tume than a uniform," he admitted.

It was the Japanese passengers who always sought him
out, asking him to recount his experiences. They were pleased
to find a Pearl Harbor survivor without bitterness toward Japan, and somewhat startled too, I imagine, to find one so pro-
Japanese. Within minutes, he had told me the qualities he saw
in the Japanese—devotion to the elderly, love of family, and
respect for education—were the values of 1941 mainland
America, the ones he had fought to defend.

When American passengers saw him with the Japanese,
they sometimes winked or shook their heads, sure that despite
his smile, he must still loathe them. Sometimes they whispered,
"Hey! How do you feel about all these Japs being on board?"
When he answered in a booming voice, "I *like* the Japanese!"
they were amazed, and disgusted. By the end of a cruise he and
the Japanese had shared war confessions and business cards, so
they would know where to send these expensive curios—these
attempts at . . . well, at what? At reparations? Reconciliation?

Hudson also exchanges Christmas cards with Kazuo Sakamaki, the Japanese midget-submarine captain taken prisoner
after the attack, and he enjoys a "delightful correspondence"
with December 7 Zero pilot Aeiichi Hayashi, and with Iyozjo
Fujita, responsible for "ground strafing" at Kaneohe Naval Air
Station. He has invited Fujita and Sakamaki to attend ceremo-

nies in Hawaii marking the fiftieth anniversary of Pearl Harbor. He was encouraged in this, he says, by a public affairs officer at Pearl Harbor and by officials at the National Park Service, which administers the *Arizona* Memorial. Navy and State Department officials in Honolulu and Washington had apparently been searching for ways to promote reconciliation by including the Japanese in the ceremonies. They liked the idea of a Pearl Harbor survivor inviting two former enemies to Honolulu, one with the symbolic distinction of being "Japanese Prisoner of War Number One."

When news of Hudson's invitations reached members of the Pearl Harbor Survivors Association, an organization of twelve thousand veterans who were present on the island of Oahu on December 7, there was an uproar. A fellow crewman on the minelayer U.S.S. *Oglala* wrote, "I was beside myself as [to] how to answer that letter stating that you want to have Sakamaki and Fujita, the pilot who bombed Kaneohe, as your *guests* at the 50th reunion in 1991. As of today I presented the idea of yours to 140 members of the Pearl Harbor Survivors Association [at a meeting of a California chapter]. So now I can answer and feel that it's not just me: 139 out of 140 think this is *not* advisable, nor very healthy for you to do this. I suggest you forget it completely. . . . Keep away from the rest of us. We do not want them at our reunion."

Hudson dismissed this as an isolated protest and was prepared to continue, despite the threat implied by the reference to his health. But then he received a letter from the national president of the Pearl Harbor Survivors Association saying, "You have caused the Aloha [Hawaii] Chapter to get up in arms with your proposal. . . . There are not many in the Association that feel the same way as you do toward the Japanese. In fact, that is one of the concerns of the local fathers, that some of our members might cause an incident while over there for the anniversary in 1991. . . . I'm afraid as the President of the PHSA

I will have to write to Mr. Anderson at CINCPACFLT [Commander in Chief Pacific Fleet] and object very strongly against your proposals. . . .Your slogan, 'YESTERDAY'S ENEMY—TODAY'S FRIENDS,' I simply do not agree with."

The Survivors' objections persuaded the Navy to withdraw its support. Hudson rescinded his invitations to Sakamaki and Fujita, writing lengthy apologies. Months later, he was still angry and surprised by his fellow survivors, but I was not. For three years I had been visiting Hawaii, searching for the physical and emotional legacies of Pearl Harbor, and I had soon learned that some wounds have yet to heal.

I had come because I was curious to see what kind of spin these legacies put on life in Hawaii, and I wanted to know how Honolulu, the only American city attacked by a foreign power since the War of 1812, had changed since December 7, 1941, and because of it. I also hoped that by looking for the shadows—or "ghosts"—of that day in the place where they should be longest and darkest, I might recognize the paler shadows haunting the mainland.

By the brutal standards of World War Two, Pearl Harbor was neither a very bloody nor complicated engagement. Unlike many other Pacific battles, tactically elaborate affairs that resist capsule descriptions, it is easily summarized. In the early hours of December 7, 1941, without a formal declaration of war, a Japanese task force containing six aircraft carriers sailed to a point 220 miles north of the Hawaiian island of Oahu, where it launched 350 warplanes. These flew undetected to Oahu, surprising the American military. During a raid lasting about an hour and fifty minutes, Japanese pilots attacked every important air and naval installation on Oahu, destroying 188 Army and Navy aircraft, most on the ground, and sinking or damaging four auxiliary ships, three cruisers, three destroyers, and eight battleships. Japan lost twenty-nine aircraft and five midget submarines, while its fleet, the strongest yet assembled in the Pacific, withdrew without being sighted, having won one of the century's most one-sided victories.

   This air raid has since become the most carefully, obsessively examined battle in military history, described in countless articles and monographs, in the 102 titles listed under "Pearl Harbor" in the Library of Congress, and in the reports of nine military and Congressional investigations, transcribed and bound into a forty-volume set. In many cases, we know which pilots sank which ships, and which gunners downed which planes. We know what happened afterward to every Pearl Harbor vessel; for example, that the light cruiser *Phoenix* was sold to Argentina, renamed the *Admiral Belgrano,* and torpedoed by a British submarine during the Falklands war, that Coast Guard cutter *Taney* was the only Pearl Harbor ship serving in Vietnam, and that Navy Tug 146 has become a tugboat in San Francisco Bay.

   Any aircraft involved in Pearl Harbor is particularly valuable. A wing section from an American P-40 fighter (or "pursuit plane" as fighters were then called) shot down on December 7 was sold in 1989 for "several thousand dollars." The crews of six American planes which disappeared during the attack are still listed as MIAs, and World War Two "archaeologists" continue searching for them. On Oahu, Ted Darcy has collected the names and curricula vitae of all Japanese pilots and accounted for all but six of the planes downed on December 7. He is looking for the rest, hoping to find one that will be the centerpiece of his projected museum. "Japanese airplane wrecks are big business now," he told me, lowering his voice and speaking in the generalities and clipped sentences of someone holding priceless information. In Texas, David Aiken has been at work for twenty-two years compiling "a full accounting of every airman airborne" and attempting "to locate witnesses to every aerial battle or flight from 0600-1310." He promises a genealogy identifying the descendants of every Japanese and American airman, who he believes are certain "to have pride in such kinship." He imagines it will become the "foundation for an organization of such airmen and their descendants similar to the Daughters of the American Revolution."

Some reasons for the obsession with Pearl Harbor are obvious. It was a foreign military attack on American soil, and the worst naval catastrophe in United States history. There is the romance surrounding spectacular military defeats such as the Little Big Horn and the Charge of the Light Brigade. There is the belief that like the assassination of President Kennedy, it was a watershed event, dividing an innocent past from a corrupt future, and most of all, there was the Cold War, causing every Pearl Harbor mistake to be scrutinized, catalogued, and sifted for "lessons" to guarantee we could never again be surprised.

My own obsession began in grade school during the 1950s, when no December 7 could pass without a bulletin board filled with yellowed newspaper clippings or a visit from a veteran. I learned Americans had been heroic, and the Japanese treacherous for mounting a "sneak attack," then an indisputable evil rather than a preferred tactic. I remembered Pearl Harbor during air raid drills, reasoning that if those poky propeller planes could have appeared without warning over Hawaii, then why not Russian jets over Connecticut?

Before going to Hawaii, I had considered Pearl Harbor solely a military affair. Newsreels, photographs, and books encouraged this by concentrating on what happened to military targets, and I imagined warships spewing fire, lines of planes exploding on the ground, gunners surrounded by rings of flame, and the band on the battleship *California* completing "The Star Spangled Banner" before breaking for cover. I pictured Marine officers emptying their revolvers at Zeros as tears ran down their cheeks, and admirals standing in their gardens, still wearing pajamas, staring in disbelief. But what I had ignored or never understood was that this had all happened on the edge of a city which has since become America's thirteenth-largest, one where 40 percent of the population in 1941 was the same race as the pilots of those dragonfly planes.

When I first arrived in Honolulu I found it difficult to believe that this modern city of almost 900,000 could have much time for the memories or legacies of a 1941 city less than a third its size. But soon I began seeing them everywhere. Bullet holes scarred buildings at Hickam and Wheeler fields, and a cave overlooking the Waialua sugar plantation held a cache of canned food and batteries, left by a Japanese teenager as emergency supplies. The teahouse patronized by spies from the Japanese consulate had changed its name and removed its famous telescope from the second-story balcony, but it still catered to homesick visitors from Japan. Resentment against Japanese investors was often voiced in a Pearl Harbor context. "They couldn't invade us, so now they're buying us." "What they couldn't do with their bombs they're doing with their yen." Or, if the speaker had a certain perspective, "We have turned their yen into bombs." And always, it was that unspecified "they," the enemy.

I found that some Pearl Harbor legacies are buried, although not very deeply. A pier at the submarine base is built around a Japanese midget submarine that was rolled into its excavation in 1942, its dead crew still inside. Backyard gardens in Japanese neighborhoods conceal a treasure of swords, kimonos, and framed photographs of Emperor Hirohito, all buried in a hurry by people ridding themselves of anything too "Japanesy." Other legacies lie submerged, and certain to survive longer than any living memory. Pearl Harbor has aircraft skeletons, pieces of blasted superstructure, a yet-undiscovered midget submarine, the wrecks of the battleship *Arizona* and target ship *Utah*—the most visible members of a ghost fleet of sunken warships lying like a rusty necklace between Hawaii and Japan—and a thick sediment of oil, grit, and shell fragments, contaminated with high levels of copper, lead, and zinc from Japanese bombs and posing a continuing ecological threat to the harbor. Pockets of 1941 air remain trapped between the *Arizona*'s closed hatches and portholes, and marble-sized drops of oil still bubble up every twenty seconds from its tanks, spreading a thin stain of 1941 pollution.

The fiftieth anniversary of a war is an urgent time for legacies and memories, a time when death has cut through the ranks of officers, leaving the memories of corporals and privates. It is a time when survivors seize a last chance to redress wrongs or reveal secrets. Fearing their battles and sacrifices are soon to be forgotten, they embark on a final binge of memorial unveiling and memoir writing, saying, "Remember us. Remember us! Remember!" But remember what? Remember how? And how do they want us to remember their enemy? By perpetuating their grudges? Or should these disappear with the only generation with a right to them?

A fiftieth anniversary is also a transitional time: when the memory of a war generation coexists with the inherited memory of their children and the ignorance of their grandchildren; when you can begin discerning what the folk memory of a war will be; and when living memory still challenges sweeping conclusions. During this time, Pearl Harbor witnesses remember bullets stitching a sidewalk, and pilots flying so low they were seen laughing or smiling. Then they stop, wondering, Did I *really* see this, or was it cribbed from a documentary? From someone else's memory? From one of the famous photographs? Or from *Tora! Tora! Tora!*, which for months in the mid-sixties was filmed across Oahu, corrupting local memory.

During this transitional time you find, among the visitors

to the memorial on the sunken battleship *Arizona*, American veterans who burst into tears, or complain about the "damned Jap tourists," standing alongside Americans who, according to a secret "blooper book" kept by park rangers, ask questions such as: "I'm a bit confused. I thought I was in Hawaii . . . then what's all this *Arizona* business?" "Can you tell me how often the bodies float up?" "So this is a Japanese ship that we sunk, huh?" "Hi! I want to check to see if the *Arizona* is in port today." "Why didn't they tow the *Arizona* to Waikiki? It'd be much more convenient to visit it there." "What time is the dolphin show?"

By the time of a fiftieth anniversary, the years have often erased commonplace recollections, leaving behind more eloquent memory flashes. A man told me he remembered racing through a pineapple field while bombs sent the fruit flying and exploding, filling the air with their sweet aroma. A woman remembered the representative of the Yokohama Specie Bank playing tennis with his family on their backyard court as smoke spiraled from Pearl Harbor. An airman remembered lying in bed, separating the slats of a venetian blind with two fingers and shielding his eyes against the low sun, then recognizing the red "meatball" circles on the wings of a Japanese plane. A pilot's wife remembered saying goodbye to her husband as a Japanese bullet flew through the window and nicked the floor between their feet, showering their legs with sparks. A boy remembered his father returning from Pearl Harbor stinking of gasoline, and experienced flashbacks whenever he filled the gas tank of his car.

Pearl Harbor flashbacks are so powerful because what happened was so unexpected. One moment a sailor was brushing his teeth, the next he was blasted into the harbor or chased by Japanese bullets. An ensign who pulled wounded sailors from the harbor still wakes up screaming, haunted by the men he failed to rescue. Twenty-seven years later, a Japanese-

American defense worker found himself escaping a Vietcong ambush in the limousine of a Japanese businessman. Seeing a fluttering Rising Sun flag on the hood, framed by mortar explosions, he screamed, "Hey, I'm an American, let me out!"

Perhaps the Pearl Harbor survivors who opposed Robert Hudson's ceremony of reconciliation suffered similar flashbacks, or perhaps they worried they might if they returned to Hawaii for the fiftieth anniversary and saw submariner Sakamaki and pilot Fujita touring Pearl Harbor in the CINCPAC (Commander in Chief Pacific Fleet) admiral's barge. This was a feature of Hudson's program he had not volunteered at first, this plan for the Japanese to enjoy a VIP tour of the harbor on the eve of the anniversary, all the while being filmed and interviewed by the world press as they cruised the sites of sunken United States battleships. On reflection, Hudson admits, he "might have gone a little too far."

His aborted ceremony is one of many failed attempts to find the right gesture or event to symbolize both Japanese contrition and American forgiveness. The Germans have been largely forgiven for their war, yet for years, Japanese and Americans have been walking forward, arms outstretched for an embrace, yet missing, their efforts at Pearl Harbor rapprochements misfiring, and too often reviving old hatreds instead of burying them. The failed reconciliations have occurred ten years after the war, or forty-nine, sabotaged by thick-skinned Japanese or thin-skinned Americans, poisoned by too much sincerity or too little.

Consider that after Emperor Hirohito died, the only American governor ordering flags flown at half-mast for his funeral was John Waihee of Hawaii, and that on hearing this, Honolulu mayor Frank Fasi, a World War Two veteran, prohibited lowering any flags on city property. Some said Waihee was toadying to Japanese investors, and Japanese-American war veterans were outraged at the suggestion he might be attempting to curry favor with Hawaii's Japanese voters by making a gesture to the Japanese imperial family.

Consider Zero pilot Makato Bando, who came to Honolulu for the fortieth anniversary accompanied by a translator and Japanese television crew, then hired a launch so he could be filmed against the specific area of the harbor he had attacked. He boarded the *Arizona* Memorial, striking poses with American survivors who had also gathered there for the anniversary. When asked about his role in the attack, despite claims of being on a mission of reconciliation, he could only manage, "When you are in the military, you have to follow your orders whether you like it or not."

Consider Mitsuo Fuchida, the Japanese commander who fired signal flares signaling the start of the attack. He returned in 1953 to lay a wreath on the wreckage of the battleship *Arizona,* only to be greeted by a "public outcry." The Navy forbade him to enter the harbor, and one correspondent wrote to the *Honolulu Star-Bulletin,* "In my opinion he took a very active part in a program of mass murder." Fuchida also protested he had only been "following orders," but his "mission of peace" was perhaps not helped by his inappropriate attire— rows of medals across the smart uniform of the Sky Pilots International, an organization of evangelical Christians he had joined after the war.

Consider the first postwar "goodwill" visit of a Japanese naval vessel to Pearl Harbor in 1953, during which several crewmen wandered into the Likelike drive-in, within minutes attracting elderly first-generation Japanese-Americans [known as "issei"] who gathered outside, bowing, and calling the astonished sailors "admiral" and "fleet marshal." For several years after the war, many issei insisted the American victory was a hoax. They organized "victory clubs" and contributed to a fund to provide entertainment for the Emperor when he came to claim Hawaii. On October 27, 1945 (prewar Japan's "Navy

Day"), hundreds of issei climbed Aiea Heights, expecting to witness the triumphant entry of the Japanese fleet into Pearl Harbor. Two years later, the president of one victory club still claimed that reports of a Japanese surrender were propaganda and that General MacArthur was a prisoner of war. By 1950, membership in these clubs had dropped, some said to five thousand, others to five hundred, but the last of them, the Hisso Kai (victory society) did not disband until 1977, and it is likely the Japanese navy's goodwill cruise of 1953 had the unexpected effect of refreshing its delusions.

Consider *Tora! Tora! Tora!*, a recreation of Pearl Harbor that gives equal narrative time to Japanese pilots and military planners. It was an expensive movie, and a dull one, but certainly not "pro-Japanese." Yet on the eve of its Washington premiere, Congressmen John Murphy (D-N.Y.) and Lowell Weicker (R-Conn.) described it as "glorifying" the Japanese and denounced the Pentagon for cooperating in its filming. "Every ethical patriotic standard is besmirched by the Hollywood-Pentagon hookup to produce and promote a film glorifying the attack on Pearl Harbor," Murphy said. Veterans' groups were also critical, still unable to accept that the attack had been a glorious success for Japan, and that any movie depicting Japanese servicemen would reflect this.

Consider that in 1988, the *Arizona* Memorial Association raised fifteen thousand dollars to move Ensign Sakamaki's midget submarine back from Key West, Florida, and display it near the *Arizona*. The symbolism was obvious: on the fiftieth anniversary, the wreckage of Japanese and American vessels would be reunited. But before it could be shipped west, a rumor surfaced that it was to be placed aboard the *Arizona*. The VFW and American Legion protested, and the scheme was canceled.

Or consider the forty-fifth reunion of veterans of the unit that dropped the atomic bombs on Japan. They gathered where they had trained, in Wendover, Nevada, to renew friendships, dedicate a "peace memorial" commemorating the unit's two thousand members and their victims in Hiroshima and Nagasaki, and listen to two speeches by Hideaki Kase, a conservative author and adviser to two former Japanese prime ministers. On opening night, Mr. Kase chose to argue the bombs had been unnecessary, since Japan had been ready to capitulate. Dozens walked out in protest, one describing himself as "disgusted." The next evening, at the peace memorial dedication, the veterans retaliated by preventing Kase from delivering his second speech and ordering the Army band not to play the Japanese national anthem.

The Japanese have been a unique enemy in United States history, hated more than any other. Before going to Hawaii, I had thought the hostility easily explained. It was racism. It seemed simple: we had made our peace with Germany because it is a Caucasian nation, but we were still "bashing" Japan because they are Orientals; Japanese investment was resented because they were a former Asian enemy, but investment by Germans was not because they were Caucasian. But in Hawaii, as I came to understand the unusual triangle of relationships between Americans, Japanese, and Americans of Japanese ancestry, I saw it was not that simple. Why did a Japanese-American woman carry fresh flowers every week to the grave of the FBI agent responsible for interning Japanese residents of Hawaii? Why were the wartime military governor of Hawaii and his chief of intelligence both celebrated by the Japanese-American community in a 1985 pamphlet "dedicated to all in Hawaii who with kindness and an understanding heart assisted the Japanese as they worked to establish a home and bright future in our islands"? And why did I hear from Japanese-Americans comments such as "Don't you ever lose sight of the fact that the Japanese of today are the same kind of 'Japs' that were in Japan in 1931. . . . Give them time, another fifteen years, and they will do the same thing they did in 1941!" and

"I'm all for the USA whipping their asses again!" and "Many [postwar] Japanese businessmen ... flaunt their money and breach their word. The best way to handle them is to get a big bulldozer and bulldoze them into the ocean. . . ."

The longer I lived in Honolulu, looking for Pearl Harbor legacies, interviewing Pearl Harbor witnesses, and reading 1941 newspapers and diaries, the more I began to suspect that the enduring American-Japanese hostility and the failed American-Japanese reconciliations were a product of both 1941 and the present—of the unique nature of Pearl Harbor, and of its ghosts. Soon I was seeing the city with a double vision, juxtaposing 1941 Honolulu with its ghosts, unable to visit a neighborhood without comparing it to its past, or to listen to a witness without connecting his memories to his current life. So I have decided to retell the events of December 5 to December 7, 1941—a weekend that was the last of peace and the first of war—by placing 1941 and 1991 alongside each other, hoping this will explain why, when bloodier battles have been forgotten, Pearl Harbor still generates such emotion.

Before leaving for Hawaii I had read about a Pearl Harbor survivor protesting the use of a Japanese-made Komatsu backhoe to excavate an addition to the national cemetery that would one day hold his remains. "Is it too much to ask that this practice to be stopped on the hallowed grounds of our national cemeteries?" he asked. "Do other Pearl Harbor Survivors feel as I do? Does 'Remember Pearl Harbor' mean anything today?" Here was a perfect example, I thought, of the excessive sensitivity of the older, wartime generation. But a few days later, I found myself in the shrine room of the *Arizona* Memorial, angry beyond all reason at a Japanese woman born at least a quarter century after a Japanese bomb had ignited the *Arizona*'s forward magazine, sinking it in nine minutes and killing 1,177 of its crew. I was reading the names of these dead crewmen carved on a marble wall, searching for the seventeen sets of brothers, when I heard a whisper of "Please, sir . . . please, sir . . . please!" I turned to face a young Japanese woman wearing a pained smile. She waved the back of her hand, motioning me to move. She wanted to pose her sister in front of this list of dead sailors, and I was in the way. I shook my head. She asked again, raising her voice and becoming annoyed. I glared, folded my arms and turned my back. Her shutter went clickety-clack, and for a moment I considered grabbing that camera and exposing the film.

Let me be clear about this. Had she been American, British, Russian, Chinese, or even German, I would have smiled and moved away, perhaps offering to take her picture in front of those names. At first, I put my reaction down to my age. I was born in 1946, in the earliest of the postwar generations, one that grew up listening to war stories and surrounded by German helmets, Japanese bayonets, and the flight jackets we wore as teenagers. For us, bravery was defined by Omaha Beach, leadership by Winston Churchill, evil by the Holocaust, and treachery by Pearl Harbor. The war we knew was immediate, its wounds raw, its issues simple. We were too close to it for historical perspective, too removed to understand its ironies or moral ambiguities. The movies we saw and the books we read were often wartime propaganda, but we were too young to separate the real from the bogus. And after watching all those black-and-white documentaries, reading those fat histories, and participating in those philosophical disputes that could never be argued without reference to Hitler, and after comparing our restless, unfulfilled generation with the one before it, perhaps it is not surprising we felt such secondhand nostalgia for a time we had never lived and a war we had never fought, nor surprising that my secondhand memories had become secondhand grudges.

The descendants of Pearl Harbor veterans have formed their own organization, the Sons and Daughters of Pearl Harbor Survivors, which has a schedule of dues, a national convention, and an executive board that flies from across the country to conduct its business in places like the Marriott Hotel of Overland Park, Kansas. But, I wondered, what business? What besides collecting dues, selling bumper stickers, and preserving the secondhand memories and grudges? A member of this curious organization declared, in the newsletter of the Pearl Harbor Survivors Association, "I am the proud son of a Pearl Harbor survivor. Although I can't smell the smoke, hear the rattles and bangs of weaponry used December 7, 1941, I feel the intensity of an emotion. . . ." Well, as I discovered that morning on the *Arizona* Memorial, I too felt an "intensity of emotion." It was not one to brag about, but perhaps if I understood it, I might also come to understand why Robert Hudson's proposal for a simple act of Pearl Harbor reconciliation had led to what might be construed as a death threat.

PART ONE

December 5, 1941

1

The Great White Ship Leaves Honolulu

EVER SINCE I READ OF THE LAST PEACETIME SAILING OF THE S.S. *Lurline* from Honolulu on December 5, 1941, the words "Pearl Harbor" can set her sailing again in my mind. Perhaps it is the symbolism of the great liner leaving peacetime Honolulu and docking five days later in wartime San Francisco, its passengers in the meantime traveling from peace to war. They still remember this abrupt change, and learning of the attack when a porter brought their morning coffee in a tin pot, the expensive silverware having been placed in storage, or when a crewman sloshed blackout paint across their porthole, with each stroke darkening their staterooms as inexorably as an eclipse. They lived for two nights in this eerie blue twilight, fully clothed and wearing life preservers, forbidden to smoke, knowing there were casualties in Hawaii, but not knowing which of their relatives or friends had been killed.

Or perhaps I like the romantic "Last Train from Paris" imagery of the *Lurline*'s departure. Although her passengers were not escaping an enemy occupation, they might have been, had the Japanese won the Battle of Midway. Nor were they escaping certain death, although had they been on Oahu, they might have been among the 2,404 servicemen and civilians killed in the raid. Instead, the *Lurline*'s sailing may be so compelling because·it separated everyone into two distinct groups: those remaining on Oahu as she pulled away from the dock, who would be strafed by enemy planes, live under martial law, see dead American soldiers and sailors; and everyone else, whose memories of December 7 would always be confined to where they were and what they were doing when they heard the news, much as a later generation would recall the assassination of President Kennedy.

So consider, as I have many times, the S.S. *Lurline,* the "Great White Ship" of the Matson Lines, as she loaded passengers in Honolulu at noon on December 5, 1941. First, consider her from a distance. Perhaps from the observation deck of the Aloha Tower, "The Gateway to the Pacific," that winked colored signals at harbor traffic, and at eight stories was the tallest building for thousands of miles. From there, several hundred feet above the docks, there was little to distinguish this "Boat Day" from others marking a liner's arrival or departure from this, the most isolated archipelago in the world. There were spiderwebs of streamers and blizzards of confetti. Reporters interviewed departing celebrities, and photographers took posed pictures. The Royal Hawaiian Band played its tearjerking melodies, hula girls danced, and local boys dived for coins from the top deck, and everywhere there were flower leis.

Earlier that day, Japanese women had gathered blossoms from slopes of the saw-toothed mountains overshadowing the harbor. All morning, elderly Hawaiian women had sat along the sidewalks leading to the docks, plucking wild ginger and plumeria from old cereal boxes, and releasing clouds of perfume as they strung the fifteen hundred leis the Hawaiian Lei Sellers Association claimed necessary for an average Boat Day. These leis were long and full, fragrant ropes of yellow ilima, and garlands of sweet mountain maile hanging as low as the knees. Today, when leis are sold from concrete stalls tucked under the access ramps to the Honolulu International Airport, this scene seems impossibly romantic, but in 1941, many longtime residents of Hawaii—known as "kamaainas"—condemned commercial lei-making as degenerate. They remembered the 1920s, when people collected blossoms and strung leis themselves, instead of paying someone to perform this labor of love.

Seen from the Aloha Tower, the Boat Day crowds of December 5 resembled earlier ones, with so many people wearing white the scene appeared as in an overexposed photograph. Women wore white cotton dresses and were shaded by white parasols. Naval officers wore dress whites and civilians wore linen suits. Nursemaids in white uniforms minded the scrubbed pink children of the kamaaina aristocracy, an elite of a hundred Caucasian families descended from nineteenth-century New England missionaries who, as the famous expression goes, "came to do good and did well." During the last half century, these families had overthrown the Hawaiian monarchy, organized the immigration of Chinese, Japanese, and Filipino laborers, and through intermarriage and interlocking directorates seized control of the land, commerce, and political life of these islands as completely as the oligarchy of any Central American banana republic. Yet within three days of this sailing, this elite would see logs rolled across its polo fields, its private school and country clubs requisitioned for barracks, and its political power, unbroken for fifty years, swept away forever.

As at any Boat Day, the crowds were in the thousands, more than seemed warranted by the departure of eight hundred passengers. But as any island dweller knows, the arrival or departure of an infrequent boat is more than a transportation event. Large Alexander and Baldwin calendars hung in most Honolulu kitchens, advertising the movements of the Matson liners, and on Boat Day, downtown office workers left their desks to see who was coming or going. Young men met every arriving liner, hoping to be first to discover a pretty girl. Beachboys from Waikiki attended every departure, serenading with ukuleles the women they had romanced. Businessmen and politicians came to make deals and exchange gossip, and the leis, hula dancers, and Royal Hawaiian Band reminded all they lived in a community unique in its history and customs, and in its isolation from the horrors of this century.

But if you were to descend from the Aloha Tower and come closer, you might notice this Boat Day was unlike any other. Her passengers might not imagine the *Lurline* would soon be zigzagging at full speed, dodging Japanese submarines, and officers embracing their departing wives might not imagine that in two weeks some would be carried aboard this ship on stretchers, but there were clues. Because of the increases in defense workers and servicemen, there were more police in evidence, and more cars clogging Fort and Bishop streets, despite the traffic lights replacing the Hawaiian policemen who until recently had directed traffic from beneath umbrellas. Because so many passengers were young defense workers, the Matson Line had arranged for two Los Angeles policemen to make the round-trip voyage on their vacation time, giving them free accommodation in exchange for keeping order. Because war with Japan was feared—although few thought it would begin in Hawaii—and 40 percent of Hawaii's population was Japanese, the authorities worried about Japanese sabotage, and so the piers were guarded by soldiers of the nationalized Hawaii Territorial Guard, who, more likely than not, were Japanese.

The *Lurline*'s sister ship, the *Matsonia*, had been turned over to the government for conversion to a troopship, and for two weeks there had been no transportation to California except a few seats on the Pan Am clippers. So there was a record number of passengers on this voyage, so many that seventy were assigned cots in a main lounge described as "the last word in maritime trimmings . . . until someone puts a keel under the Louvre and floats it." There were a record 350 letter pouches and 7,000 bags of parcels, more American diplomats and Pan-American Airways employees than usual, evacuated from the Orient because of the danger of war, more stowaways, more people without leis, since they had not been in Hawaii long enough for anyone to make an event of their departure, and more women than men, including sizable contingents of prostitutes and military wives. Some had decided only at the last minute to leave, and some would discover, when the *Lurline* docked in San Francisco, that during this voyage they had become widows.

There were Japanese-Americans on the passenger list—a young Army officer who would probably suffer some embarrassing moments, and families sailing from a place where their incarceration in a concentration camp was unlikely to a place where it was certain. Usually, the *Lurline* filled several staterooms with starlets and socialites. On this sailing, there was only Miss Marjorie Petty, who modeled for her father's drawings of the scantily clothed "Petty Girl" in *Esquire,* and who had been in Hawaii three weeks, chaperoned by her mother and chased by photographers. More numerous were the defense workers, returning home after shocking Honolulu by being the first haoles (Caucasians) seen to engage in heavy physical labor, and after turning Hawaii into America's "Fist in the Pacific," or so it was said. Because these workers did not consider this home, and many were glad to be departing after months of loneliness, you could see at this Boat Day something unthinkable only a year before, people leaving Hawaii with dry eyes.

It is easy to conclude everyone must have *known* war was coming. Why else the crowding? The stowaways? The Army wives? The panicked prostitutes, who, more than anyone, were

sensitive to the military mind? And there were passengers on
this sailing such as Mrs. P. R. Sellers, who remembers that "our
husbands had been telling us for some time they were concerned," and that her husband, then at sea on the carrier *Enterprise,* wanted her "out of there." Yet Mrs. Sellers was in the
minority. Most wives were leaving because their husbands worried a war in Asia would restrict travel from Hawaii to the
mainland, and many kamaainas were leaving on vacation and
business trips, confident of being able to return. Bob Stroh's
father, a salesman for Primo beer, was taking his family along
on a West Coast business trip, never imagining they would be
stuck in California for three years, nearly penniless, their property in Hawaii requisitioned by the Army. Stroh recalls this
sailing as a "glorious occasion" because he was allowed to
throw confetti, and remembers the *Lurline* surrounded by
clouds of colored paper and streamers.

If this sailing reflected anything, it was the confusion
reigning in Honolulu during this last week of peace. Assembled on the pier were those leaving because they feared war,
and those staying for the same reason; those departing because they thought war was remote, and those remaining for
the same reason. This same uncertainty was reflected in Honolulu's newspapers. If you wanted to prove everyone should
have known war was imminent, you could pick out headlines
such as "London Cries U.S.–Japan 'War,'" "Kurusu [a special Japanese envoy to Washington] Bluntly Warned Nation
Ready for Battle," "Pacific Zero Hour Near," "U.S. Army
Alerted in Manila—Singapore Mobilizing as War Tension
Grows," and "U.S. Demands Explanations of Japan Moves—
Americans Prepare for Any Emergency; Navy Declared
Ready." If you wanted to prove peace was equally likely, you
could point to "Japan Called Still Hopeful of Making Peace
with U.S.," "Japan Parries Open U.S. Break," "Hirohito
Holds Power to Stop Japanese Army," "Further Peace Efforts

Urged," and, on the day before the attack, "New Peace Effort Urged in Tokyo—Joint Commission to Iron Out Deadlock with U.S. Proposal."

The *Lurline* passenger best symbolizing these contradictions and the curious combination of nervousness and overconfidence characterizing Honolulu on December 5 was Colonel Tetley of the Army Signal Corps, commander of the Army's aircraft warning system in Hawaii. Radar had arrived in Honolulu in November 1941, but was largely ignored or treated with contempt by military and civilian authorities, despite the important role it had played the year before in the Battle of Britain. Fearing they might ruin scenic vistas and defile mountains sacred to the Hawaiian people, Governor John Poindexter and the National Park Service both refused Tetley permission to install radar sets on mountain peaks, where they would have been most effective. The commander of the Army's Hawaiian Department, General Walter Short, believed the five mobile radar stations that Tetley put into operation were simply good training tools, and not important enough to operate twenty-four hours a day. But in the lower ranks there was great enthusiasm for the new device. Tetley remembers his radar operators as "exceptional people, the brightest young men from Signal Corps, the kind of people who are now arbitraging on Wall Street or designing programs in Silicon Valley. They all had good learning curves and active minds, and soon became impatient with all the training. I told them not to, because, I remember saying, 'One of these fine days you're going to see some nice big blips. . . .' "

When Tetley's whiz kids plotted a Japanese attack in their training exercises, it was always carrier-based, and coming at dawn. They expected an attack at Thanksgiving, and when it failed to materialize, Tetley thought Oahu was "okay until Christmas." Still, he was dumbfounded when he and his liaison officer Coastal Artillery Antiaircraft were ordered to San Francisco at that sensitive time to observe how radar stations there handled a simulated attack by carrier-based planes against the San Francisco Navy Yard.

He decided to use the opportunity to evacuate his wife and infant son to the mainland. He was so convinced an attack was coming he had already prepared his household goods for shipping. The only accommodations available were in first class, but he took them anyway. As they waited for the *Lurline* to sail, his wife met the Pan Am and State Department employees being evacuated from Wake and Midway islands. "Why are they pulling people back from Asia and the islands?" she asked. "For the same reason you're on this boat," he said.

But Tetley was the exception. Most of civilian and military Hawaii considered the chances of a Japanese raid as remote to impossible. Certainly none of the civilians arriving in Honolulu two days earlier on the *Lurline* believed they had sailed into a potential war zone. If a raid was expected, would two football teams from the mainland have arrived on the *Lurline* on December 3? The team from Willamette University was scheduled against the University of Hawaii on December 6, while San Jose College would play on the 13th. Or would Hollywood cameramen have come to film scenery as background for *To the Shores of Tripoli,* a historical drama about the first Marine Corps victory? Or would the noted European war correspondent Joseph C. Harsch have arrived intending to catch the Pan American Clipper on December 7 and spend the winter reporting from Japan?

Earl Thacker, a local transportation executive, had told reporters meeting the *Lurline* on December 3 the opinion in Washington, D.C., was that "there will be no war with Japan" and that "the Japanese do not want to fight America and the present attitude is bluff," although "if the Japanese military want a fight, the United States is fully prepared for them." And Frank Atherton, chairman of the board of Castle and Cooke, said he "believed some plan could be worked out to avoid it [war with Japan]."

Walter Dillingham, who came from a wealthy and influential Honolulu family, remembers nothing sinister about the *Lurline*'s last peacetime crossing to Honolulu. "A normal *Lurline* voyage except there were no pretty girls," he says. "Most of the passengers were defense workers who came to the main dining room—which was a very plush place—with rubber bands around their sleeves and wearing sweat-stained hats." He had paced the deck wondering "why the damned boat didn't get home faster," and recalling the parties when the *Lurline* brought the Hawaiian students back home from vacations, and "the band played Hawaiian music that seemed to keep time to the roar of the ship." He was so confident Hawaii was safe he proposed via radiophone to his girlfriend, who was temporarily in San Francisco. "You're going to have a problem getting back to the Islands," he told her, "because the military are not letting people on the boats now unless they're bona fide citizens of Hawaii. Perhaps you should tell them you're about to be one because you're going to marry me."

The most complacent—perhaps "deluded" is more accurate—of the arriving of *Lurline* passengers was Brigadier General Howard C. Davidson, commander of Wheeler Field's 14th Pursuit Wing, the fighter planes assigned to intercept any airborne attack on Oahu. A formation of fighters buzzed the *Lurline* in his honor, and on the pier he announced that during a tour of mainland airfields he had been most impressed by a Seattle exercise in interceptor maneuvers. Because of the presence of eight thousand volunteer civilian "spotters," he said, "attackers were seen and reported long before they could get in close, and reports piled into defense headquarters in plenty of time for the interceptor flight squadrons to rise and meet them." He promised that "the scheme will probably be duplicated here soon with a local setup of volunteer civilian 'spotters' who, during wartime, keep an eye peeled for the approach of enemy air raiders."

It is difficult to imagine a plan less suited to Hawaii's geography, or more useless to its defense. Davidson's own command at Wheeler Field was only nine miles from the north shore and twelve from the south. Civilian spotters standing at water's edge would provide less than five minutes' warning. But on December 3, after his fighters completed their aerial tricks over the *Lurline,* they were disarmed and rolled into a tight antisabotage formation on the exposed tarmac, making it impossible to arm and launch them all in under four hours.

Not until late on the afternoon of December 5, after a five-hour delay occasioned by the last-minute arrival of military families, did loudspeakers in the *Lurline*'s corridors sound "All ashore going ashore." Like every departure from Hawaii, this one now unfolded in an atmosphere of hysteria, melancholy, and recklessness. Strangers embraced, laughter became hoarse, corridors filled with cigarette smoke, and staterooms were choked with the thick perfume of flower leis. It was customary for men to demonstrate their love by running down gangplanks at the last second, then racing to Diamond Head Lighthouse to wave a final goodbye, or hiring speedboats to escort the *Lurline* from the harbor, cutting dangerously across her bow. All this and more happened on December 5, which even by Boat Day standards is remembered as being memorably frenetic and sad. The delayed departure had made the stateroom parties more boozy and emotional than usual, and tears were even seen in the eyes of those veterans of countless Boat Days the Royal Hawaiian Band.

Finally the *Lurline* blasted her whistle a last time, the band played a last "Aloha Oe," people shouted "Goodbye . . . see you in a month, six months, a year," and men, even men in uniform, wept. Passengers threw streamers toward friends on the pier, forming a colored spiderweb that straightened, tightened, and, just before breaking, appeared to tie her to the dock, and this peaceful day, forever. Outrigger canoes followed her to the mouth of the harbor. Bombers from Hickam Field circled overhead, their bellies just feet above the water, and fighters from Wheeler swooped across her decks, their pilots waggling their wings in a last farewell to their wives.

Some passengers tossed their leis overboard, the legend being if they washed ashore their owners would return to Hawaii. Although if they wished to do this as civilian passengers on the *Lurline,* they would have to wait until April 21, 1948, when this liner, now a symbol of happier, more innocent times, would be welcomed back to Honolulu by sirens, fireboats spitting geysers, fleets of canoes, tugboats, and yachts, fifty thousand cheering spectators wearing—as requested by the governor—"bright aloha prints," a plane towing an "Aloha *Lurline*" banner, girls in canoes scattering flowers, an eighty-foot lei, and whatever other merriment Honolulu could devise to recreate a prewar Boat Day and convince itself life would resume as before, which was, of course, utterly impossible.

The day after arriving in Honolulu, I visited the Aloha Tower and, beneath it, the pier used by the *Lurline* on December 5. On such short notice, I had been unable to find someone who had sailed on the *Lurline* or witnessed her departure. But I started here anyway, because in a new city I like taking my bearings from the top of a tall building, and although Honolulu now boasts its own small fist of skyscrapers, their top floors, in the custom of such places these days, are monopolized by offices and private clubs. Despite all the construction and progress, despite the Aloha Tower going from the tallest building in a horizontal city to one of the lowest in a vertical city, it is still the highest point in downtown Honolulu open to the public. It is scheduled to become the centerpiece of the kind of redeveloped waterfront that offers T-shirts, ice cream, and fake gas lamps in place of stevedores and ocean liners, but for now it is a backwater in a city with few of those. Although used by infrequent cruise ships, its piers and customs halls have the look of being abandoned around 1959, when jets began cutting air time to the West Coast by half. Their walls are peeling and spotted by leaks, and faded travel posters promise an unrecognizable low-rise Honolulu.

Right after the war, some Hawaiians tried transferring their Boat Day rituals to the airport, and before the days of jumbo jets and terrorism, they succeeded. Family groups accompanied passengers onto the tarmac to embrace, cry, and present leis. The Hawaii Visitors Bureau organized Operation Aloha, in which hula students, musicians, and transportation firms were said to be "cooperating to give airport aloha." In 1948, a magazine reported, "When the great plane's doors swing open, the fragrance of a lei, the beauty of a brown-skinned girl and the melody of an island song indicate at once that this is Hawaii." But today, arriving at Honolulu International Airport has, as one kamaaina told me, "all the excitement of a trip to Safeway." Instead of crossing thousands of miles of empty ocean, then seeing the humpy green outline of the Koolaus and the winking lighthouse on Makapuu Point, you fly for hours with the shades pulled, watching a movie and a medley of commercials. Unless you have a window seat, you may land without seeing more than a flash of green. Only when you are in the airport, watching visitors receive an assembly-line aloha, a lei, and quick kiss, from glassy-eyed teenagers in grass skirts, do you know you are in the middle of the Pacific.

The day I visited the Aloha Tower, a cruise liner had docked at Pier Nine. She was the *Canberra,* a creaky British vessel that calls once or twice a year. From the upper deck of the arrivals hall I saw plastic chairs facing a swimming pool surrounded by Astroturf. When I asked the sunburned Australian and British passengers where they had just come from, one said, "We've come from, oh dear, where *have* we come from. . . ." It turned out to be San Francisco.

My 1939 guidebook to Honolulu described the Aloha Tower this way: "Rising from the heart of the city, at the central docks, it provides a lofty and convenient view platform from which the malihini [newcomer] can get his bearings. . . . One mounts this tower gratis, in a self-operating elevator, to the observation gallery, which is open to the sky and the view on every side." I took this same elevator to the top to compare views. Looking "makai" (toward the sea), my book promised, I would see "the harbor channel, and the open sea, probably with craft, large and small, enlivening the scene." Fifty years later, except for a procession of jets making their approach to the airport, this scene remained unchanged.

The old view west, toward Pearl Harbor and Ewa, had been of a small industrial neighborhood dominated by the Dole cannery, its steel water tank painted to resemble a gigantic pineapple. In 1941, this tower was the tallest structure on the horizon, and stretching beyond had been a green carpet of cane fields and Pearl Harbor. Although the pineapple was still there, it was now almost lost against Honolulu Airport and the Aloha Stadium, industrial parks, car dealerships, malls, and housing developments—the hot sprawl common to any American city. It looked as if one of Oahu's dormant volcanoes had erupted, spewing a lava of concrete. Patches of cane field were only visible in the far distance, beyond Pearl Harbor, but even they will soon be plowed under for a "second city" that will push the lava field of concrete clear across the island.

My book said, "Waikiki direction leads the eye coastwise by several boulevards . . . to Diamond Head." But now I saw only the architecture of fast cars and fast deals: expressways, multilevel parking garages, and a crowded cemetery of tombstone hotels that blocked most of Diamond Head. Sun skipped off tin roofs and the tops of cars stalled in freeway traffic, and instead of green and tropical, Waikiki looked bleached and hot.

If you looked north and inland from the Aloha Tower in 1941, you saw a compact, low-rise city of palm trees, red-tiled roofs, and stores shaded by tin awnings. You saw the granite banks and trading houses of the haole elite, the rococo Iolani Palace, and the Nuuanu Valley, squeezed by the slopes and ridges of the Koolaus. Honolulu was then a small colonial city, more of a Singapore than a Seattle, a place where people woke to mynah birds and drifted down to beaches to swim at sunrise, and where children, even wealthy children, went to school barefoot. It was a city of short workdays, pink stucco, and polo fields, of louvered windows, hibiscus hedges, and open patios leading to houses that were difficult to black out and impossible to lock, an architecture spectacularly unsuited to war.

The Honolulu I saw resembled the Singapore of 1990, a dense island city where the automobile, a construction frenzy, mass tourism, and greed had shrunk gardens, felled palms, raised the temperature, and quickened the pace, casting long, rectangular shadows over parks and beaches. Beneath me, traffic on the multilane Nimitz Highway threw up a continuous roar, cutting off the Aloha Tower from the rest of Honolulu. A glass wall of office buildings blocked the view inland, but if I moved my head, I could just make out, between the twin white marble towers of the Amfac Building, and beyond two blue skyscrapers, a block of the old Fort Street commercial district, a corner of Bishop Street, most of Chinatown, and slivers of green mountain—fleeting glimpses of the city the *Lurline* left behind on December 5, 1941.

2

Vice-Consul Morimura Sees
the Sights

ON THE SAME DAY, AND PERHAPS AT THE SAME TIME, THAT pursuit pilots flew over the *Lurline* to salute their departing wives, Vice-Consul Yaeashi Morimura of the Japanese consulate in Honolulu was observing Wheeler Field and Pearl Harbor from the passenger seat of a Piper Cub, counting planes and warships, and searching for the barrage balloons rumored to have arrived from the mainland. Morimura was in fact Ensign Tadeo Yoshikawa of the Imperial Japanese Navy, a wispy, boyish-looking man who, since arriving in Honolulu under diplomatic cover nine months earlier, had become the most effective and important spy in a world with many contenders for that title.

Spying on Pearl Harbor from a commercial sightseeing plane while dressed in linen trousers and an aloha shirt was in keeping with Yoshikawa's style. He checked out the depth of Kaneohe Bay by taking a glass-bottomed excursion boat, accompanied by several young women from the consulate. Disguised as a Filipino laborer, he washed dishes in the Pearl Harbor officers' club while eavesdropping on conversations. He went swimming at the mouth of Pearl Harbor to look for

submarine nets, avoiding detection by scattering moss on the
water and breathing through a reed. He purchased rounds of
drinks in sailors' bars, and traveled as a tourist to Maui to
inspect the anchorage at Lahaina, staying at a hotel owned by
a Japanese alien with a glass eye. He hiked through the for-
ested hills and cane fields of Aiea Heights, with their unob-
structed views of Pearl Harbor, memorizing ship movements.
He joined a Japanese fencing club popular with American servicemen, becoming known as an "attentive listener." He
spent evenings carousing with the consulate staff at the
Shuncho-Ro teahouse on Alawa Heights, romancing geishas
and observing Pearl Harbor through a high-powered telescope that its owners had thoughtfully installed on a second-
floor balcony. He did not know how to drive, so he was
chauffeured by a shabby Japanese-American taxi driver
known as Johnny the Jap, who spoke only pidgin, yet after
the attack was discovered to have an expert knowledge of antitorpedo nets and naval guns.

He had two agents under his command: a lazy German
playboy named Otto Kuehn, who was related by marriage to
Heinrich Himmler and was under FBI surveillance, and the
chief chemist of the Honolulu sake brewery, who was in the
habit of drinking too much of his own product and boasting
that his father-in-law was a Japanese admiral. He had decided
not to recruit agents from among the Japanese residents because he thought them "just trash" and "insufficiently educated," an attitude that continues to be expressed, although
more subtly, by some of today's visitors from Japan.

Yoshikawa was an unlikely combination of dedication and
recklessness, not unlike the Japanese businessman you see in
Honolulu now, who puts in a serious, productive day, then
goes to a karioke bar for an infantile binge. He was frequently
drunk, often entertained girls in his quarters overnight, and
wrote sugary love poems to the Shuncho-Ro geishas, boasting

the first joint of his left index finger was missing "on account of love." Yet, he was careful and methodical in his intelligence gathering, varying his clothing so he would not be remembered, never carrying binoculars or a notebook, never taking photographs, and always relying on maps printed by the Hawaii Visitors Bureau. "The first rule of information collecting," he told one consulate employee, "is no get caught."

Add up the teahouse, telescope, drunken sake chemist, German playboy, glass-eyed hotel owner, and missing finger (a device used by Alfred Hitchcock in *The 39 Steps* to identify a German spy), and Yoshikawa becomes a spy out of a radio serial or Hollywood B film, a caricature of a Japanese spy, a comedian's Japanese spy, the most obvious Japanese spy in the world. Yet he was never caught, or even identified as an agent by a hundred-odd FBI and military intelligence agents operating in Honolulu.

Yoshikawa used diplomatic cables to file his reports on the number of ships in Pearl Harbor and the reconnaissance activities of American aircraft. A September 24 cable from Tokyo had ordered him to place an imaginary grid over Pearl Harbor, dividing it into five areas, and report regularly on which warships were anchored where. After the attack, this cable became known as the "bomb plot" message because of its obvious value for planning an air raid on Pearl Harbor. The American military had broken the Japanese diplomatic codes, and Yoshikawa's messages were deciphered by top-secret Navy and Army units in Washington collectively known as Magic. Yet, after being processed in Washington, the "bomb plot" message, like much of the intelligence transmitted by Yoshikawa, was filed and forgotten, not considered important enough to be communicated to military commands in Hawaii. This happened because of bureaucratic rivalries and the military's obsession with secrecy, and because it was not believed information of tactical or operational military value could be

found in the routine communications of minor Japanese diplomats.

Yoshikawa transmitted his most valuable espionage to
Lieutenant Commander Suguru Suzuki, who arrived in Honolulu on November 1, 1941, aboard the Japanese *Taiyo Maru*,
disguised as a ship's steward. The *Taiyo Maru*, the last Japanese liner to call at an American port, had been sent via a
northerly route, to chart the course that Admiral Yamamoto's
strike force would use a month later. Its other mission was to
collect intelligence material that Yoshikawa could not easily
cable to Tokyo. Suzuki feared arrest by American counterintelligence agents, so he met aboard ship with the Japanese consul, Nagao Kita, slipping him a ball of crumpled rice paper
bearing ninety-seven questions such as "Are there antisubmarine nets at the entrance of Pearl Harbor?" "Each week, the
fleet goes to sea. Where do they go; what do they do, particularly aircraft carriers?" "This is the most important question:
On what day of the week would the most ships be in Pearl
Harbor on normal occasions?"

Back at the consulate, Yoshikawa provided detailed
answers, many of which proved essential to the last-minute
planning and timing of the attack. He reported aerial reconnaissance to the north was "poorly organized" and "downright
bad," and identified Sunday as the day most ships were in
harbor and their crews most relaxed.

Despite dozens of FBI, customs, and military intelligence
agents at the gangplank and customs hall, and despite searches
of departing passengers so thorough that the *Taiyo Maru*'s
sailing was delayed several days, consulate staffers succeeded in
smuggling maps, Yoshikawa's answers, and copies of "Souvenir of Honolulu" photographs on which Yoshikawa had divided Pearl Harbor into numbered squares aboard ship
concealed in rolled-up newspapers (copies of these were later
found in the cockpits of planes downed during the attack).

Because American counterintelligence believed the greatest danger to Hawaii's security came from its Japanese residents, consulate employees were given only cursory inspections, while Japanese-American and alien Japanese passengers were carefully searched.

In the final ten days, Tokyo increased its demands on Yoshikawa. On November 28, he was ordered to "report upon the entrance or departure of capital ships and the length of time they remain at anchor." On November 29, he was told, "We have been receiving reports from you on ship movements, but in future you will also report even when there are no movements." (A clue Japan was interested as much in the ships that remained in harbor as in their sorties.) On December 2, his Tokyo control instructed him, "Advise me whether or not there are any observation balloons over Pearl Harbor or if there are any indications that they are likely to be used. Also let me know whether or not the battleships are protected by antitorpedo nets. . . . In view of the present situation, the presence in port of the battleships, aircraft carriers, and cruisers is of the greatest importance. Hereafter report to me daily to the utmost of your ability." On December 4, he was ordered to "wire immediately the movements of the Pacific Fleet subsequent to [December] 4." This is why the next day found him making a penultimate "information-collecting" expedition.

After his sightseeing flight on December 5, Yoshikawa drove to the Pearl City peninsula, buying a soda pop from a stand conveniently situated opposite the Pearl Harbor gate. He then returned to the Japanese consulate and drafted a cable to Tokyo reporting, "(1) During Friday morning . . . the three battleships mentioned in my message #239 arrived here. (2) The *Lexington* and five heavy cruisers left port on the same day. (3) The following ships were in port on the afternoon of [December] 5: eight battleships, three light cruisers, sixteen destroyers . . ."

Like every coded message sent by the Japanese consulate since December 1, a copy of this one was made by the manager of the RCA office in Honolulu and given to Captain Irving Mayfield of naval intelligence. These Japanese diplomatic cables were priceless intelligence. They contained obvious clues to the attack and were ungarbled originals, delivered on the day of their filing. But Mayfield had no one on his staff capable of deciphering this diplomatic code. Neither he nor Admiral Husband Kimmel, Commander in Chief Pacific Fleet, nor any Navy or Army officer on Oahu knew of the existence of Magic in Washington, which could have easily deciphered these messages, and several days too late did so. Instead, on December 5, he took this and the other Japanese consulate messages of the last several days to Commander Joseph Rochefort, who headed the naval communications intelligence unit on Oahu responsible for trying to intercept and decipher Japanese naval codes. Because Rochefort's unit was busy attempting to discover the location of the Japanese carrier groups, Yoshikawa's cables were given a low priority and assigned to Farnsley Woodward, an inexperienced young warrant officer. Neither Woodward nor anyone in Rochefort's group had any experience with the diplomatic code, so on December 5, he began the task of breaking it from scratch.

Fifty years later, the importance of the cables passing between Tokyo and the Japanese consulate in Honolulu is widely recognized. Besides giving the Japanese task force crucial information about Oahu's defenses and the ships in harbor, they provided the last, best clue that Japan was preparing a surprise attack. In his book, *And I Was There*, former fleet intelligence officer Edwin T. Layton concludes that any of Yoshikawa's cables "would, at the very least, have brought an increase in the level of alert on Oahu. Air patrols would have been stepped up, and Kimmel might well have reversed his decision not to send the battle fleet to sea."

All the incriminating cables passing between Tokyo and the Japanese consulate in Hawaii during the first week in December were intercepted and sent to Washington for deciphering by the top secret Magic program. Yet by the morning of December 7, only one had been decoded and translated; the rest sat in low-priority in boxes. And the only one that was translated, the revealing December 3 "lights" cable, was discounted as unimportant for a reason which underlines the prejudices of 1941.

The "lights" cable had been transmitted from the Honolulu consulate to Tokyo on December 3. It described an elaborate system devised by Yoshikawa's bumbling German Agent, Otto Kuehn, to signal intelligence to offshore Japanese submarines with lights placed in the dormer windows of Kuehn's beach house (although at the time he had it rented to two Army couples), stars and numbers displayed on the sail of his boat (although he did not own one), bonfires lit on high points in Maui, and radio want ads such as "Beauty Parlor Operator Wanted," and "Chicken Farm for Sale."

Although Kuehn did not know an attack was imminent, the intelligence officer in Tokyo who requested that such a code be devised did know, and had Oahu's defenders seen this cable, it almost certainly would have rung alarm bells. Being a visual system, it assumed the presence of Japanese vessels in Hawaiian waters and indicated a strong interest in the Pacific Fleet anchorage.

On December 6, unknown to Mayfield and Rochefort, the "lights" message was deciphered in Washington, and awaited only translation into English, a process that might be delayed several weeks for such "deferred" category documents. Dorothy Edgers, the only woman among the Navy Department's cryptographic section's six Japanese-English translators, chose it from a half-dozen similar intercepts. Three years later, she told a court of inquiry, "At first glance, this seemed more interesting than some of the other messages I had in my basket. I selected it and asked one of the other men who were also translators working on the other messages whether or not it shouldn't be done immediately." Edgers had been employed in the section only three weeks, but she had lived in Japan for thirty of her thirty-eight years, and held a diploma authorizing her to teach Japanese to Japanese pupils at the high school level. Yet, as a novice in the cryptographic section, she was not trusted to translate top-priority work, such as cables transmitted in the "purple" code used by the Japanese embassy in Washington.

Although Edgers was supposed to quit at noon on Saturday, and although one of her superiors said the "lights" message did not warrant any special attention and would keep until Monday, she decided the message *was* important and continued working on her translation. She showed a rough version to Commander Alwin Kramer, the chief of the section, who criticized her for staying to work on a "deferred" intercept, saying he did not think the message was of "sufficient importance." He made some trivial changes in her translation—to make it more "professional," he would later testify—and said, "This needs a lot of work, Mrs. Edgers. Why don't you run along now? We'll finish the editing sometime next week."

She protested, saying the intercept should be disseminated immediately. "You just go home, Mrs. Edgers," he replied. "We'll get back to this piece on Monday."

She stayed nonetheless, finishing the translation and giving it to the chief clerk. On December 8, it sat on Commander Kramer's desk, waiting for him to make it more "professional." Today, when you examine the "lights" message story, and the justifications Commander Kramer manufactured later to excuse himself, it seems obvious that the principal reason Edgers's suspicions were dismissed and her translation ignored was that she was a woman.

The story of how radio intelligence data from the Japanese consulate in Honolulu, such as the "lights" message, was misused in the months and days preceding Pearl Harbor is a maddening, complicated one. Historians and former officers have chronicled this saga of bad luck, and of rivalries between the Army and Navy, and between staff officers in Washington and those in Honolulu. At fault was an obsession with secrecy that kept the local commanders in Hawaii from even knowing about Magic, much less receiving crucial information from it. There was too much faith placed in technology—on the technical side of intercepting and deciphering—and too little analysis and interpretation, and too much confidence that the ability to read Japanese diplomatic correspondence would protect the United States from any surprise military action.

Less attention has been paid to the larger flaws behind these shortcomings. An obvious spy like Yoshikawa enjoyed such success largely because of the perception, shared by counterintelligence agents in Honolulu and cryptographic officers in Washington, that the staff of the Japanese consulate in Honolulu were bumbling amateurs, unable to produce valuable intelligence. Although in 1941 the government had closed all German and Italian consulates, Japanese consulates everywhere were permitted to remain open. Appeasement was partly responsible for this, since it was feared closing these consulates would upset Japanese-American negotiations, but so was the delusion that Japanese diplomats were harmless. German spies were assumed to be efficient and dangerous, but Japanese spies had the image of being small, bespectacled, easily identified, and slightly ridiculous.

There is no written evidence of anyone suspecting Yoshikawa of being a spy. No file was opened on him, and he was never named by intelligence officials testifying at the nine Pearl Harbor investigations. Yet forty years later, J. Harold Hughes, an FBI agent at the time of the attack, would claim, "We all knew he was a spy." Hughes said he had broken silence because "I'm just so tired of reading this kind of story about 'Master Spy' Yoshikawa. It just isn't so, by dang." He also declared the FBI had spotted Lieutenant Commander Suzuki when he arrived on the *Taiyo Maru*, although there is again no evidence to confirm this. Hughes argued that none of Yoshikawa's information "had any bearing on the attack," and that there had been no great change in Yoshikawa's routine in the last week indicating the attack was coming, statements that are both contradicted by every known fact.

Another formal naval intelligence officer, Don Woodrum, told me Yoshikawa's spying had not mattered much because "he collected mostly negative information, such as that there weren't any sub nets, or any long-range reconnaissance on weekends. People were suspicious of him, but suppose he had been followed, what would you really have seen?"

Yoshikawa might have been caught had counterintelligence agents employed Japanese-Americans as informers. Many local Japanese worked as cooks, secretaries, and drivers in the consulate, where Yoshikawa's erratic habits, lack of official duties, and interest in intelligence gathering were widely known. In hearings convened a month after the attack, Navy intelligence chief Mayfield said, "It has been my experience, [with] which I believe the other two investigative agencies [the FBI and Army] agree, that to investigate a Japanese is exceedingly difficult and can really only be done by another Japanese." Yet when asked, "Aren't there amongst those American-Japanese some persons whom you could trust as American agents?" Mayfield answered, "I have not found one."

The FBI had only one Japanese-American staff member, and he was a translator. Yet the FBI agent in charge of the Honolulu office, Robert Shivers, admitted being unable to gather information about Japanese activities from Caucasian sources. He had tried, even making a tour of the islands and asking Caucasian businessmen and plantation managers about the Japanese. "I got just about as many different answers as the number of people I talked to," he said. "So far as I could learn the haole [Caucasian] populace in Hawaii was not in a position to give any accurate information about the Japanese populace [since] there had been very little intercourse between the two. . . . To a large extent the average haole does not know . . . the Japanese mind, and for that reason he did not know what was going on within the inner circles of the Japanese community."

Yoshikawa's task was also made easier by the military's obsession with the loyalty of the local Japanese. A month after the attack, Admiral Reeves of the Roberts Commission asked a young naval intelligence officer named George Kimball, "Is it possible, then, that both the Navy and the FBI may [have] concentrate[d] on subversive activities among the Japanese populace and have both overlooked the espionage activity?"

"I think there has been that tendency," Kimball admitted. "The FBI called that internal security, to go after people . . . who were strongly pro-Tokyo who perhaps would be dangerous in the event of a war. . . . Of course, a good Japanese agent is not going to be actively pro-Japanese and offensively so. So, I think perhaps they may have overlooked some of the most important ones. . . ."

And in 1943, Captain Mayfield conceded, "The type of investigation indulged in was well suited for the purposes of internal security, that is, determining whether certain persons in wartime would likely be loyal to or sympathize with the cause of, or give to, nations at war with the United States. It was not suitable for counterespionage purposes."

In the last days before Pearl Harbor, instead of searching for Japanese spies by staking out obvious Pearl Harbor observation points, such as Pearl City and Aiea Heights, counterintelligence was preoccupied with the question of who among

Hawaii's 160,000 residents of Japanese ancestry should be detained in the event of war. FBI agents composed elaborate organization charts showing connections between Japanese religious, social, business, and educational groups and the Japanese consulate. They listed every Japanese-controlled corporation and trade organization and named all the Japanese consular agents, language school principals, Shinto priests, and staff members of the Japanese consulate, omitting only Vice-Consul Tadashi Morimura.

In late November 1941, Army intelligence officers and FBI agents spent weeks compiling lists of potential detainees—German and Italian aliens, and "residents of the Territory of Japanese descent, all of whom would be considered dangerous to the security of the islands under certain circumstances." An Army intelligence report boasted, "Representatives of this office and the FBI carefully scrutinized the list of Japanese residents," concluding that fifteen hundred posed a potential security threat. These were divided into an "A" group of five hundred believed dangerous to the internal security of the United States," and a "B" list of "doubtful" loyalty, who would be kept under tight surveillance.

Lieutenant Colonel George Bicknell of Army intelligence reported that during November, "individual investigations of persons suspected to be dangerous to security were intensified with all available trained personnel being assigned to this highly important requirement." Right up until December 7, counter-intelligence agents worked twelve and fourteen hours a day, seven days a week, checking the addresses of targeted detainees. They prepared small maps showing the exact location of their rural residences, even making arrangements to cut telephone service to their homes so they could not warn friends, and to stage riot squads at key intersections on the assumption other Japanese might attempt to set them free. On November 23 and 30, agents made a "reconnaissance" of detainees' homes, familiarizing themselves with their neighborhoods, and according to an Army report, "Detailed instructions were drawn up for each squad, including the most minute details. . . ." The detainee lists were revised for the last time on December 1, then forwarded to the chiefs of military intelligence and the FBI on December 4, just before Ensign Yoshikawa embarked on his last weekend of espionage.

3

George Akita Delivers a Speech

IN THE DAYS BEFORE PEARL HARBOR, NO ONE WAS MORE CON-
cerned with what "Americanism" was and how it could be
attained than young Japanese-Americans, so it is not surprising
that a fifteen-year-old Japanese student at Farrington High
School named George Akita should win the ten-dollar first prize
in the fourth annual speech contest of the Aloha chapter of the
Daughters of the American Revolution (DAR), held at seven-
thirty on the evening of December 5 in the McKinley High
School auditorium. The contest's theme was "Americanism," a
word that now sounds dated but that was no joke in 1941 for
Japanese-Americans wishing to prove their loyalty. It was not
enough, they knew, to vote, pay taxes, serve in the Army, and
observe patriotic holidays. "Americanism" was also required,
which, like every "ism," was an all-encompassing way of living
and thinking, reflecting a knowledge of American history and
geography and a taste for approved books, movies, and sports.

The theme of Akita's prize-winning speech was "American
Citizenship and National Defense," and it ended, "From tropical Hawaii to the rock-bound shores of Maine, from the snow-
clad plains of the Dakotas to sunny Texas, let us, Americans

all, rally around the Stars and Stripes in the defense of our way of life. With the love of democracy burning in our hearts and minds, we cannot fail—we must not fail."

Did he really believe this? Did he really think he was an American like any other? Apparently he did, if the following description of December 7 from his diary is any proof: "Planning to stay at Central [the school where he was assigned as a student civil defense volunteer] tonight. Mom didn't want me to go. She was afraid. Pop told her that no matter how young I am since I was a citizen of America I have to help America whenever I am able to. Even to die for America. I like his attitude. . . . I guess we Japanese are in for it now. Especially Mom and Pop, they're aliens. But the U.S. Government has promised not to molest the nationals unless they by their actions and deeds make themselves detrimental. I have faith in the U.S. Government."

It is enough to make you cry. Like most Japanese residents of Hawaii, Akita and his parents were not interned, but 110,000 mainland Japanese were, and on December 5, many of them must have believed in "Americanism" as fervently as he did.

It is possible he won the DAR contest fairly (the year before he had won the *Honolulu Star-Bulletin* oratory contest on the Constitution), and that his speech was better than "What Is Americanism?" by Christine Weatherby, or ""Americanism Marches Onward" by Irene Makaiau, or Peggy Engstrom's "I Am an American." But it is also possible that he won (and that Tereu Masatsugu won second place with "A United America") because in these final months of 1941, the DAR judges were as obsessed as the military with the loyalty of Hawaii's Japanese, and believed it their patriotic duty to encourage it.

In considering the dilemma of young Japanese-Americans like Akita, it is useful to recall how, just forty years earlier, Honolulu's electric trolley cars caused an epidemic of broken

bones among Japanese customers, who, after forgetting to press
the stop button, departed with several traditional, deep-bowed
alohas, grandly stepping off backward into space. Such acci-
dents were so commonplace the Rapid Transit Company
mounted a public education program directed at the Japanese.
But by 1941, transit company officials and passengers could be
heard complaining about the loud conversation and boisterous
manners of the children and grandchildren of those overly cour-
teous trolley departees. And it was also possible to see, riding
the city's new electric buses, children shushing parents who
dared speak Japanese in public, and looking embarrassed if
their parents made a "deep-bowed aloha" or engaged in any
display considered too "Japanesy."

By 1941, the distance between the first and second generation of Japanese immigrants had become greater than even the
usual wide gap America drives between immigrant parents and
their offspring. The issei—first-generation immigrants—were
still Japanese citizens, prevented from becoming American by
discriminatory laws, while the nisei—second generation
immigrants—had American citizenship, or were dual citizens
but almost wholly American in their attitudes. The issei wanted
their children to study Japanese, follow traditional codes of
etiquette and familial piety, and adopt the Yamato spirit, which
taught loyalty to the Emperor and the uniqueness of the Japanese people, values the nisei found inimical to their crash program of "Americanization." The issei spoke English poorly, if
at all, while the nisei spoke Japanese poorly, forcing many
families to communicate in pidgin. Children slept on beds while
their parents used futons, sat in chairs while their parents rested
on zabutons, and used American dressers while their parents'
kyodis stood in another corner of the room. Some issei parents
encouraged the Americanization of their children, believing
they should adopt the customs of their country of residence,
but the parents were often appalled at the results. They spent

holidays alone while their children attended school dances; they heard sons adopt American slang and saw daughters holding hands with boys who called them "sweetheart."

The determination of the nisei to "Americanize" themselves now seems touching and quaint, but soon it would make a difference between freedom and imprisonment. In the winter of 1942, "loyalty hearing boards," set up to determine which Japanese internees should be released, favored those who demonstrated "unbridled Americanism." The boards seemed unable to define what this was, but they knew what it was not—anything smacking of Japan. "Are you truly an American citizen, or are you partly loyal to Japan?" one board member asked a detainee. "It seems by reason of the fact you act Japanese, and you have all the habits and customs of the Japanese indicates you are not wholeheartedly American."

Other ethnic groups in Hawaii also judged the Japanese by the extent of their assimilation, considering the retention of any Japanese customs as prima facie evidence of disloyalty. An essay written by an Army wife for the War Records Depository at the University of Hawaii is a good reflection of this loathing for anything Japanese: "Above, little silver planes dodged out antiaircraft fire. Even my gentle Hawaiian friends cheered the puffs as they neared those fiendish little silver emissaries of Hirohito. Even these Polynesians, the most loving of all peoples, have not learned to love their Japanese neighbors. The polite Japanese smiles had long ago been learned to be nothing more than masks of deceit in many cases. They had come to the islands years ago, these people of Nippon, but most of them still slept on their wooden pillows, wore their colorful but awkward kimonos, ate their rice and drank their sake wine, read their Japanese newspapers and sent their children to long hours of language school. . . . Yes, they had remained a thing apart; they did not know the meaning of assimilation, and here was eloquent proof."

Imagine the obstacles niseis like George Akita faced in trying to prove their Americanism. Here they were, living in great numbers among servicemen sent to defend Oahu against an enemy looking exactly like them. No matter how many patriotic speeches they gave, rallies they attended, or hours they spent becoming civil defense wardens, they were still suspected of disloyalty.

The Japanese of Hawaii had once been encouraged to raise hogs, a job other races scorned as demeaning, causing them to branch into collecting garbage to find scraps to feed their animals. Yet by 1941, they were accused of using this enterprise as an excuse to rummage through the refuse of military families, looking for discarded national secrets. They were criticized for being clannish and shirking the responsibilities of American citizenship, yet if they ran for public office they were denounced for trying to colonize Hawaii for Japan. They were attacked for not becoming more assimilated, yet many plantations encouraged the erection of Shinto temples and subsidized the entertainment of visiting Japanese priests, dignitaries, and military officials as a way of improving the morale and productivity of their laborers. Meanwhile, the Hawaii Visitors Bureau promoted the preservation of Japanese dress and customs as a quaint "attraction," and the same haole housewives who feared being poisoned by their Japanese servants took lessons in flower arranging, decorated their walls with Japanese prints, and encouraged their maids to wear kimonos.

In 1941, one's opinion of the loyalty of Japanese residents depended more on race, money, and politics than on objective fact. Supporters of Hawaiian statehood depicted them as red-blooded Americans; opponents described them as untrustworthy aliens who might "take over" the state. A haole with pleasant relations with his Japanese servants might argue for their loyalty, while Koreans or Chinese, whose homelands had been occupied by Japan, were convinced of their treachery.

Plantation owners claimed 99 percent of their Japanese laborers were loyal, but Navy and Army officers argued that left sixteen hundred potential saboteurs and fifth columnists.

So strong and so accepted was the dislike of the Japanese in Hawaii that even those who defended their loyalty sometimes felt compelled to express their distaste for the Japanese as a people. Thus a retired general who described them as "law-abiding and quiet, and industrious and provident and thrifty and not quarrelsome" to the Army Pearl Harbor Board added, "They are not very pretty to look at." And the author of "Our Hawaii Is Absolutely American" in the December 1939 issue of *Paradise of the Pacific* qualified his praise for their loyalty by saying, "Now I wish to deny emphatically that I am holding a brief for the Japanese. My natural bias is rather against that race."

The Japanese knew summary conclusions about them were wrong, and that supporters or detractors could easily find individuals to prove their prejudices. They knew of splits in their community invisible to outsiders: antagonism between Okinawan and mainland Japanese, and between recent immigrants who considered themselves more cultured and the pidgin-speaking kamaaina Japanese. They knew that while many nisei had joined the ROTC at the University of Hawaii, others had returned to Japan for college, where they were drafted into the army; that while most niseis were loyal, some had been embittered by racial discrimination; and that while many issei were loyal to the Emperor, others felt little attachment to Japan and, if it had been possible, would have become citizens.

Despite these divisions, and despite the confusing signals from Caucasian Hawaiians, the Japanese of George Akita's generation tried to prove their "Americanism" in ways now seeming fanatical, and heartbreaking. In the months preceding Pearl Harbor, their efforts gained intensity. Japanese youths joined the Army in numbers exceeding their proportion of the

population, and at the 1941 Armistice Day parade, the Ha-
waiian-Japanese Civic Association contributed the most impressive display of all, a float carrying grim-faced AJA (Americans
of Japanese ancestry) soldiers from Territorial Guard in World
War One uniforms, standing against a background of machine
guns, trenches, a no-man's-land of dirt, and a banner saying,
"We Did It in '17, We'll Do It Again." Another Japanese-
American civic group sponsored a patriotic rally advertised as
a "unique outdoor ceremony in which children of all races
unite in demonstration of their Americanism." Japanese leaders
formed a Committee for Inter-Racial Unity in Hawaii to advise
the FBI how to maintain racial harmony in the event of war and
sponsored an annual New Americans Conference, which met
for six days in July 1941 in the Honolulu YMCA, passing
resolutions calling on AJAs to renounce their dual national
status, announcing, "We Americans do hereby most solemnly
pledge and reaffirm our undivided allegiance and loyalty to the
United States of America," and issuing a report full of slogans
such as "Sincere Loyalty Is the Keynote" and "Find a True
Man and Know True America."

Throughout 1940 and 1941, individual Japanese proclaimed their loyalty and "Americanism" in numerous public
letters and articles. Miss Anne Kuaoka wrote an essay, "No
Less American," which ended with this pathetic sentence: "It is
deplorable to have enemies of these fair islands bear malice
against this racial group [the Japanese] which is so sincere in its
multitudinous endeavors to live up to the standards of its white
brothers."

A Japanese-American reporter for the *Honolulu Star-
Bulletin* named Lawrence Nakatsuka wrote a twenty-part series examining problems faced by young Japanese in Honolulu
and exhorting them to become better Americans. "There are
many American-Japanese who are not worthy citizens of this
country," he said. "They have failed to prove to other Ameri-

cans by actions and words that they are truly trustworthy coun-trymen." He urged Japanese to avoid Japanese clubs and "learn to associate more freely with other nationalities." He told ad-miring stories about Japanese-Americans, like "Hazel the shop-girl," who were "positive and aggressive in their stand as American citizens." He raged against the public use of Japa-nese, saying he had been "embarrassed and infuriated on many occasions when the first-generation Japanese, in public places, have used Japanese indiscriminately," and advising his readers "to use the Japanese language only when it is necessary and one is positive other Americans won't be slighted or made suspi-cious." He cautioned his generation against being overly influ-enced by their parents, saying that "too many Hawaiian-born Japanese are dominated by their parents, who are 'dyed in the wool' Japanese nationals."

For niseis such as Nakatsuka and Akita, the days before Pearl Harbor were a precarious time when they were struggling to convince haoles of their "Americanism" while battling their parents over their abandonment of Japanese culture. The at-tack would catch them at a bad moment, suspended between the Japanese customs they had rejected and an America that still rejected them. The tricky position they found themselves in on December 7 explains much of what happened later, and why in 1991 many felt compelled, out of habit or because Japan was again making things difficult for them, to prove their "Americanism" all over again.

4

From Walter Dillingham's Window

A NEWSPAPERMAN VISITING HONOLULU IN 1893 REPORTED more of its citizens wearing evening dress than in any other American city. A half century later, this was still the custom, so it was not surprising that the evenings of December 5 and 6 should find Walter Dillingham wearing a dinner jacket. After all, as he told me, his family was so prominent that when President Roosevelt visited Hawaii in 1936, the only man he cared to meet was Dillingham's father. The airport was named for his mother's cousin, Commander John Rodgers, the first man to fly to Hawaii from the mainland. And when the Prince of Wales visited Hawaii, he borrowed Dillingham's polo clothes. "My claim to fame," he said, "is that the Prince of Wales wore my polo helmet and breeches."

He cannot remember why he wore a dinner jacket on December 5, but he knows on December 6 he attended a party at the north shore plantation town of Haleiwa. He had been living there all week, because he was a reserve officer in the Army Air Corps and his pursuit squadron had been engaged in two weeks of gunnery practice at the Haleiwa airstrip. He brought dinner clothes to these exercises because, he says, "in those days if you were going anywhere you always wore a tuxedo." Nowadays almost no one in Honolulu, including members of families like the Dillinghams, wears a tuxedo very much, and the city has gone from being one of the most formal—as colonial outposts always have been—to the most casual place in the nation. Fewer than a half-dozen restaurants require a tie, senior executives and attorneys come to work in aloha shirts, and even funeral notices specify "aloha wear."

When I met Dillingham, I discovered there was no better place from which to appreciate how Honolulu has changed since 1941 than his sixteenth-floor office at 1750 Kalakaua Avenue. This is a shimmering blue skyscraper across the Ala Wai canal from Waikiki, one of many buildings that by deflecting trade winds and heating the atmosphere have made its own central air conditioning essential. Dillingham's office was determinedly old-fashioned, a reproach to everything outside its windows. There was an ancient manual typewriter, a dusty globe, stacks of old newspapers, and the tax files of a partner who had committed suicide. Because Dillingham disliked air conditioning, the room was boiling hot.

The effect was disorienting. I sat perspiring and surrounded by the furnishings and clutter of forty years earlier, while through an open window I saw modern Waikiki, a neighborhood largely shaped by Dillingham's ancestors and now largely owned by the Japanese. Before his family's company, Hawaiian Dredging, reclaimed Waikiki in the 1920s, 85 percent had been a waterland of duck ponds, rice paddies, and taro patches. Now I saw hotel skyscrapers, and the multilevel Ala Moana Shopping center, originally developed by the Dillinghams and the largest in the world when it opened in 1959. Although much of what Walter Dillingham saw from his windows resulted from the labors of other Dillinghams, the view did not please him. "Too many people, too many buildings, too many cars," he said. "We need a moratorium on the number of new cars that can be licensed on this island, and I wouldn't want to see any more development either. If we have more places for people to sleep, where are they going to find room to walk on the street? Oh, Jesus, it's terrible. . . . I liked it better in the old days when you got dressed up in a tuxedo to go to the Royal Hawaiian."

As I listened to him tell how the first wave Japanese bombers rocked the house in Hickam Field where he had recently lain sleeping in his rumpled tuxedo, I tried imagining Honolulu as he did, forever comparing the prewar city to its present incarnation. From his office, Honolulu appeared now to be an American city like any other, where anything, good or bad, might happen. But as I listened to what he and others remembered of 1941 Hawaii, I began realizing it must have been difficult for them to imagine anything bad happening in a place so beautiful, and that if there was ever a "fifth column," undermining Hawaii's defense, then that fifth column was Hawaii herself.

Because the Islands have changed so much, it is easy to overlook how their beauty unhinged the purpose of their defenders. Headlines may have said, "Japan Prepared to Strike Over Weekend," and cables from the Navy Department may have declared, "This dispatch is to be considered a war warning," but when their recipients looked out windows and up from breakfast tables, they saw paradise.

They rose to soft, flower-scented breezes, and the kind of morning that promises renewal. They ate papaya or mango from backyard trees, and took cool showers, because in this climate—perhaps the world's most perfect—many houses lacked water heaters. On weekends, women dressed in loose-fitting muumuus or, because Japanese fashion and culture were admired, kimonos. Men wore aloha shirts, a recent invention of a local Japanese tailor, who made them from the colorful silk fabrics used for children's clothing in Japan. On weekdays people worked in the mornings and relaxed in the afternoons. After the attack, a captain commanding a field artillery battery at Schofield Barracks told the Army board of inquiry, "Because it was in the tropics we did very little work in the afternoon. It was just the opposite of a warlike attitude."

Almost everyone woke smelling and seeing flowers. Hedges of hibiscus and morning glory flowered underneath jacaranda and poinciana trees. Cut flowers decorated parlors and bedrooms. Crimson and white oleanders were so fragrant they stopped pedestrians in their tracks. Lavender blossoms fell from shower trees, carpeting streets and lawns. Orchids bloomed in ramshackle hothouses, or in coconut shells hanging from backyard monkey pods. Purple and rose-colored bougainvillea climbed over stone walls and blanketed houses, making them appear to be in flames.

Imagine Oahu without the roar of the Lunalilo Freeway, without glittering jets, buzzing jet skis, or carpets of roofs covering mountain slopes. Imagine a low-rise little city buried under palms, banyans, and flowering shrubs, with little to distract the eye from the lurid green cane fields or volcanic cliffs eroded by rain and wind into fantastic folds, like some thick, velvety curtain.

On the mornings of December 5 and 6, as on most mornings, trade winds blew strong across Oahu, bringing the landscape alive—rippling cane fields, shaking palm fronds, and stirring up surf. The sky was clear, the light sharp, and the air fresh. In the afternoon, clouds piled up across the Koolaus, releasing gentle showers that threw up rainbows and drifted on wind currents down the Nuuanu Valley, falling from a clear sky on Honolulu streets, so predictably that trolley stops were known as "first shower," "second shower," and "third shower" stops.

In 1941, Honolulu was a pleasant and prosperous city. The Depression had left it largely untouched, and a defense boom was making it rich. Gardens and foliage planted at the turn of the century had matured and grown, and palm trees towered over telephone and electric poles, creating tunnels of unbroken shade. Regulations prohibiting outdoor billboards and posters were so strict that Libby could not even write its name on the outside of its pineapple cannery. The less attractive necessities of urban life, the factories, pumping station, electric plant, and piers, were confined to a circle a mile and a half from City Hall. The largest buildings were the fine Greek Revival office buildings, the airy, superbly designed public schools, and the sturdy white Congregational churches, set on lawns resembling New England greens. The homes of wealthy haoles were unpretentious, and according to one traveler, even the poorest neighborhoods resembled "slums that have wandered off into a garden."

In 1941, there was not a single practicing psychiatrist in Hawaii—the profession was apparently considered unnecessary in paradise. Crimes were infrequent and minor. A front-page newspaper story appearing after Thanksgiving 1941 titled "Crimes Keep Police Busy over Holiday" described a "crime wave" consisting of a stolen car, a man pummeled by sailors in a street brawl, an attempted suicide with a pocketknife, the theft of a piggy bank, and the theft of bananas from Mr. Issya Tanimoto's front-yard tree.

Oahu was still rural, a place of taro patches and stray pigs, sugar camps and empty beaches where Hawaiians netted fish. An airman stationed at Wheeler Field saw pineapples and pink mountain ranges. A sailor looking north from a battleship moored in Pearl Harbor saw watercress fields, boys with fishing poles, and a rattletrap sugar mill; looking east, he saw the naval base, a reassuring world of perfect green lawns and officers with white gloves and calling cards making social rounds.

In 1941, people were already complaining that Waikiki was "ruined" and "overbuilt," a "honky-tonk" without charm.

A 1940 article in *Fortune* magazine said local residents "contemptuously stay away from the visitor's compound around Waikiki." But since the Ala Wai drainage canal, which had transformed Waikiki from marshland to resort, had only been completed in 1928, it might be more accurate to say that during these last prewar months, Waikiki was at its best, nicely balanced between the smelly backwater it had been and the skyscraper resort of hookers, time-share barkers, and bewildered Japanese honeymooners it would become. It was still slightly bohemian, with room for bungalows and fishermen's shacks, picket fences, and vacant lots. There were no traffic lights, every cottage had a garden or lawn, and it was quiet. In the evening, you heard strolling musicians, surf, and the clang of a trolley; in the morning, a muffled radio, the clink of milk bottles, and a distant car. Palm trees leaned at crazy angles over flowered lanes, and traffic detoured around banyans permitted to grow in the middle of a highway. From the air, it appeared to be a carpet of trees, occasionally broken by a peaked roof. From the sea, it resembled a coconut plantation sprinkled with hotels.

The biggest hotels in Waikiki were the stately Ala Moana and the flashy Royal Hawaiian, soon to become a symbol of "Old Hawaii," even though its art was French, its cherubs Italian, its carpets from Tunisia and Trenton, and its Moorish architecture inspired by Valentino's *The Sheik*. The only cinema in Waikiki had clouds floating across its ceiling, imitation palms planted along walls, and murals depicting scenes from Hawaiian history. Patrons wore dinner jackets, and the souvenir program from its 1936 opening proclaimed that its "sheer beauty" was "a complement to all Hawaii."

In 1941, Honolulu was still a city where people advertised for a "Hawaiian yard boy who can sing, dance, and play the guitar," taxi drivers used call boxes attached to palm trees, and you requested a favorite driver by name. It was a city where at eight o'clock, a siren ordered minors off the streets; where beachboys had names like Hankshaw, Steamboat, Panama, and Tough Bill, but played the ukulele and tucked hibiscus blossoms behind their ears; where policemen sometimes wore leis and sat on high stools under umbrellas, waving at friends as they pulled "Stop" and "Go" levers; and where Pete, the famous "Hula Cop," who directed traffic with the arm motions of a hula dancer, was honored by a downtown plaque thanking him for having "smiled his way into the hearts of the people." The most serious civic nuisances were a lack of shade trees along Kalakaua Avenue and bad-mannered children on the trolley buses. Politicians wore white suits and panama hats, and promised the moon in several languages. Hostesses descended from early missionaries served Hawaiian food on their best china, used ti leaves as tablecloths, and sang the doxology before dinner.

Despite its huge military installations, defense workers, and servicemen, it was a peaceful and quiet city, compared to those on the mainland, and deserving of its 1941 advertising slogan—"A World of Happiness in an Ocean of Peace." On December 5, posters bearing that slogan decorated hotels, travel agencies, and restaurants. They showed native Hawaiians dressed in flower capes and leis, and said, "You can pin a definition on the peace of Hawaii. It is tangible, universally desired, even though almost universally discarded elsewhere. It explains in one word the overwhelming trend to Hawaii. Here life is lived as it was meant to be lived, happily, close to flowers and warm surf." And, no doubt, they reassured Hawaiians that here, on these remote islands, they were safe.

Honolulu's small-town customs also made war seem impossible. Doors were so seldom locked that house keys had been lost years ago, a fact reflected in the title of the first Charlie Chan mystery, *House Without a Key*. At bars and parties, people entertained themselves by singing. The piano was popular. Children gave recitals, and servicemen played in hotel parlors, for the fun of it. People believed in "being a good American," and men spoke the language of the country club locker room. Listen to how Walter Dillingham's uncle expressed himself to the Army board investigating the Pearl Harbor attack: "I didn't like the cut of his jib"; "Well, golly, I said to myself, if there is anything in God's world I can do . . ."; "I think he is a clean-cut, straightforward, hard-hitting man."

Young people were relatively chaste. "People then just did not go around jumping in and out of one another's beds," the descendant of an old missionary family told me. The young women "were virgins when they were married, and now in rehashing our lives, so many of us seem to comment on how incredibly pure we were, and how the boys didn't expect a lot and make it difficult. It just wasn't something you did."

But Honolulu was not a perfect paradise, not Eden on the eve of destruction. By December of 1941, it was already suspended between its past and future, changing in ways that would leave it resembling mainland cities. You could already see, all at once, what it had been, and would become: see its easygoing past coexisting nervously with the housing shortages, traffic jams, and suburbanization caused by the defense boom. By December 1941, this boom had increased the population 10 percent in a single year, while construction expenditures had risen tenfold in two years. Retail sales were up by a half, sixty new trolley buses were running on seven new lines, and the boys who once dived for quarters off passenger liners earned twenty dollars a day in Pearl Harbor's workshops. The new wealth and hustle was reflected in crowded sidewalks, shopping districts spreading into residential suburbs, and a fad for speedy weddings. The liners were bringing so many fiancées of servicemen and construction workers that a competition arose to see who could marry the fastest on arrival. The record holder, a Mr. Jack Doolittle, boarded the *Lurline* on the pilot boat and upon landing rushed Verona Merrill of Arizona to the license bureau, completing the formalities within a half hour.

The changes in Honolulu were most evident to kamaainas returning after a long absence. Patricia Morgan, a college student coming home in July 1941 after a year away, noticed, "The air seemed charged with activity: the slow Hawaiian tempo had speeded up. As we drove through town there were more cars, traffic was thicker . . . many more soldiers and sailors were in the streets than I have ever seen in Honolulu before. There were new grills, new cafés, new dance halls, new stores. . . . The people in the street look different, the buildings are new, the smoke of industry is heavier in the Hawaiian sky. Still, the old Honolulu is here, and the combination of carefree Hawaii and mainland efficiency is far from uninteresting."

By tradition, most kamaainas greeted every change and wave of immigrants with dismay, insisting the "best" time for Hawaii had been ten, twenty, or thirty years earlier, just like the "old-timer" in the 1925 *The House Without a Key,* who complained, "I knew Honolulu in the glamorous days of its isolation, and I've watched it fade into a . . . copy of Babbitt-ville, USA. The waterfront's just a waterfront now—but once, my boy! Once it oozed romance at every pore."

In 1941, most kamaainas disliked the changes brought by the defense boom. An editorial in the December 1941 *Paradise of the Pacific* said, "Old landmarks are disappearing. There is a faster tempo in the business community. . . . The number of traffic mortalities is appalling. The kamaaina sees few of the old faces. . . . It was not like that ten years ago—five years ago." Another article complained of "thousands of men and women, new to Hawaii, new to the life of Hawaii," who had "swarmed" into the city, bringing with them "the Mainland's rush and crush, hurry and bustle," and concluded, "The old . . . has gone, never to return."

But even the booming economy could not change Hawaii's

reassuring geographical isolation. Those arriving from the West Coast had traveled almost five days by liner across empty ocean, without sighting island or reef. Those who came on the Pan Am Clipper had been aloft for fifteen hours over an ocean marked only by cloud shadows. Despite this isolation, Caucasian Hawaiians took a keen interest in the war in Europe—instead of the closer one in China—and had founded a British War Relief Society, which raised funds, rolled bandages, and collected Christmas presents for bombed-out British children. The same front page of the *Honolulu Star-Bulletin* that reported Navy Secretary Frank Knox declaring that the Orient was "a vast powder keg potentially ready to explode with a roar that will be heard across the Pacific" also featured a photograph of a local debutante holding chrysanthemums to be used as decorations for the British War Relief Ball. One local matron, a Mrs. Philip Kahala, adopted a European refugee dog, a German shepherd going by the name of Kenos von der Misenger who was said to crawl under a bed at the sound of "Hitler" and had been sentenced to death by Nazi authorities in Denmark for eating too much. At a time when Jewish refugees found it difficult to enter the United States, he was shipped halfway around the world at Mrs. Kahala's expense.

Hawaii was reminded of the European war by newsreels, freighters from the Middle East that arrived marked by shrapnel, and passengers on the Pan Am Clipper. Almost every day one of these planes brought celebrities, diplomats, and generals from the West Coast or the Orient. On November 12, Japan's new special envoy to Washington, Saburu Kurusu (who would be meeting with Secretary of State Cordell Hull as Japanese planes returned to their carriers on December 7), arrived in Honolulu on a Clipper en route to Washington. He was met by a crowd of journalists and dignitaries, but became so flustered he fled into the ladies' room and gave a news conference there. His comments were bland, but afterward one of his fellow

Clipper passenger revealed, "Kurusu appears to have little hope for an amicable settlement of the issues." Also stopping on the Clipper was the Soviet Union's new ambassador to Washington, Maxim Litvinov. He arrived on December 4, went into seclusion in his hotel room, refused a dinner in his honor by the Chamber of Commerce, and would say only, "I am happy to be in your beautiful islands." (Years later, it was suggested that Stalin, and perhaps Litvinov too, knew of Japanese war plans, so perhaps there was more than fatigue behind his refusal to meet anyone.) One journalist saw the shadow of war in his shabby suit and unglossed shoes, but like all reminders of war brought on by the Clipper, it departed Honolulu the next morning.

The wars in Europe and China reinforced Hawaii's complacency by sending it refugees and expatriates whose very presence confirmed the Islands' status among the world's safe places. Suddenly there were European playboys who kept pet chimpanzees and banded together into a motorcycle gang, a princess who worked as a taxi dancer, and counts with dubious titles. Many worked as chefs and waiters in the hotels, or survived on small remittances funneled through Hong Kong banks.

Hawaii's physical isolation was matched by a cultural one that, for all the territory's flag-waving, made it seem an exceptional place, not quite American and existing almost outside time. Hawaii had its own singular obsession with flowers, which had originated with native Hawaiians, been adopted by other races, and found its most feverish expression on Lei Day, when leis decorated everything from car radiators to the straw hats of Japanese gardeners.

Hawaii had its own peculiar history. A half century earlier, before American sugar planters engineered a coup leading to its annexation as a United States Territory, it had been a Polynesian kingdom, and evidence of the toppled monarchy was still visible. Elderly Hawaiian men sweeping grass in front of the

Iolani Palace, now the office of the territorial governor, ha
performed this service for King Kalakaua and Queen Liliuokalani. A Hawaiian employee of the Sans Souci Hotel could
not be broken of the habit of removing his hat, standing at
attention, and shouting "Ka moi! Ka moi!"—The king! The
king!—whenever Governor Poindexter made an appearance.
Only ten years earlier in 1931, the daughter of Hawaii's de-
posed queen, Princess Kawananakoa, had thrown a luau for
the visiting king and queen of Thailand. According to the
Honolulu Advertiser, "The pomp and pageantry of a fallen
kingdom was displayed in all its panoply . . . in a colorful
reproduction of an ancient Hawaiian court. . . . Arriving guests
found 18 stalwart Hawaiian youths wearing red capes and
malos and bearing spears like the young warriors of old, lining
the driveway to the house. They stood beside flaming torches
which lighted up the grounds. . . . The Princess was a striking
figure in a black lace *holoku* with gorgeous feather lei. . . .
Softly muted music filled the beautiful home throughout the
evening." (In 1960, the grandson of this Thai king visited
Honolulu. None of the descendants of the monarchy was invited to the dinner given in his honor by Hawaii's governor at
Washington Place, the former home of Queen Liliuokalani, and
the evening's entertainment was furnished by the Dixie Cats
Jazz Band.)

In 1941, native Hawaiians had no political or economic
power. Their culture—which has since seen a revival—was de-
caying, their language lost, and their lands expropriated. They
lived on the margins and in the shadows of Hawaiian society,
comforted by their large families and wrapped in nostalgia for
a romanticized past. Even their music had been stolen by haole
artists and turned into hapa-haole (half-haole) ditties like "The
Cockeyed Mayor of Kauanakakai" and "When Hilo Hattie
Does the Hilo Hop." Their dance, the hula, had been subjected
to attacks by missionary families as late as the 1920s, with

itor denouncing it as a "vile obscenity" and the
ɔnolulu *Advertiser* condemning it as represent-
ʌsness of old Hawaii" and promising to "wipe
ɪe hula] . . . from the fair name of Hawaii."
ɒut by 1941, the hula was one of many Hawaiian customs
that, with the encouragement of the "visitor industry," had
been adopted, and sometimes trivialized, by the Islands' other
racial communities. Native Hawaiians may have lived on society's margins, but their customs still exerted influence on Hawaii's atmosphere. No custom had more influence than the
spirit of "aloha," the Polynesian tradition of friendliness and
generosity. As "aloha" spread to other ethnic groups, through
intermarriage and its promotion by the tourist industry, it also
came to connote a certain *mañana* attitude. In this bastardized
form it was absorbed by newcomers in the military services,
encouraging the postponement of unpleasant tasks and decisions and further convincing them that nothing bad could happen on these relaxed and beautiful islands.

PART TWO

December 6, 1941

5

Omens Are Seen

SOME REMEMBER DECEMBER 6, 1941, AS A LATE-AUTUMN SATUR-day like any other, when Honolulu was preoccupied with Christmas and football. Because of Hawaii's climate and Asian population, Christmas had always been less celebrated than on the mainland. Wreaths were fashioned from cellophane, tinsel looped through backyard trees, and many street-corner Santas were Japanese. But in 1941, homesick defense workers and servicemen insisted on a more traditional, and commercial, Christmas, and so gaily wrapped presents hung from palm trees in the Sears Roebuck parking lot, a canopy of colored bulbs had been strung over Fort Street, and, on the last Sunday before the Japanese attack, at the same time the *Honolulu Advertiser* was warning, "JAPANESE MAY STRIKE [in Asia] OVER THE WEEK-END," it was also sponsoring the arrival of Santa Claus. He circled the city in one of the silvery planes of the 86th Observation Squadron, before landing in Kapiolani Park to the screams of three thousand spectators, leading to the *Advertiser* to conclude that "an all around richer Honolulu . . . [is] ready for the merriest Christmas on record."

On the afternoon of December 6, 10 percent of the city's

population of 250,000 packed Honolulu stadium to watch
the University of Hawaii play the Willamette Bearcats. Civilian and military authorities saw a connection between football and patriotism, and one Honolulu company had
sponsored an essay contest with the topic question "How
does football promote national unity?" It was won by a Corporal Harry F. Dittmer, Jr., of Philadelphia, whose essay,
"How Football and Americanism Define True Democracy,"
declared, "Football makes one think of America. Democracy
makes one think of America. And . . . we find they both define true Americanism."

The game was sponsored by the Shriners, and its halftime
show was lavish and patriotic. Fireworks exploded, and a miniature parachute floated to earth carrying the Hawaiian flag.
Fourteen marching bands paraded across the field to "Hawaii
Pono." They played the Shriner anthem, "I'm Forever Blowing
Bubbles," and a Shriner flag fell from a rocket. They played
"The Stars and Stripes," and another rocket was launched,
although this time, as one report put it, it seemed "to hesitate
and malfunction before it unfurled its patriotic symbol." Those
looking for further portents would later mention the cardboard
tank that circled the grounds once before breaking down in
midfield.

December 6 is also remembered as a day of exceptional
beauty, even for Hawaii, with clear skies and puffy clouds over
the Koolaus. The words most often used to characterize it are
"calm" and "still," and it reappears in some memories with the
clarity of sharp Pacific sunlight, while in others it is a slow-
motion day, with time stretched like taffy.

Compare it with August 31, 1939, the day before the German attack on Poland that precipitated the European war. Even
if Poland had learned of this attack beforehand and its army
had not been taken by surprise, the outcome of that battle and
that war would have been little affected. But in Hawaii, history

would have been changed in important ways if cables had been
deciphered, telephone calls made, and intelligence properly
evaluated on December 6. Although Oahu was not the impregnable fortress described by the press, the United States was also
not Poland, facing German panzers with cavalry, and there
were enough planes and warships on hand to blunt a Japanese
attack, inflicting serious losses. Had American forces not been
so humiliated on December 7, more than the first six months of
the Pacific war could have been affected. If you believe, as I do,
that the humiliation of Pearl Harbor contributed to the will-
ingness to drop atomic weapons on Hiroshima and Nagasaki
and is responsible in part for current attitudes toward Japan,
then December 6 was a last chance to avoid more than a single
day of carnage.

Even today, some who were on Oahu on December 6
continue reexamining it, breaking it down, and slowing time,
much as a captive repeatedly imagines his last day of freedom.
As they do this, they discover omens, real and imaginary. The
belief that December 6 was littered with portents may arise
from the conviction that catastrophes always come with some
warning, that just as earthquakes are preceded by screeching
birds and nervous animals, so too must Pearl Harbor have had
its harbingers. Thus, it is remembered that Hawaiian women
sitting on the lawn of the Kawaihao Church saw morning
clouds pile up and take the form of a monster, with a long
tongue lashing from side to side. One woman reported the
miracle to the wife of Honolulu's mayor, and the story circulated all afternoon, making it impossible to dismiss as invented
after the attack. Nor can anyone say the story of unusual clouds
over the Big Island on November 27, the same day the Japanese
task force sailed into the North Pacific, was concocted later. On
November 28, 1941, the *Honolulu Star-Bulletin* reported,
"What to most Big Islanders today was just a nice bright sunny
morning, to old time Hawaiians was ominous of impending

woe. Native legend has it than when Zeppelin-shaped clouds hang over Mauna Kea and Mauna Loa some catastrophic event is due."

Although jokes about Japanese attacking Hawaii had been made for years, those made on December 6 are remembered as premonitions. Thus we know that as Commander Roscoe F. Good strolled past the naval headquarters building on his way to lunch, he looked at Battleship Row with its line of double-moored warships and remarked, "What a beautiful target that would make." We know that as the wife of Captain James W. Chapman reached a point in the Kamehameha highway where all of Pearl Harbor was spread out below, she said, "If the Japanese are going to attack Hawaii, this would be the ideal time, for there sits the entire Pacific Fleet at anchor." Lieutenant Commander Edwin Layton, upon hearing "The Star-Spangled Banner" played in the Royal Hawaiian Hotel ballroom, experienced a sudden urge to shout, "Wake up, America!" And while returning home from a charity dinner dance, General Walter Short, seeing the lights of the warships and dry docks blazing in Pearl Harbor, remarked to his wife, "What a target that would make!"

If on December 6 a Japanese resident offered a drink to a serviceman, it is remembered as an omen, evidence the Japanese had been somehow tipped off. If a Japanese person appeared excessively nervous or calm, sullen or happy, well, that too was suspicious. Author Catherine Mellen later considered it sinister that her Japanese maid announced she would not be coming back to work on Sunday, December 7, because, as she wrote in her unpublished autobiography, "five men from the island of Kauai were arriving to spend the weekend at her home (already filled to overflow with her family). When I asked who they were she said she . . . thought they were friends of her husband. She was greatly agitated so I did not press for further information but that night I wrote in my diary: 'I am sure she is not a traitor but this news does alarm her because her home is near enough the waterfront to be of importance. . . ."

Mrs. Mellen also found it suspicious that her Japanese yardman should appear on December 6 bearing a large package, and she wrote, " 'A Christmas gift,' he said, nervously. Amazed at this early arrival of a Christmas present I opened it to find a full assortment of expensive toilet articles. His previous gifts had never exceeded one dollar."

A month after the attack, Governor Poindexter declared that on December 8 the city's rice supply was discovered to be "unusually short." He added, "Our investigation showed that these Japanese merchants, or some of them, when customers would come in to buy a sack of rice, would tell them, 'You better buy two sacks.' Now, that may have been due to either one of two reasons: one, of course, that they had advance notice of what was coming; the other was the rising price of rice. . . . But, anyhow we know that most of them did; they accepted that advice and instead of buying one they bought two . . . so that it aroused my suspicion. . . ."

When the Roberts Commission convened in Honolulu on January 5, 1942, to investigate the attack, its members had already heard rumors that, as one said, "certain Japanese places of refreshment were serving free drinks to white people on the night of December 6." The commissioners were particularly suspicious of a party thrown by a Mr. Otani to celebrate the opening of his Chinatown fish market, even though the FBI and naval intelligence had already stated there was no evidence of Japanese barkeeps serving free drinks to "white people" on December 6.

The chief of the Honolulu Police Department testified to the Roberts Commission that serving free liquor at the Otani opening was "a custom of the islands here." In 1944, the Army board investigating Pearl Harbor concluded, "The attack was such a surprise to the Japanese residents themselves that they were stunned and incoherent for a few days . . . [and] stories of maids, garbage collectors, small merchants and laborers [knowing beforehand of the attack] can be dismissed as idle talk and the product of fantastic imagination." But despite all these forceful denials, and although it defies logic that Japanese Consul General Kita would have had no warning while a Japanese bartender would, Mr. Otani was arrested and interned, and decades later I was to hear and read numerous stories of how, throughout the evening of December 6, the Japanese of Hawaii had thrown wild parties and bought drinks for sailors.

Some of the 1990 echoes of these stories said to "prove" the Japanese in Hawaii had been warned were so faint it was unclear whether a speaker believed that they knew in advance or, like those jittery pre-earthquake animals, that they were simply sensitive to the vibrations. I heard, for example, of the Yokohama Bank in Honolulu refusing to execute transfers during the last week of peace, and of family servants who left work on the evening of December 6, never to be seen again. Other echoes left no doubt of Japanese treachery. One Pearl Harbor survivor described a tavern near Schofield Barracks providing free drinks for anyone in uniform on December 6, a tavern later "proved" to be owned by a commander in the Japanese navy. Another survivor claimed, "A Lt. Commander, retired from the Japanese Navy . . . invited all the pilots in the American Armed Forces to attend a Hawaiian luau at Wahiawa. Plenty of food, liquor, music, and beautiful girls were provided to entertain our pilots far into the wee hours of the morning. Most of our pilots were still drunk [on December 7], and not capable of flying their planes if they could have gotten them off the ground."

You might imagine what is remembered, or saved, from the Honolulu newspapers published over this weekend would be articles warning of war with Japan, or copies of the *Honolulu Star-Bulletin* extra of December 7 saying, "WAR! OAHU

BOMBED BY JAPANESE PLANES." Instead, I heard about an advertisement appearing on an inside page of the *Honolulu Advertiser* on December 5 (and two days earlier in the *Star-Bulletin*). It was placed by the Japanese-owned Hawaii Importing Company of 215 North King Street, announcing "Fashions by the Yard—Look! Our Silks on Parade," and gave the price per yard for silks with exotic names like Tip-Hi, Cantona, Jungo, and Yippee.

On December 8, FBI agents searched the home of the manager of Hawaii Importing. In downtown Honolulu, its employees were besieged by Caucasian customers asking for the advertised fabrics by name, then leaving without making a purchase. People descended on the offices of the *Honolulu Star-Bulletin,* rummaging through trash piles and searching for a copy of this famous "silk ad," now considered conclusive evidence that Hawaii's Japanese residents had been warned.

"Those of us who had thrown out our papers dashed madly over the landscape snagging whatever discarded copies we could find, not hesitating to rob our neighbors' garbage cans if our own were empty," wrote Margaret Yates, the wife of a Pearl Harbor naval officer, in an introduction to her 1942 book *Murder by the Yard,* a mystery premised on the "silk ad" being a Japanese code. When Mrs. Yates returned to the mainland two months later, "bearing my own copy as if it were printed on gold leaf," she found the West Coast flooded with copies, and "sleuths, amateur and professional, were burning the midnight oil and coming up with as many answers as there were decoders."

Some "decoders" claimed the advertisement warned Japanese to stay home on December 7, explaining why so many Japanese maids and gardeners reportedly called in sick. Others insisted it was a code enabling Japanese spies to report on which warships were in Pearl Harbor. One man "decoded" the ad for me, explaining that the dot over an *i* was "the symbol of the Rising Sun of Japan," and the "yard" in "Fashions by the Yard" represented the U.S. Navy Yard. I was also told letter combinations in the silk names represent battleships, so "Cantona" is the *California*, "Romaine" is the *Nevada*, and "Matelasse" is the *Maryland*—or the *Tennessee*, or the Mutual Telephone Company of Honolulu—and Silk Broadcloth means "broadcast," the price of "$1.15 yd." is a clue to the date—since its three numbers add up to seven—and a black background represents "black clouds for the bombing" or, according to another version, "clouds at dawn."

I heard about the "silk ad" from a survivor in Honolulu, a Navy veteran in my hometown in upstate New York, and from a mainland teenager who admitted knowing only two things about Pearl Harbor—that President Roosevelt knew about the raid in advance, and that the Japanese of Honolulu did too, since they were tipped off by a newspaper advertisement.

A copy of it was mailed to me pressed in pages of *I Was at Pearl Harbor,* a self-published book sent by its author, John E. Ollila, a Navy veteran of the attack. "Look in the back of this paper against the light and see 'raids,' " Mr. Ollila had written along its bottom. I held it to the light. I turned it upside down. I placed it opposite a mirror. I was supposed to notice that "fashions" had been written in a tricky script that, when reversed, became "raids." But I only saw ".ƨnoiʜƨɒᖸ" Mr. Ollila's book devoted a chapter to the ad. "No one wanted to admit that the silk sale advertisement existed or that there was any truth to it, just keep it HUSHED UP!!" he said. "You will have to see this advertisement decoded, as it was shown to myself and others and then find your own answer to this mystery which has eaten at me for forty-two years."

I received another copy from Richard Van Dyke, a photographic archivist in Honolulu who had an envelope stuffed with them and boasted of possessing the original negative.

"Turn it backwards, to the light," he suggested. "Can you see it? How 'fashions' becomes 'raids' spelled backwards?"

The "silk ad" was one of many rumors of Japanese treachery. They were spread by Navy wives like Mrs. Yates, by racists using them as justification for the internment of Japanese-Americans, and by magazines like *Collier's* and *Time,* because they made a good story. "Last week Honolulu was fluttering with stories of fifth column activity," said the January 5, 1942, issue of *Time.* "One story was that a display advertisement in a newspaper, ostensibly pushing bargain sales of silks, was actually coded instructions to spies. . . . There were many others, and the average Honolulu citizen did not know which was true and which false, but he did know one thing; fed on tolerance, watered by complacency, the Jap fifth column had done its job fiendishly well and had not been stamped out."

Of all the Pearl Harbor rumors, the "silk ad" has enjoyed the greatest longevity, because it comes with proof, a piece of paper you can "decode." It has made no difference that the "code" has neither logic nor pattern, no difference that it was inconceivable for Japan to have risked the success of its raid just to prevent Japanese residents of Hawaii from being injured, no difference that an identical advertisement appeared a year earlier in the same newspaper, and no difference that within weeks, FBI agents had punctured the "silk ad" story and were refusing even to interview the man who designed it. Despite all this, it has become an article of faith that this advertisement proves the disloyalty and treachery of Hawaii's Japanese, proving as well that Pearl Harbor was the result not of Japanese bravery, skill, and tactics, but of subversion and sabotage.

6

The Submariners' Wives Throw
a Party

KATHY COOPER REMEMBERS THE EVENING OF DECEMBER 6 AS
a time of anticipation and butterflies. She and Bud Cooper had
been apart almost continuously since being married in August,
and the next morning her husband's submarine, the *Pollock,*
was scheduled to dock at Pearl Harbor after an absence of two
and a half months. Because she was so looking forward to the
reunion, the evening seemed particularly long, leaving details
engraved on her memory. She remembers attending a party for
the wives of *Pollock* officers. Their conversation dwelt on two
subjects: the possibility of war with Japan, and the possibility
of sabotage by the Japanese of Oahu. She worried about the
first because her father, who was in charge of naval construction projects in the Pacific, believed the United States was preparing for certain war. Like their husbands, she and the other
wives feared war but assumed it would start in Southeast Asia,
and be quickly won by the Navy. The wife of Bud Cooper's
skipper, Mrs. Stanley Moseley, told the other women at the
party not to worry because "we can lick the Japanese with our
hands tied behind our backs."

"Not one of us," Kathy Cooper says, "worried about them

attacking us here." Instead, they worried about Japanese spies in Honolulu, and passed the evening trading stories about the suspicious behavior of their servants. Even a casual question about the proposed guest lists at their parties—a question from a Japanese maid such as "Was Mr. So-and-so there too?"—was considered a devious method of discovering which ships were in harbor.

Now, after spending a lifetime in Hawaii and watching it evolve from a segregated colonial society into a multiracial one, and after raising eleven children and having two marry native Hawaiians, Kathy Cooper seems amazed by the racial fears of 1941. "Two of our grandsons are part Hawaiian," she says, "but I can remember back then school friends telling me they were forbidden to play with someone because she was rumored to have Hawaiian blood."

Hawaii is probably the most successful multiracial society on earth. The rate of mixed marriages is the highest of any American state or foreign country. Over half the children are of mixed ethnic parentage, and at any public gathering you see the kind of idealized multiracial mixture usually confined to UNICEF posters. Private schools that in 1941 excluded Orientals except for carefully chosen tokens have a student body reflecting the population. The Japanese have progressed from being forbidden to work for the telephone company or operate a streetcar to dominating the state's economic and political life. One congressman and both senators are Japanese, and Japanese control of the state bureaucracy has led to charges of discrimination against other races. If you compare what passes for "racial tension" in Hawaii with the tensions afflicting other multiracial and multinational societies, Hawaii's would scarcely register on even the most sensitive instruments. All of which makes it difficult to imagine the racial fears of the prewar years, and to forgive the submariners' wives for scrutinizing their servants for evidence of disloyalty.

At the time of the attack, Kathy Cooper had been living for several years in Honolulu and had a mature understanding of the Japanese community. But consider Hawaii from the perspective of the other submariners' wives. Most had arrived only recently, sent here because of possible war with Japan. Yet they found themselves in a territory where 40 percent of the population was racially Japanese, the third-largest overseas Japanese population in the world, after China and Brazil, and in a city that, outside of Japan, was the most Japanese city on earth. Moreover, one quarter of the territory's 160,000 Japanese were first-generation Japanese and continued to be Japanese subjects, while two thirds of the second generation held dual citizenship. The wives soon learned that many Japanese residents supported Japan's war against China, buying Japanese war bonds, sending "comfort bags" of blankets, shoes, and candy to Japanese soldiers, and collecting money for the Japanese Red Cross to buy a hospital ship, which somehow instead became a bomber named the *Hawaii*.

They discovered that Japanese owned half the restaurants and food stores, built most houses, repaired most cars, and worked behind the counters of most retail shops. Japanese fishermen with fast boats and powerful shortwave radios caught all the Islands' fish. Lunch wagons served American coffee and doughnuts, but they were owned by Japanese and topped with overhanging Japanese roofs. So numerous were the Japanese customers and enterprises that they could discriminate against other races, and for every classified advertisement seeking "Haole fountain girls for the Waikiki Milk Bar," there were ones saying, "Night Cashier—Japanese" for the Times Grill, "Automobile Mechanic—Japanese preferred—OK Service Station" and "Barbecue Inn, prefers Oriental."

The submariners' wives found themselves living in a city with dozens of Japanese teahouses, two fish-cake factories, two shops selling nothing but kimonos, and the only sake brewery outside Japan. There were movie theaters showing only Japanese movies, two Japanese-language newspapers, a Japanese Chamber of Commerce, Japanese professional and charitable associations, associations to strengthen the bonds between Japanese from the same prefecture, and language schools where 85 percent of all Japanese children went after school to receive instruction in Japanese language and culture. On Japanese holidays, skies filled with paper kites and banners, and when a circus paraded through town, the clowns were met with silent stares from Japanese spectators, who considered it rude to laugh in public.

The largest Oriental neighborhood was known as Chinatown out of habit, but Japanese and Filipinos far outnumbered its Chinese residents. When the wives went there they saw Japanese women carrying children on their backs, wearing silk kimonos in brilliant pinks and purples and sandals or straw slippers. They saw bathhouses, Shinto shrines, Buddhist temples puffing smoke, and alleyways so narrow tenement balconies almost met overhead. They saw garish foreign signs, restaurants displaying photographs of the Emperor, crowded neighborhoods where more than a hundred people shared a latrine, and small stores which never seemed to close, where babies crabbed across wooden floors, moonfaced children ate pink gelatin candies, and families sat behind curtains eating rice and clicking dice and dominoes. They smelled incense, fish, and soiled baby, heard firecrackers, languages they could not fathom, and gongs floating down the Nuuanu Valley from the Buddhist temple. And after hearing, seeing, and smelling all this, they can perhaps be forgiven for wondering if Japanese living this way might feel more loyalty to Japan than to the United States, for worrying that people displaying photographs of the Emperor might pass information about American ship movements to one of the many Japanese consular representatives in Hawaii, for succumbing to the fear of servants, which is a common feature of colonial societies on the eve of insurrection or war, and for being afraid that if war came, the same employees who demanded a holiday on the Emperor's birthday might creep into their bedrooms with knives.

As it turned out, none of these fears came close to describing what actually happened on December 7 when, instead of charging into haole neighborhoods waving samurai swords, or slinking toward piers and bridges with satchels of dynamite, the Japanese of Hawaii began to dismantle their former lives so feverishly that within two days most of Honolulu's signs of Japanese culture and influence had vanished as surely as if sucked into a tornado.

What would have seemed even more fantastic to the submariners' wives was that they would have to wait until they were grandmothers before they could again walk down a Honolulu street and see signs written only in Japanese, and restaurants and shops catering almost exclusively to Japanese patrons. In 1991, these new Japanese neighborhoods include the most expensive real estate in the nation—the Kahala beachfront and several blocks on Kalakaua Avenue in Waikiki largely catering to Japanese visitors. These are places where anyone worrying that the Islands will become a Japanese "colony" can find sufficient visual evidence to support a new generation of anti-Japanese fears and prejudices, ones which bear an uncanny resemblance to those circulating in Honolulu on the eve of Pearl Harbor.

7

Alerted for Sabotage

HAWAII'S MILITARY LEADERSHIP ALSO BELIEVED THAT IF WAR broke out in Asia, the Japanese shopkeepers, maids, and gardeners of Oahu would attack them with guns and dynamite, destroying aircraft on the ground, slapping mines to the hulls of warships, and blowing bridges and electric lines. They believed it even though there had not been a single case of sabotage, and despite the insistence of Colonel George Bicknell of Army intelligence and of other officers who knew the Islands well that "there were no indications of any widespread plans involving sabotage or subversive activities." They believed it because they thought it axiomatic the Japanese had a race loyalty superseding citizenship, place of birth, or residence. They believed it for the same reasons their wives did—because of Honolulu's manifestly Japanese atmosphere, and because, according to chief of military intelligence Kendall Fielder, "just the mere fact of approximately 160,000 people of Japanese extraction would lead us to believe that a certain number of them would be loyal to the Japanese empire." They believed it because of racism, because of the traditional American obsession with subversion, and because since they considered a direct Japanese attack on

Hawaii so foolhardy as to be impossible, sabotage was the only threat they could imagine. (The senior Walter Dillingham told the Army Pearl Harbor Board, "I think the officials of the Army and Navy, from statements made by them—and I discussed it with a great many over a period of several years—[had] . . . the feeling that the most serious thing that could happen to us in the event of war would be what the [local] Japanese would do, whether we would be knifed in bed. . . .")

The commander of the Hawaiian Department, General Walter Short, was so obsessed with sabotage that when he received Message No. 472 from the War Department in Washington on November 27, informing him, "Negotiations with Japan appear to be terminated to all practical purposes. . . . Japanese future action unpredictable but hostile action possible at any moment," and ordering him to "undertake such reconnaissance and other measures as you deem necessary," he took it solely as a warning against sabotage. He immediately called his "Number 1 Alert," described as "a defense against sabotage, espionage, and subversive activities without any threat from the outside." He could have called a Number 2 Alert, which included a defense against air, surface, and submarine attack, or a Number 3, "a defense against an all-out attack . . . as if there was a possible attempt at landing in sight."

Within an hour of receiving the War Department warning, Short answered he was "alerted to prevent sabotage." This reply went across the desk of numerous Washington staff officers, including Army Chief of Staff General George Marshall and Secretary of War Henry Stimson, and none thought to compare the two messages and inform Short his sabotage alert was not what they intended. This omission was justifiably seized upon by Short and his defenders as mitigating his responsibility, and Marshall later admitted, "That was my opportunity to intervene and I did not do it." Stimson, however, made the point that Short's reply "certainly gave me no intimation that . . . being 'alerted to prevent sabotage' was in any way an express or implied denial of being alert against an attack by Japan's armed forces. The very purpose of a fortress such as Hawaii is to repel such an attack, and Short was the commander of that fortress."

A month after Pearl Harbor, Short still believed his sabotage alert had been justified. When asked by the Roberts Commission, "In other words, there were no troops in your command ready for war at that moment?" he answered, "No, sir. They were ready for uprisings. They were—we were definitely organized to meet any uprising or any act of sabotage. . . ." During the 1945 Congressional hearings he testified, "We can't tell what would have happened if we hadn't held a tight rein over them [Hawaii's Japanese residents]. I think the feeling was that if there had been any real success to the Japanese plans, that anything might have happened." A senator asked, "What do you call a success if December 7, 1941, wasn't [one] . . . ?" To which Short replied, "A landing on the island of Oahu. They immediately would have had an army of thousands, a fifth column of thousands, ready to support them."

Most of Short's staff and subordinates agreed that sabotage was the main danger they faced. The commander of the Army Air Forces on Hawaii, Major General Frederick Martin, told the Army Pearl Harbor Board he had been confident there would be no Japanese strike, "because if it failed, it meant such a reduction in their striking power they would be confined to their home islands from then on." Instead, in December 1941, he believed the most probable danger came from "the Japanese population of the islands."

Martin's attitude is particularly surprising, since he was coauthor of a widely circulated March 1941 report which proved to be an eerie description of the Japanese attack. In it he warned, "A successful, sudden raid against our ships and Naval installations on Oahu might prevent effective offensive action by our forces in the Western Pacific for a long period." He predicted, "A declaration of war might be preceded by: 1. A surprise submarine attack. . . . 2. A surprise attack on Oahu including ships and installations in Pearl Harbor . . ." and said that "such an attack would most likely be launched from one or more carriers which would probably approach inside of three hundred miles," and that "in a dawn air attack there is a high probability that it could be delivered as a complete surprise. . . ." But despite predicting all this, and despite recognizing the theoretical possibility of a surprise Japanese air raid, like most staff offices on Oahu, Martin was so confident Japan was intimidated by American military power, and so concerned with local saboteurs, that he could not bring himself to believe such a raid was a realistic probability.

Because the Army was alerted only against sabotage on December 6, ammunition was boxed and locked to prevent its theft by local Japanese, leaving many batteries unable to return fire during the first fifteen minutes of attack. Because of this alert, the commanders of Wheeler and Hickman fields moved their warplanes out of protective revetments, disarming them and massing them closely together in the middle of the open tarmac, making them easy to guard against Japanese saboteurs, but excellent targets for an enemy air raid. Thirty minutes would now be needed to disperse them, even longer to arm and send them into the air. As it would turn out, if anyone "sabotaged" Oahu's defense, it was General Short himself, and if there was a "subversion," it was practiced by an army subverting its own defenses.

The Navy was equally sabotage-conscious, holding drills and posting guards on ships. On November 27, Admiral Kimmel had received a warning from the Navy Department couched in even stronger terms than Short's. "This dispatch is to be considered a war warning," it began. "Negotiations with Japan looking toward stabilization of conditions in the Pacific have ceased and an aggressive move by Japan is expected within the next few days." Sent to naval commands across the Pacific, it reported that Japanese movements indicated "an amphibious expedition against either Philippines, Thai or Kra Peninsula or possibly Borneo," and ordered "an appropriate defensive deployment." But because it did not specifically mention Hawaii, because the Navy Department had not provided Kimmel with the decrypts of the radio intelligence data, including Yoshikawa's "bomb plot" message identifying Hawaii as a possible target, and because Kimmel believed "an air attack on Pearl Harbor or anything other than a surprise attack was most improbable," he failed to make the most "appropriate defensive deployment"—long-range aerial scouting.

Afterward, Kimmel and his supporters argued there had been a shortage of planes and spare parts, making it impossible for the Navy, which had the responsibility for long-range patrols, to mount a full 360-degree sweep of the waters surrounding Hawaii. This, however, is no excuse for sending no patrols at all. A year earlier, General Martin's report on the danger of a surprise carrier-based attack had identified the waters northeast of the island as the most likely avenue of attack (because of favorable prevailing winds). With the planes available, Kimmel could certainly have sent patrols over the most likely areas. The reason he did not was probably that although he and his staff could imagine a Japanese air raid on Hawaii as a theoretical possibility, they were so confident Japan was intimidated by America's military superiority they did not accept it as a realistic one. And this is why, despite the Navy's "war warning" and the Army's warning of "hostile action possible at any moment," the only extraordinary military measures being taken on Hawaii on December 6 were directed against imaginary civilian saboteurs.

The first military event of December 6 was a 2:00 A.M. alert, coming when Captain James Shoemaker, commander of the Ford Island Naval Air Station, woke his men to repel a simulated sabotage attack. He had planned the drill two days earlier, after a meeting with Rear Admiral Claude Bloch, commandant of the 14th Naval District, which had been specifically called to discuss measures necessary to defeat sabotage attacks by the Japanese residents of Oahu.

Several hours later, during morning inspection at the Kaneohe Naval Air Station, Commander Harold Martin urged vigilance against sabotage, saying, "Men, I have called you together here this morning to tell you to keep your eyes and ears open and be on the alert every moment. You are probably the nearest into a war that you will ever be without actually being in it." He had been warned the day before, he said later, "that the possibilities of sabotage were unusually imminent."

The destroyer *Helm* was moored alone in the west loch of Pearl Harbor, having returned the day before from a week of gunnery exercises and escort duty. One of its officers, Victor Dybdal, told me, "We came here for rest and relaxation and considered ourselves safe, and protected by the Army. We very seldom even manned our guns in port . . . but everyone was thinking sabotage; everyone was suspicious of the local Japs. We saw Army sentries on all the bridges and we had sentries posted on our ships, usually on the fantails to look out for swimmers. It was slightly ridiculous, because our sentries didn't know how to fire rifles. We had so many false alarms that we took guns away from our sentries and gave them whistles. On other ships they gave the sentries unloaded rifles and locked the ammunition behind a pane of glass on the quarterdeck. If they were sure saboteurs were approaching, they were to break the glass and load their rifles."

The Army antiaircraft unit assigned to protect Ford Island from an enemy air attack was based fifteen miles and a ferry ride away, at Camp Malakole on Barbers Point. Every day its men had to truck their guns to Pearl Harbor, stopping to pick up ammunition kept in an arsenal to prevent its theft by local Japanese. Upon reaching Ford Island they had to reassemble the guns and set them in emplacements. But December 6 was the first weekend in months they did not perform even this laborious exercise, remaining instead at Camp Malakole, their guns without ammunition and broken down in pieces. "We had all been on alert for so long," former Corporal Myron Hayes said, "and particularly after Thanksgiving there was a general loosening of that alert." But the sabotage alert was not relaxed, and on December 6 a Camp Malakole guard saw two Japanese fishermen swimming near a boat anchored fifty yards offshore. He unholstered his .45, pointing it, and warning he would shoot if they came closer. They retreated, and a machine gun was hurriedly assembled and mounted on the beach to repel other "fifth columnists."

At Hickam Field, machine gun emplacements and slit trenches were dug to repel a land-based attack by saboteurs, but nothing was done to protect against an aerial attack. On the morning of December 6, the base commander, Colonel William Farthing, called a meeting of officers to discuss measures in place to guard aircraft against sabotage. One man attending it remembers, "By this time security against sabotage was almost an obsession."

At Wheeler Field, U-shaped revetments had been built to protect its fighter squadrons from an air raid, and before General Short's November 27 antisabotage alert, planes had been parked in them, dispersed along the length of the runway. Afterward, they were all gathered on the apron, fitted together nose to tail in a reverse T formation, so that a single rifleman could guard them. A Wheeler Field pursuit pilot named Gus Ahola, who still lives on Oahu, remembers jokes in the officers' club about "how one guy could take a pass and get thirty planes in our squadron with a single bullet." But he admits the bullets they really feared were from Japanese civilians hiding in the underbrush and pineapple fields and he "never imagined that Japanese planes would attack us, no way."

On December 6, Wheeler Field took further antisabotage precautions. Ammunition was removed from planes and locked in hangars, and regulations requiring controls in unattended planes to be left locked continued in force. (In a Number 2 or Number 3 alert, planes were left unlocked.) These locks were cumbersome metal collars that fitted over the joystick and were attached to a seat by four cables ending in S-hooks. A pilot "locked" a plane by adjusting his seat until the cables were taut. He unlocked it by easing his seat forward, then pulling the rudder pedals forward to provide some slack. "Even on a bright sunny day, with no urgency and no one looking over your shoulder," Ahola remembers, "it was difficult to take those goddamn things apart."

When I came across Ahola's name I had assumed he was native Hawaiian. It sounds Hawaiian, and is "aloha" spelled backward. The Army Air Force made the same mistake in 1941, assuming he belonged to the former Hawaiian royal family—because what other native Hawaiian could become an officer?—and when he arrived from the mainland, an official military greeter provided the welcome usually accorded a VIP. He is instead a second-generation Finn from Minnesota who enlisted to see the world and escape northern winters. He made a career of the Air Force, retiring as a colonel and returning to live in Hawaii, where he has at last come to resemble a native Hawaiian, with white hair, mahogany skin, and a laconic but intelligent manner.

In 1941, the only highway from Honolulu to Wheeler Field was the narrow Kamehameha Highway, a two-lane road dipping like a roller coaster into canyons and gullies. The bored pilots turned it into a racetrack. "You'd recognize another guy on that road," Ahola said, "toot your horn, and away you'd go." He and I drove up to Wheeler Field on the same Kamehameha Highway, now an ugly, but patriotic, stretch of six-lane divided road, bordered by the Pacific outposts of virtually every fast-food franchise in the country, all flying American and Hawaii state flags—bigger than the ones on Fifth Avenue or at the Capitol—which have replaced rows of palms on some Hawaiian roads.

We skirted Pearl Harbor, passing the old Pearl Harbor Tavern, a barnlike bar and restaurant popular with enlisted men during the war and now owned by Japanese nationals. High wooden fencing contained condominium developments, as if they were landslides threatening to bury the road. "This didn't exist in 1941," Ahola said. "It was like being out in the country: just sugar mills, plantation towns, and Pearl Harbor. Ever since I moved back, the temperature in Honolulu has been rising, because of this."

As we entered Wheeler Field, he said that on the evening of December 6, he and his roommate had been giving a party, playing cards, drinking coffee, and showing home movies to their girlfriends. "My God, what a way to spend *that* evening," he said, amazed at the innocence of those pleasures. He remembered driving his girl home, then passing Pearl Harbor and being dazzled by its warships, moored in ponds of yellow light and "lit like Christmas trees." Another pilot passed him, tooting his horn as a challenge. They raced back to the base in their convertibles, speeding two abreast, screaming around corners and falling into dips, their headlights sweeping across empty cane fields.

Before turning in, he detoured to the runway to admire his squadron. He saw thirty planes, grouped in a tight antisabotage square and illuminated by searchlights, "almost as if they were in prison." He was overcome with feelings of pride, and thought, "We must be the best squadron in the Pacific, with the best training, the best pilots, and the best planes."

This is what I remembered thinking as a boy, that because

our planes and pilots were American, they had to be the best, and they were destroyed on the ground only because the attack was a surprise. We had been defeated by Japanese treachery, not Japanese skill. When I saw the old newsreels and photographs of orderly rows of fighters and bombers exploding in flames, I was angry at the Japanese, at fate, but never at us. Blake Clark's *Remember Pearl Harbor,* an excellent eyewitness account, was published in 1942, and remained for many years the most widely read reconstruction of the attack. It was the first book I read about December 7, and from it I learned that "Alert Number Three—against attack by air, which calls for dispersion of grounded planes, had not been ordered [because] . . . diabolical luck was with the Japanese."

Torpedoman Second Class
Robert Hudson, 1942
COURTESY OF ROBERT HUDSON

BELOW: Robert Hudson displays his
Pearl Harbor memorabilia, c. 1989.
COURTESY OF ROBERT HUDSON

Admiral Husband E. Kimmel (*center*), Commander in Chief of the U.S. Pacific Fleet in 1941, conferring with his chief of staff, Captain William Smith (*right*), and his operations officer, Captain W. S. DeLany   OFFICIAL U. S. NAVY PHOTOGRAPH

Lt. Gen. Walter C. Short, commander of the Hawaiian Department   NATIONAL ARCHIVES

TOP LEFT: Lt. Col. George W. Bicknell, the intelligence officer who was suspicious of the Mori call
COURTESY OF DOROTHY BICKNELL

TOP RIGHT: Lt. Comm. Victor A. Dybdal, who was on board the USS *Helm* on December 7, 1941, and almost fifty years later took the author on a tour of Pearl Harbor
COURTESY OF VICTOR DYBDAL

Lt. Donald Woodrum, a young naval intelligence officer on December 7
COURTESY OF DON WOODRUM

Lt. Gus Ahola waves from the cockpit of his fighter several months after the attack.

Sgt. Bob Kinzler at Schofield Barracks in 1941

ABOVE: Larry Nakatsuka, the first reporter to arrive at the Japanese consulate on December 7
COURTESY OF LARRY NAKATSUKA

Richard Ishimoto, who served in the U.S. Army in the Pacific during the war, and fifty years later found himself working for his wealthy Japanese neighbors in Black Point
COURTESY OF RICHARD ISHIMOTO

Sue Isonaga, who still reveres the memory of FBI agent Robert Shivers
COURTESY OF SUE ISONAGA

RCA messenger Tadeo Fuchikami poses on his motorcycle several years after the war.
COURTESY OF TADEO FUCHIKAMI

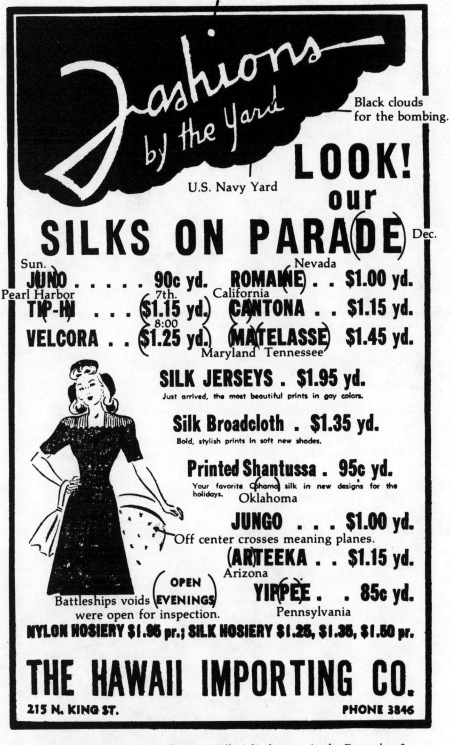

Dot is the symbol of Rising Sun of Japan.

Fashions by the Yard

Black clouds for the bombing.

U.S. Navy Yard

LOOK!
our

SILKS ON PARADE

Dec.

Sun.

JUNO . . . . . 90c yd.

Nevada

ROMAINE . . $1.00 yd.

Pearl Harbor   7th.

TIP-IN . . . $1.15 yd.

California

CANTONA . . $1.15 yd.

8:00

VELCORA . . $1.25 yd.

MATELASSE $1.45 yd.

Maryland   Tennessee

SILK JERSEYS . $1.95 yd.

Just arrived, the most beautiful prints in gay colors.

Silk Broadcloth . $1.35 yd.

Bold, stylish prints in soft new shades.

Printed Shantussa . 95c yd.

Your favorite Ophama silk in new designs for the holidays.

Oklahoma

JUNGO . . . $1.00 yd.

Off center crosses meaning planes.

ARTEEKA . . $1.15 yd.

Arizona

OPEN EVENINGS

YIPPEE . . 85c yd.

Battleships voids were open for inspection.

Pennsylvania

NYLON HOSIERY $1.95 pr.; SILK HOSIERY $1.25, $1.35, $1.50 pr.

THE HAWAII IMPORTING CO.

215 N. KING ST.   PHONE 3846

A decoded version of the famous "Silk Ad" that ran in the December 3, 1941, *Honolulu Star-Bulletin* and was widely believed to be a coded warning to Japanese agents and sympathizers in Honolulu

REPRINTED BY PERMISSION OF THE *HONOLULU STAR-BULLETIN*

Aerial view of a peaceful Pearl Harbor in October 1941, two months before the attack. BELOW: View of "Battleship Row" taken by a Japanese plane at the start of the attack. Notice shock waves in the water caused by exploding depth charges.   OFFICIAL U.S. NAVY PHOTOGRAPHS

has been eased slightly, and that now there is a fairly good reason to hope that there will be no major conflict in the Pacific, at least for the next few weeks. . . ."

They would also be spared the front-page news that Secretary of the Navy Knox had released a report declaring that "the United States already is the world's greatest naval power as a result of the 'greatest program of expansion attempted by any navy in world history.' " Or from reading, at the same moment Japanese carrier-based planes were pounding Pearl Harbor, a magazine supplement feature titled "AIRCRAFT CARRIER—Hard-Hitting Weapon for Uncle Sam in the Pacific," which started, "By sea and by air the Navy is in fighting trim. Carrier-based aviation, which has undergone wide development in tactical scope and strategic concept, is destined to play a major role when the signal comes. . . ."

The appearance of this article on December 7 was not an extraordinary coincidence. The feature the week before had been "Nothing Can Stop the Army Air Corps." Its lead paragraph, set over a photograph of Lieutenant Joe Glick and his fighter—which was almost certainly destroyed on the ground at Wheeler Field—began, "And why? Because it's men like Joe Glick, typical red blooded American youth who comes from the coal mines, the corn fields, from all America, to learn to fly by the seat-of-his-pants. Fair weather and foul, good or bad breaks, the thousands of Joes keep-em flying!" And a few weeks before that, you could have read about how Pearl Harbor's destroyers "proved unquestionably in their war games that they are ready for what may come. Ready with the latest battle equipment—and ready with men who are trained to know it'll be a short fight but a hot one—and victory and death are the only rewards."

Overconfidence is often listed as one of many failings leading to the catastrophe. But the more you explore the attitude of the civilians and military—both on Hawaii and on

8

"The Supreme Overconfidence of a Great Athlete"

AT 8:00 P.M. ON DECEMBER 6, THE HONOLULU *ADVERTISER'S* presses broke while printing copies of the next day's edition. The next morning, *Advertiser* employees considered this a catastrophe, since it allowed their rival afternoon paper, the *Honolulu Star-Bulletin,* to publish the first "War Extra!" And several days after that, the broken presses were blamed on sabotage, with the wife of one newspaperman writing, "Details of the [sabotage] were given to my husband a few days afterwards by an employee of the newspaper who described it as an act of revenge for the paper's bold stand on the situation in the Orient."

But there were compensations. Not finding their paper in its accustomed place the next morning, *Advertiser* subscribers would spend several minutes peering into hedges and walking to the end of driveways, and would therefore see the black smoke and aerial acrobatics, sights they might otherwise have missed. More important, *Advertiser* subscribers would be spared from reading the December 7 front-page story headlined "U.S. SURE PACIFIC WAR IS NOT LIKELY," which began, "Official Washington believes that the tension over the Far Eastern crisis the mainland—the more it seems calling this state of mind overconfidence is a kindness. Better to describe it as deluded or arrogant. Examples make for painful reading, because its proponents were so totally wrong you feel embarrassed for them, and for unsettling reading, because you may find yourself thinking Pearl Harbor was divine retribution for such hubris.

Listen to Melvin J. Mass, a congressman from Minnesota and colonel in the Marine Corps Reserves who, upon returning from active duty in Hawaii, told his colleagues in Washington, D.C., on September 3, 1941, that "Japan is deathly afraid of the American fleet," and that American air and sea forces in Hawaii could defend themselves "against any combination of forces that might challenge our interest."

Listen to Andrew J. May of Kentucky, chairman of the House Military Affairs Committee, who released a press statement on December 1, reported in the Honolulu newspapers the following day, urging President Roosevelt to tell the Japanese that unless they renounced their ambitions for an empire in southeast Asia, "the United States will blast them off the land and blow them out of the water."

Or listen to Secretary of the Navy Frank Knox, who told a private gathering in Washington on the evening of December 4, "But I want you to know that no matter what happens, the United States Navy is ready! Every man is at his post, every ship is at its station. . . . Whatever happens, the navy is not going to be caught napping."

Journalists were equally guilty. The *New York Times Magazine* pronounced Oahu "Our Gibraltar in the Pacific," the "hub of our strategic universe," and boasted of its submarine nets (there weren't any), its planes swinging "far and wide to seaward searching, searching" (there was no long-range reconnaissance on December 7), and its "men beside the Army's 16-inchers, half hidden in the jungle growth near Barbers

Point" (Barbers Point resembles a desert more than a jungle, and ammunition kept there was usually kept locked).

A June 1941 article in *Collier's* magazine titled "Impregnable Pearl Harbor" reported on military exercises in Hawaii said to prove "how quickly the billion-dollar fist that America has built in the Pacific could deliver a smash. The Army's Hawaiian division . . . can be at their posts within thirty minutes, if they're not there already. The Pacific Fleet . . . [is] always within a few minutes of clearing for action." The author assured readers that "to the extent that we know how many fighting ships and planes Japan has, we're kept pretty well informed where they are and what they're up to. . . . Our Pacific battle forces are not exactly groping around in the dark.

"Ships can be sunk. Planes can be downed. . . . But neither the Army nor the Navy believes that there is any power or combination of powers existing today that can prove it in the islands.

"In the continental United States there may be some doubt about our readiness to fight, but none exists in Hawaii. Battleships . . . plow the ocean practicing gunnery, wary as lions on the prowl."

The blackest humor is found in *Our Billion Dollar Rock,* in which the author described "what this mighty defense base would look like and act like if it were called on to repel an attack." He then explained, "Although this was to have been a 'surprise' attack, listeners and sound amplifiers in mountain recesses have heralded the enemy. The word is hurried from observation posts. Curtiss pursuit hawks whip into the air . . . to meet the invader. Meanwhile, antiaircraft guns from a dozen emplacements have found the range and are knocking enemy planes out of the sky . . . Promptly, or battleships would wheel into action against the enemy. . . . Whatever the strength of the invading enemy, he would soon know he had been in a battle. For Oahu is ready."

You cannot just dismiss such boasting as careless journalism or a mainland fantasy. It was repeated in wire service dispatches and printed in the Honolulu papers, and believed there as well. It created a closed system, in which mainland delusions reinforced those of the Islands, which in turn magnified those of the mainland, so that as December 7 approached, the arrogance and boasting grew exponentially. It reached some kind of peak in a speech delivered on December 6 (and reported that same afternoon in the *Honolulu Star-Bulletin*) by Senator Ralph Brewster of Maine, who claimed, "The United States navy can defeat the Japanese navy, any place and at any time."

Listen to what was being said by the military and civilian residents of Hawaii, who you might think would have known better. The commander of the Hawaiian Department in 1940, Major General Charles Herron, announced, "Oahu will never be exposed to a blitzkrieg attack. This is why: we are more than 2,000 miles away from land whichever way you look, which is a long way for an enemy force to steam. And besides, it would have to smash through our Navy."

Honolulu's own magazine, *Paradise of the Pacific*, boasted in its May 1941 edition, "The island of Oahu is so thoroughly ringed with defenses, it would be impossible for hostile planes to come over the island. Their approach would be detected long before they were in striking distance, and if they ever got over the city, the army and navy would make quick work of them before they returned to their bases—presumably ships at sea."

An editorial the same month in the *Star-Bulletin* said, "This week a high officer of the U.S. Army remarked that he knows of no place under the American flag safer than Hawaii— more secure from the onslaught of actual war."

Hawaii's Japanese-Americans were also confident. They feared an American-Japanese war in Asia, but believed Hawaii was too strong and distant to be menaced. Seiyei Wakukawa, who for many years had traveled to China to cover the Sino-

Japanese War for the local Japanese newspaper, *Nippu Jiji,* admits, "I never imagined [the Japanese] would be so stupid as to attack America directly." And on December 4, George Akita led a discussion at his high school on the topic "Can Hawaii Be Attacked?" and reported later in his diary, "The answers were mostly no's. They say that our navy is too strong. The distance too much. Japan can't even conquer China. Japan's power has depleted etc. etc."

A Japanese raid was considered so improbable and suicidal it had become a long-standing joke. One kamaaina woman told me, "My father and I would stand outside on the lanai and whenever we saw a funny boat offshore we'd say, 'Here come the Japanese,' in the same way you'd say to a child, 'Here comes the bogey man.' " A Marine bugler on the *West Virginia* recalled eating dinner several days before December 7 with his father, a chief petty officer based in Pearl Harbor, and having his father warn him, with a smile, "If you see any of these local Japanese fellows wearing gas masks, you be careful." A tongue-in-cheek *Paradise of the Pacific* editorial declared, "Says one 'school of guessing' the Japanese might get a number of airplane carriers within a few hundred miles of Honolulu, then swoop over the city (from an 'unexpected' angle) and drop bombs on forts, barracks, government buildings . . . unavoidably smiting, here and there, a hospital, a hotel or two, shipping, a few private homes (mansions and 'little grass shacks'), and possibly the headquarters of the Hawaii Visitors Bureau . . . and even the Japanese consulate itself. Possibly! . . . . Not too probable!"

On December 6, no one on Oahu was more overconfident than the military. Richard Sutton, a young ensign who witnessed the attack from Admiral Bloch's veranda, remembers, "We had the supreme overconfidence a great athlete has who has never been beaten—we all thought we were invincible."

Bob Kinzler, a former soldier at Schofield barracks, says

the Japanese were taken so lightly that when General Short put the base on alert against sabotage, "we changed from khaki-colored shirt to olive-colored, and spent the week lying on the ground and squeezing the triggers of our empty rifles—'Click!'—in preparation for our marksmanship tests the following week. That was the extent of our alert."

Naval intelligence officer Don Woodrum admits, "Like everyone else I thought they'd go into Southeast Asia. Japan is so far away it never occurred to me they'd hit us here." And in an article published on one of the Pearl anniversaries, he wrote, "What never crossed the threshold of consciousness was the possibility of a hit-and-run attack on the fleet at Pearl Harbor. . . ."

Bernard Clarey, executive officer on the submarine *Blowfin,* which returned to Pearl Harbor from patrol on December 5, remembers, "We expected to relax in Hawaii, and we always thought that the real danger came during our patrols."

Bud Cooper says that on his submarine, "we believed [the Japanese] couldn't really sail a ship without going aground. We had a very low regard for their ability." Aboard his sub was a Navy commander who was hitching a ride to Hawaii from the West Coast, and who, when news of the attack came over their radio, stood as if in a trance saying, "I just can't believe it . . . I just can't believe it . . . I just can't believe the Japanese could do it."

At a staff meeting ten days before the attack, Admiral Kimmel asked Captain Charles McMorris, his fleet war plans officer, "What do you think about the prospects of a Japanese air attack?" McMorris answered, "None, absolutely none." And on December 6, when Joseph C. Harsch asked Kimmel, "Is there going to be a war out here?" Kimmel answered he was confident there would be no war because the Germans had failed to take Moscow and "that means that the Japanese cannot attack us in the Pacific without running the risk of a two-front war. The Japanese are too smart to run that risk."

Fleet intelligence officer Edwin Layton wrote that on December 2, 1941, when he admitted to Admiral Kimmel he was unsure of the location of two Japanese carrier divisions, "the admiral then looked at me, as sometimes he would, with a stern countenance and an icy twinkle in his penetrating blue eyes. 'Do you mean to say they could be rounding Diamond Head and you wouldn't know it?' "

On the morning of December 6, Admiral Pye, the battle force commander in Pearl Harbor, told Layton, who had just raised the possibility of a Japanese move against the Philippines, "Oh, no. The Japanese won't attack us. We're too strong and powerful." Layton rightly believed the attack on the Philippines would come the next day, although he admits, "Even if Kimmel was inclined to share my fears about an attack on the Philippines, any thought that the Japanese might also hit Pearl Harbor at the same time was far from our minds."

The best summary of Oahu's overconfidence can be found in a report written after the war by Colonel George Bicknell of Army intelligence. "Practically every person on the island of Oahu had been lulled into a sense of false security through the constant reiteration of the belief that the defenses of the island made it practically impregnable," he said. "In addition, it had been constantly stated that Japan, as a military and naval power, amounted to nothing when pitted against the superior equipment, personnel and tactics of our own army and navy. Our own naval personnel had made it a common practice of belittling the Japanese navy. Many times it had been stated that the Japanese fleet would be simply and easily annihilated if we started an offensive against them. . . .

"Little was actually known about Japanese air power although, again, there were many stories about the poor quality of Japanese aircraft, the lack of proper equipment, and the alleged fact that the Japanese made poor aviators and would never be good as occidentals in this field. Stories of Japanese having such poor vision that their flying ability was hampered, and tales of other physical characteristics which prevented them from ever becoming truly proficient in handling aircraft were common and many times retold."

There was a connection, of course, between the arrogance of December 6, and the search for scapegoats that began on December 8. The rumors that Japanese-American fifth columnists and saboteurs had helped the attackers were attempts to explain a defeat that was otherwise unexplainable. The pre-attack arrogance of the military also served to magnify the post-attack humiliation, since, as any "great athlete who has never been beaten" knows, there is no greater disgrace than to be defeated by an opponent you have previously denigrated. This is one reason why the psychological wounds of Pearl Harbor are cut so deeply into so many memories, and why the healing skin is so thin and easily punctured.

┌─────┐
│ *9* │
└─────┘

Mrs. Mori Talks to Tokyo

THE FBI RECORDED EVERY RADIOPHONE CALL BETWEEN HONO-
lulu and Tokyo, and on the afternoon of December 5, as the
Lurline sailed for California, it fell to Thomas Flynn, most
junior of the Honolulu agents, to sit in a cubicle in the FBI
office in the Dillingham Building, monitoring these calls. Since
he could not understand Japanese, and since conversations were
scrambled to prevent eavesdropping, what he remembers most
about the famous "Mori call" is not its content, but the details
surrounding its recording—copying it onto a brittle 78-rpm
record, and the byplay between the Honolulu and Tokyo operators. "Good morning, Honolulu. Good morning, Honolulu. . . . I have two tickets [calls]," the Tokyo operator said in
a tinkly Japanese voice. The Honolulu operator coldly cor-
rected her, answering "Good afternoon," because the time
zones were different and because, Flynn says in a disapproving
voice—evidence he now regards this prejudice as outdated as
the 78-rpm records—"she didn't like Japs."

The call was placed by a Mr. Ogawa, a reporter at the
Tokyo newspaper *Yomiuri Shinbun*, to Mrs. Ishiko Mori, a
Japanese alien living in Honolulu. She was married to Dr. Mo-

tokazu Mori, a prominent Japanese-American dentist, and worked as a stringer for *Yomiuri*. Ogawa had cabled on December 3, announcing he would call two days later to interview influential members of the Japanese-American community. But, wary of ties with Japan, all the people Mrs. Mori approached refused to participate, leaving it to her to answer Ogawa's dangerous questions.

"Are airplanes flying daily?" he asked.

"Yes," she replied. "Lots of them fly around."

"Are they large planes?"

"Yes, they are quite big," she said. It was an answer that Army Intelligence agent George Bicknell would soon consider highly significant, since "big planes" indicated long-range reconnaissance missions during daylight hours.

Many of Ogawa's questions concerned the Oahu's defenses. He asked: "Do they put searchlights on when planes fly about at night?" "I hear there are many sailors there, is that right?" "Do you know anything about the U.S. fleet?" Mrs. Mori answered with information available to anyone in Honolulu, including diplomats at the Japanese consulate.

When Ogawa asked, "What kind of flowers are in bloom in Hawaii at present?" the counterintelligence agents who later read the transcript suspected a code. And when Mrs. Mori answered that "the hibiscus and poinsettias are in bloom now," they believed she was reporting on the movement of specific battleships.

After the attack, Mrs. Mori and her husband were interned, but never charged with espionage. Their loyalties, however, have little to do with the real importance of this call. It was significant on December 6 not for information it communicated to Tokyo but for the warning it should have given Oahu's defenders. Because if they really believed someone in Tokyo was interested enough in Hawaii's defenses to invent such a flower code, and to pay two hundred dollars for a fifteen-minute call, they should have concluded Hawaii was in danger of attack.

FBI agent Robert Shivers read a transcript on the morning of December 6, judged it suspicious, and telephoned Captain Mayfield and Colonel Bicknell. Mayfield was out, and later that day, when the Mori call was described to him by an assistant, he called it "interesting," but not urgent.

Colonel Bicknell took it seriously. The day before, he had learned the Japanese consulate was burnings its papers. At a staff meeting the next morning he told colleagues this was "a most interesting fact" and "very significant in view of the present situation," and he claimed afterward it was a "definite indication that the end of peaceful relations was near." The Mori call confirmed his belief something was about to happen. He wondered why a Japanese newspaper would spend so much for a transpacific call, later explaining, "While nothing could be clearly defined as manifestly dangerous to security, the general tone of the conversation, when considered in the light of recent events, filled my mind with dread." He told Congressional investigators in 1945, "I still feel it was highly significant . . . putting it together with the information that we already had, that the Japanese consul was burning papers . . . a message of this type did, and still does, seem highly significant to me."

After reading a transcript of the call, Bicknell called his superior, Lieutenant Colonel Kendall Fielder, demanding an immediate audience with General Short. At 7:00 P.M. on December 6, Bicknell, Fielder, and Short met on the porch of Short's residence at Fort Shafter. Bicknell argued he knew Mori, suspected Mori, and was "rather positive that it [the call] meant something." He concluded the call was "highly suspicious," and indicated that "something was 'in the wind.' "

Fielder and Short were impatient. They were already late for a party at Schofield Barracks, and their wives sat in a nearby car, wearing formal dresses, upset at this further delay. Short argued it seemed like "quite an ordinary message" and "presented quite a true depiction of present-day life in Hawaii which a newspaperman would require for an article." He handed back the message, leaving Bicknell with the impression he and Fielder believed he was "perhaps too 'intelligence-conscious' . . . and that possibly there was nothing very much to get excited about."

Bicknell returned to his office, studying the transcript for another hour before going home. Today, his widow's strongest memory of December 6 is his frustration at no one taking the Mori call seriously, and her most vivid memory of December 7 is of her husband standing on their terrace in Aiae Heights, mumbling about "poinsettias" and "hibiscus" as battleships burst into flames below.

After the attack, the Mori call was important only for the Moris, who spent four years in an internment camp because of it, and for numerous Pearl Harbor investigators, who saw it as more damning evidence of the failures of the Hawaii Command. The 1946 Congressional investigation concluded, "The Mori call pointed directly at Hawaii," and described the failure to take it seriously as "inexcusable." It did not matter if the call was a genuine attempt at espionage, it still should have been "of greatest significance to responsible commanders in Hawaii."

When I first came across this story I was certain the Moris had been grievously wronged—interned on flimsy evidence, and because of their race. It seemed too fantastic that the Japanese command would risk revealing their intentions by asking such questions over an open line, and after the war, nothing had been found, either in the archives in Tokyo or in interviews conducted by occupation authorities, to indicate the Moris were spies. I was further persuaded of their innocence by Don Woodrum, who remembers sitting in the FBI offices on December 6, debating the significance of the Mori call. He believes it was simply an attempt to gather background for a story about Honolulu, which did appear several days later in *Yomiuri Shinbun,* and thinks it likely that "someone at the paper had a whiff of what was going to happen, heard a rumor of an attack on Hawaii, and thought it would be cute to have a background story ready to go."

I was also impressed by Mrs. Mori's replies to a newspaper interview published in 1957, on the sixteenth anniversary of the call. "I'm sure now that he [Ogawa] knew something big was going to happen here," she said. "He was laying the groundwork for a big scoop, feature and color copy when it happened." Her explanation for her involvement with the Japanese newspaper was poignant. She had traveled to Honolulu in 1929 from Japan to stay with a family friend, Dr. Iga Mori, and soon fell in love with his son. They married and had children, but American immigration laws prevented her becoming a citizen and required her to travel to Japan every two years, staying there a year before returning to American territory. After several such heartbreaking separations, she discovered she could remain in the United States if she was a diplomat, missionary, international merchant, or journalist.

Even had this article not described Mrs. Mori as a "vibrant, highly intelligent person," it was easy to admire her. It had taken courage to leave Japan and marry with the knowledge she would be separated from her family every two years, and I liked her honesty. In 1957, she admitted she had not become an American yet but suggested she might: "Gradually I am learning to love America the most and when my heart tells me I am sincere, I will become a citizen." When asked if she had spied for Japan, she laughed and said, "Of course not. I loved Japan, I still do, but I was never disloyal to the United States"— which is as true an expression of the conflicted emotions of Japanese aliens in Honolulu as you are likely to read.

Yet, the more I labored to convince myself the call had

been innocent, the more I began doubting it. There was the matter of the transcript, which was exactly as Colonel Bicknell described it, "very irregular and highly suspicious."

Mrs. Mori had said, ". . . It seems that the fleet has left here." (Actually only the aircraft carrier task forces had left.)

"Is that so?" Ogawa asked. "What kind of flowers are in bloom in Hawaii at present?"

Bicknell thought this exchange might be an "open code," one of the "most commonly used methods of passing on information." He believed it suspicious only two of the many flowers then blooming in Hawaii were mentioned, and that Ogawa appeared confused by Mrs. Mori's reply. He concluded, "Well, when the fellow in Japan who was talking did not catch the significance of the poinsettias undoubtedly the so-called secret code, or whatever they had, was not working properly."

If Bicknell had been among the many officers who suspected every Japanese resident of being a spy or saboteur, it would be easier to dismiss his suspicions. Instead, he was a longtime resident of Hawaii who repeatedly defended the Japanese community against charges of disloyalty or sabotage, often voicing the opinion that "we would never have any sabotage trouble with the local Japanese."

There is also the troubling question of who spoke with Ogawa on December 5. Mrs. Mori said she persuaded her husband to be interviewed, and the transcript appears to confirm this. At the end, Ogawa says, "Best regards to your wife," and Mori replies, "Wait a moment please?" But then hangs up. Both Shivers and Bicknell testified the speaker was Mrs. Mori, not her husband. (Presumably Ogawa had said "Best regards to your wife" before heavy static misled him into thinking he was speaking to a man.) Bicknell told the joint Congressional investigation, "As I remember the original record, it was a woman's voice. We may be mistaken. It may have been Dr. Mori himself. But he denied that he had the conversation and said it was his wife who did the talking when we examined him." If you examine the transcript closely, it points to Mrs. Mori. Ogawa opens by saying, "I received your telegram and was able to grasp the essential points." The voice identified as "H" for Honolulu does not dispute this, and since Mrs. Mori was the correspondent for *Yomiuri* it makes sense that she would have sent this telegram. But why would she later lie about taking the call, shifting suspicion onto her husband? Or why would he lie, placing his wife in danger?

I was told the Moris had died. They were not listed in the Honolulu phone directory, but I knew their former address, 702 Wylie Street, and went there hoping its current residents might remember them. Wylie Street is in Alawa Heights, an older Honolulu neighborhood of modest bungalows and predominantly Chinese and Japanese residents. The Moris' former home was an exception, a big rambling white elephant set on a corner lot, distinguished by its circular driveway and a porte cochère. Parked outside were three rusting commercial vans saying "DRAIN BRAIN—A. Breitinstein, Sewer and Drain Cleaning Service."

Mr. and Mrs. Breitinstein said that after living here twenty years, they had recently closed their business and were preparing to retire to Oklahoma. The downstairs rooms were jammed with packing crates, files, and plumbing tools, but I could still make out the Moris' legacy—a circular Oriental window, a teak dining-room table, a huge Japanese tub in the bathroom, built-in curio cabinets, and the spacious parlor where they had staged receptions for visiting Japanese dignitaries. "We often feel," Mr. Breitinstein said, "as if we are living with the Moris' ghosts."

"We definitely have had ghosts," Mrs. Breitinstein added, explaining the house was haunted by a lady, perhaps Mrs. Mori, or her daughter. The spirit had made its first appearance while her own daughter and Japanese son-in-law had been visiting from Japan. Their half-Japanese granddaughter had been the first to claim seeing a "lady" in her room. Their grandson saw her next. Then their daughter complained of waking up paralyzed, unable to move her hand to the telephone to call for help. The experience lasted twenty minutes, repeating itself two weeks later. The Breitinsteins hired a Japanese priest from the nearby Buddhist temple to perform an exorcism. He spent an hour upstairs, laying out plates of rice and fruit, lighting candles, and praying. But the ghost reappeared five years later, again during a visit from their daughter and Japanese son-in-law. The priest was summoned back and this time performed his exorcism throughout the house.

It made sense for Mrs. Mori to haunt the Breitinsteins. They were Japanophiles who had lived in that country many years, afterward choosing Honolulu because of its Japanese atmosphere. They had never met Mrs. Mori, yet believed she had been a Japanese agent, or at least an active sympathizer. Their best source of information was their neighbor Mrs. Wan, a Chinese schoolteacher who, before dying, had repeatedly insisted the Moris were spies, saying she had seen them rush into the street on December 7, shouting "Banzai!" and waving on the Japanese planes.

I was suspicious of Mrs. Wan. Although some of the forty thousand Japanese aliens in Hawaii on December 7 may have secretly rejoiced, few could have been foolish enough to make a public display, particularly if they were Japanese agents. The Japanese invasion of China had created tensions between Japanese and Chinese communities in Hawaii that survived the war, and I had already come across too many other similar "Banzai!" stories. In one version, an elderly Japanese man dressed in a kimono stood on his rooftop waving at the planes; in another, he waved a Japanese flag; in another, a samurai sword; and in another, he threw off his kimono and revealed the dress uniform of a Japanese naval officer.

Mr. Breitinstein said he had more convincing evidence. While running speaker cables for his music system underneath the house, he had discovered antenna wire, leading to more wire, and more, three hundred feet in all, a ground bounce for transmitting shortwave signals. "And on that much wire," he said, "you can bounce signals a long way." While searching for a plumbing leak, he found wire in what he called "the Moris' secret room." He showed me how the ceiling of a kitchen passageway had been dropped to create a small room reached through a sliding panel. Inside, he said, had been the sort of electrical connections necessary for a shortwave radio. But I still wondered if this proved anything. Perhaps Dr. Mori or his son had been ham radio enthusiasts. It was a common passion in the thirties and forties among the Japanese of Hawaii, who used shortwave sets to keep in touch with friends and relatives in Japan. This was why Marine Corps detachments sent into Japanese sugar camps like Aiea to hunt saboteurs described them as being a "forest of aerials."

Shortly after Pearl Harbor, Short and Bicknell discussed the Mori call once more when Short, nervous about his cavalier dismissal of it, said, "Well, Bicknell, you couldn't prove anything by that, that it meant anything." To which Bicknell answered, "Well, I still can't prove anything by it . . . and we never will be able to."

I felt much the same way. Had the Moris been Japanese agents, or innocent dupes in Ogawa's attempts to collect background for this "scoop"? Had Mrs. Wan witnessed their reckless demonstration of Japanese loyalty, or made it up? Why had one of them lied about who had taken the call? And why the secret room? The Mori call was like many Pearl Harbor mysteries—the more you learned, the more difficult it was to "prove" anything. Many of these mysteries, both important and trivial, such as "Why did a Navy commander disappear while walking in the hills overlooking Pearl Harbor several months before December 7?" and "Did a Japanese pilot land on a golf course during the attack, just feet from Admiral Kimmel's Japanese caddy, as this caddy has always claimed?" will probably remain forever unsolved. And the nervous uncertainty produced by such mysteries, and by many unsettled Pearl Harbor disputes and unreconciled combatants, is precisely the atmosphere that favors the appearance of ghosts.

10

Ensign Yoshikawa's Last Cable

ENSIGN YOSHIKAWA DROVE TO AIEA HEIGHTS TO SPY ON THE fleet, and then spent the rest of the morning of December 6 locked in the telegraph room of the Japanese consulate on Nuuanu Avenue. At 1:00 P.M., he responded to Tokyo's urgent request for information about "observation balloons" and "anti-mine nets" with a cable reading, "In my opinion the battleships do not have torpedo nets. . . . At the present time there are no signs of barrage balloon equipment. In addition, it is difficult to imagine that they have actually any. . . ." He then added a personal observation that might easily have changed history.

Although he did not know for certain if or when Japan would attack Pearl Harbor, the urgency and nature of Tokyo's requests for information in early December indicated it was a possibility, and so, perhaps hungover from a late evening at the Shuncho-Ro, or perhaps elated by the casual attitude of Oahu's defenders, he made a breathtaking error, adding to his penultimate message the gratuitous comment "I imagine that in all probability there is considerable opportunity left to take advantage for a surprise attack against these places."

His cable was immediately intercepted by monitoring stations in Hawaii and San Francisco and sent to Washington for decoding by Magic. A copy was also passed to Navy intelligence by the RCA office in Honolulu. But since it came from a source already dismissed as unimportant, in neither case was it decoded and translated in time.

In the afternoon, Yoshikawa visited Pearl City and Aiea Heights again to count warships. At 9:00 P.M., sitting alone in a darkened consulate, with the sky outside illuminated by the reflected glare of Pearl Harbor's lights, he dispatched a final ship-movement report that ended, "It appears that no air reconnaissance is being conducted by the fleet air arm."

Nineteen years later, Yoshikawa remembered this evening in romantic and heroic terms, recalling a "clear tropical night," taro fronds that "stirred gently in the breeze," and the "coral rock of the consulate drive shimmering faintly in the moonlight." "In truth, if for only a moment in time," he said, "I held history in the palm of my hand."

After being repatriated to Japan in August 1942 with other interned Japanese diplomats, Yoshikawa was ignored, serving out the war at the same rank on the general staff. In 1945, fearing prosecution as a war criminal and frightened after seven naval officers involved in spying on America were sentenced to long jail sentences, he went into hiding in a forest, risking starvation, becoming an apprentice Buddhist monk, and supporting himself by making candy. Two years later he surfaced to open a filling station, soon discovering that "people who knew of my past said I was a very great patriot, or they avoided me. A funny thing about a spy. No one seems to trust him, not even in his own country."

His anonymity ended in 1960 when, broke and out of work, he wrote a book about his experiences in Honolulu and promoted it on television. Billing himself the Pearl Harbor "master spy," he was soon busy teaching the techniques of industrial espionage to Japanese executives. He returned to Honolulu in 1961 to appear on a Walter Cronkite documentary commemorating the twentieth anniversary of the attack, and was later hired as a technical adviser for *Tora! Tora! Tora!* The Japanese government, however, still refuses to reward or acknowledge his exploits, and his request for a pension was denied by an official who said, "You must be some kind of child to think that we will ever acknowledge your activities in Honolulu. The government of Japan never spied on anyone."

Whenever Yoshikawa reminisced about his life in Honolulu and his return to the city in 1961, he described his residence there as the happiest times of his life. "I found Hawaii a most beautiful place," he told one American reporter. "It also made me want to see the rest of the United States. Do you think I would be received favorably in the United States? Do you think I could obtain a good job there?"

In 1981 he was operating a plumbing business, and still hoping to revisit Hawaii. He told a journalist from the *Honolulu Star-Bulletin* he planned to come the following year for his seventieth birthday. But illness forced him to cancel the trip, and he has since suffered a stroke. If he does manage a last return, he will find most of his former haunts substantially changed. The Japanese consulate has been remodeled and expanded from the original two-story concrete block. The garden where diplomats burned Japanese codes on December 6 has been altered by trees planted to honor postwar visits by the imperial family. A 1972 tree commemorating "the reversion of Okinawa to the mother country" is the only reminder of the war.

If he were to take his favorite drive down the Kamehameha Highway to Pearl City he would see strip malls, shopping centers, and the Pearl City Mall, whose vast asphalt-and-concrete precincts are connected by a monorail. Pearl City peninsula is now a restricted area of naval housing, and the service station with a view of Pearl Harbor once owned by the talkative Mr. Sumida has been replaced by self-service gas stations where clerks sit mute in plastic boxes, gesturing for payment in advance before turning on the pumps. The highway's once-fine view of Pearl Harbor is blocked by "Muumuu Factory Direct to You," "BoPeep Sheepskin Seats," Funway Rental's "Samurai Jeeps," and Japanese car dealerships, their acres of Nissans and Toyotas further enlarging the trade deficit.

But at the Shuncho-Ro teahouse, now advertised as "Honolulu's oldest," Yoshikawa is remembered. It has changed its name to the Natsunoya teahouse, but remains a sprawling two-story wooden house sitting on a bluff overlooking Honolulu. Its cream-colored dining rooms are shabby but clean, with worn linoleum and tatami mats smelling faintly of dirty socks. All but one of its 1941 geishas has been pensioned, and the balcony from which Yoshikawa observed Pearl Harbor has been enclosed in glass, while the trees in front have grown taller, blocking some of the view. Still, I could see in a minute that Pearl Harbor is too distant to be observed clearly through even a strong telescope. Spying was a pretext; Yoshikawa had come here for drink and romance.

The Natsunoya is still selling its view, promising Japanese visitors "a spectacular panorama." Instead of Pearl Harbor, its patrons see the Japanese-owned office buildings of downtown Honolulu and the Japanese-owned hotels of Waikiki. This view is also featured in the Natsunoya's handsome but unsettling brochure, which shows lines of black Japanese characters poised like lines of falling bombs above Honolulu's skyline.

I was given a tour by a headwaiter who complained that ever since Japanese companies had purchased many Waikiki hotels and equipped them with Japanese restaurants, fewer groups made the twenty-minute drive to the Natsunoya. Now the teahouse depended on "deluxe kinds of tourists" who arrived by taxi and knew about its history. They insisted on knowing where Yoshikawa had sat and where the telescope had been. Here at the Natsunoya, at least, he was famous, a hero to his countrymen.

If Yoshikawa ever does return to Hawaii, he may find Americans even more suspicious of Japanese spies than in 1941. Consider, for example, the case of Mr. Takashi Morimoto, an employee of the Nissan Motor Company whom the Japanese-American Cultural Center of Los Angeles placed as a boarder with a local family. He stayed with them six weeks, a quiet and polite guest who worked hard at improving his English. Only afterward did they learn from a newspaper article that he had been observing them as part of a Nissan research project, secretly filling up pages of a notebook before going to sleep, photographing their house from dozens of angles, and accompanying them on trips to shopping centers, not to be helpful as they had assumed, but to see how they parked, loaded, and drove their car. They were furious, charging he was not, as Nissan claimed, simply an innocent "researcher," but a corporate spy, and they sued for invasion of privacy, fraud, trespass, breach of contract, and unfair business practices. But ask yourself: If Morimoto had been a German working for BMW, or a Swede from Volvo, would they have sued? (And would Volvo or BMW have come clean from the start, identifying this as a "research project"?) And also ask yourself: Was it a coincidence they filed their lawsuit on December 7, 1989?

11

A White River Flows Down Hotel Street

THE EVENING OF DECEMBER 6 IS USUALLY DESCRIBED AS "still" or "peaceful," words evoking Christmas Eve, and implying a world catching its breath before a great event. Drive around Honolulu now on a Saturday night and you smell exhaust and hear automobiles braking, accelerating, and sending up a hum from the interstate. But on December 6, Honolulu was a city humming to music, to swing bands on jukeboxes, fox-trots played by orchestras at the Ala Moana and Royal Hawaiian hotels, and slushy Hawaiian music coming from the radios of partying sailors and lonely guards. There was a "Battle of the Bands" in the Naval Receiving Station at Pearl Harbor, at which battleship orchestras competed in playing "I Don't Want to Set the World on Fire" and "Take the A Train." The band of the U.S.S. *Arizona* won second place, and its reward was sleeping late the next morning, meaning not a single man would survive. A group photograph was taken of this band on December 6 (or perhaps at a similar competition on November 29; no one is sure), and while most photographs of the time show a blur of khaki or white, in this one band members have removed their hats and sit near the camera, revealing their innocent high school faces. Perhaps I am unsettled by their shipmates, sitting behind them in dress whites and already a ghostly presence, or the proud way they hold up their trombones and clarinets, but if I had to choose the most poignant Pearl Harbor photograph, this would be it.

Today, Honolulu's lighting is harsh, and its sodium lamps, spotlights, and security floodlights swallow more gentle illuminations. But in 1941, it was a city of deep shadows and soft light. Campfires flickered at beach picnics, and bare bulbs swung from backyard trees. At dusk the ocean turned purple, the surf became luminescent, and you could see the lanterns of Japanese sampans, the glowing portholes of moored freighters, and luau torches flickering where parties were already underway.

The evening *Star-Bulletin* of December 6 carried a front-page story by Lawrence Nakatsuka titled "Baby Boom Hits Hawaii, Stork Calls Every Hour," describing a sudden upswing in births attributed to the defense boom. He speculated that Honolulu's citizens sensed the danger of war, and quoted an expert as saying, "There is . . . a natural urge to produce off-spring before being shot to pieces," which may also explain why, believing a war in Asia was imminent, the citizens of Honolulu come across as restless on the evening of December 6, attending numerous dances and parties and determinedly searching for fun.

At the Japanese consulate, Kita was throwing one of his frequent stag night for the city's leading citizens. Admiral Kimmel had been invited, and although he had attended on other occasions, this time he refused, one of few decisions made this day for which he would later be grateful. Colonel Bicknell also declined, perhaps because he remembered Kita's earlier functions as "really wet parties, [with] a bottle of scotch at each place and a geisha girl pouring it out." One such gathering had ended with the geishas tossing a local businessman in the air in a blanket.

At the University of Hawaii there was a party for the Willamette football team, and a junior-class dance attended by many of the young niseis who would be returning tomorrow to defend the university against enemy paratroopers. Many prominent islanders were at an engagement party for the son of former Governor Lawrence Judd. The Lau Yee Chai restaurant of Waikiki, the self-proclaimed "Most Beautiful Chinese Restaurant in the World" with its mahogany screens, carp pools, and miniature backyard mountain, was having a belated harvest moon festival. Pilots from Wheeler and Hickam fields danced at the Hickam officers' club, dressed in white dinner jackets, their wives in long dresses, following the base rule that officers and their wives wear formal clothes after 5:00 P.M. Dorothy Anthony and her husband, Garner, a prominent Honolulu attorney, were throwing a party at the Pacific Club for two of his former Harvard Law School friends posted to Hawaii with the military. "We all knew war might break out in Asia, because all the big newspapermen stopped here on their way," she remembers. "But that night you couldn't have gotten anyone at that party to say war would come to Hawaii."

On the sixth day of every month for the last six, a young lieutenant from the *Arizona* and his wife, Jim and Jinny Dare, had been throwing a champagne party to celebrate their monthly wedding anniversary. Ruth Flynn, then the personal secretary to Robert Shivers of the FBI, remembers that of December 6 as the gayest of all. It was held in a cottage on the grounds of the Halekulani Hotel and attended by young officers from the *Arizona* and several destroyers. Even though tomorrow she would feel the FBI office in the Dillingham Building sway from nearby explosions, it is this party she appears to remember in most vivid detail. "My friends and I would often go to the *Arizona* in the evenings when she was in port to watch movies on her fantail," she told me. "Or we would go to the monthly *Arizona* dances at the Ala Moana. At those parties the enlisted men had permission to dance with the officers' wives or dates. I became acquainted with so many enlisted men I could not walk down Kalakaua Avenue without having someone from the *Arizona* say hello."

She had earlier eaten a supper of Chinese food washed down with zombies, with a man she disliked. She returned home to receive phone calls every five minutes from Lieutenant Bucky Walsh of the *Arizona,* who threatened to continue calling until she agreed to attend the Dares' anniversary party. She gave in and went. "There were lots of women, but not enough," she remembers. "This mob of young officers had been at sea for weeks, and when they saw Bucky walking up the path with a female, one of them grabbed me and flung me over his shoulder like a sack of potatoes. That was how I made my entrance." After a short while she felt ill, perhaps from the Chinese food and zombies, and Walsh walked her home, making a date to attend the nine-o'clock mass at St. Augustine's in Waikiki. He told her he was going back to the *Arizona* but later changed his mind, returning to the party. "When it was over," Ruth Flynn says, "the Dares insisted he spend the night in their cottage, and that's why he's alive today."

Many officers did return to the *Arizona.* "Now, when friends visit from the mainland," she says, "I can't bear to take them to the *Arizona* any longer. It's gotten to be too much, looking at that list of names and seeing so many people I knew." And I think this may explain why she and other Honoluans remember December 6 so well, because it was the last time they saw their friends alive.

While officers drank and danced in hotel ballrooms and private parties, enlisted men entertained themselves in the taverns, shooting galleries, and pool halls lining Hotel Street, a

thoroughfare running through the commercial center of Honolulu into Chinatown. Throughout the afternoon and evening of
December 6, buses and rattletrap taxis had raced down a two-
lane highway connecting Pearl Harbor and Honolulu, past the
burned-out wrecks of similar taxis, and by sunset, a white river
of sailors was flowing down Hotel Street.

The men squinted into the falling sun, bored, waiting for
something to happen. They stood slouched under stuttering
fluorescent bulbs, smoking and laughing, cartoon sailors with
flapping pant legs and caps pulled over one eye. They bought
silver daggers, fringed satin pillows saying "I Love You Mother
o' Mine," photographs of bare-breasted women holding up
patriotic slogans, and monkey-pod carvings that today bring
two hundred dollars in Honolulu curio stores. They squan-
dered money at shooting galleries, on Skee-Ball and pinball,
and on throwing baseballs at milk cans. They sat bare-chested
under naked bulbs as Filipino tattoo artists pricked their skin.
They drank too much, then sobered up with coffee at cafés like
the Black Cat Café, the Bunny Ranch, Lousy Lui's, and Swanky
Franky, which made so much money selling hot dogs to servicemen that it became the foundation of the Spencecliff restaurant chain, purchased by Japanese interests four decades
later.

Most of all, they wanted women, and finding none, they
paid for them. Honolulu had always been a city of lonely men.
First came New England whalers, who had brought venereal
diseases that decimated the native population. Then Chinese
laborers, who sent back photographs to be pasted onto those of
their families, the only way they could be reunited. Then Japanese plantation workers, who had chosen "picture brides"
from albums. Then Filipino cane cutters, who were prohibited
from marrying and had patronized the taxi-dance halls. And
finally came the 100,000 servicemen of December 1941.

Because almost seven million tourists a year now pay

dearly to vacation in Hawaii, it may come as a surprise that in 1941 many servicemen loathed the place. Some had not seen their families for almost two years. They pursued the lonely-man pastimes of beer drinking and cardplaying, fought with local youths they called "gooks," and sat on shoreline rocks, heads in hands, staring toward San Francisco. Their suicide rate was higher than on mainland bases, and in October 1941, one despondent soldier the newspapers described as a "human bomb" threw himself from the roof of the University Cinema onto the orchestra seats.

You might expected someone like Bob Kinzler to have fond memories of his Army days at Schofield Barracks, since he later settled in Hawaii, serving in the Army Reserves until 1962 and sending one daughter to West Point. Instead, he remembers the "pathetic sight" of soldiers lining up outside whorehouses and that "with ten dollars a month in pay there was nothing for a private to do but take walks." "We had no contact with the Asian population except through the Japanese lady barbers," he says, "and civilians thought we were just a bunch of bums who couldn't get jobs so we had enlisted in the military."

This was why lonely soldiers paid to embrace Filipino taxi dancers whose heavy eye shadow melted down their faces like tears, why they dropped money in Hotel Street photographic studios, paying to wrap their arms around girls in grass skirts who clicked on smiles as they ignored whispered pleas for a date, and why they joined the double lines stretching around the block from houses of prostitution that advertised on matchbooks—"The Bell Rooms—Give the Bell a Ring!"—and were so efficient that nearby taverns sold tokens good for a screw, and customers were separated into three-dollar (hard and ready) and five-dollar (clothes off) lines.

Despite the prostitution, then known as "white-slave traf-fic," despite neighborhoods with names such as Tin Can Alley, Blood Town, Mosquito Flats, and Hell's Half Acre, and despite the sneak thieves and pimps, there was a certain innocence to Hotel Street, and a certain sense of order and propriety that has since vanished. "Wholesome fun for the lads and a place to spend their money without too much exploitation," said *Paradise of the Pacific,* and that was not too far wrong. Most blocks had lei shops filled with Hawaiian women stringing flowers. Amusement arcades offered games of skill out of a state-fair midway, souvenirs were testimonials of love for mothers or sweethearts, and the most popular activity was spinning out a beer or Coke while flirting with a waitress. The taxi-dance halls were heavily varnished, barnlike rooms reminiscent of church halls, where liquor was prohibited and dancers forbidden to leave until collected by their mothers or husbands. Prostitutes were given weekly blood tests by city doctors, and in what was either shrewd policy or kindness, many women offered a discount to the Filipino cane cutters, who could not afford full price.

Hotel Street now runs through a Honolulu neighborhood that closely resembles its 1941 photographs. It is still a narrow street fronted by low stucco and granite buildings and shaded by tin awnings. But if you come closer, you can see it is being gentrified. Antique stores and boutiques coexist with dives and strip clubs still exhaling their halitosis of cigarettes and stale beer. Inside them are lizardy men with fading tattoos, Filipino toughs with needle tracks, and hookers wearing splotches of heavy pancake makeup, perhaps to camouflage AIDS blemishes. Every patron is cursed by an ugly cough, a limp, a damaged eye, or a scar. In its death throes, Hotel Street is a place for bottom-of-the-barrel fun, as nasty as a run-over dog, thrashing, snarling, and snapping its jaws, a neighborhood that would shock the lonely sailors who tried to wring some last fun from it on December 6.

That evening appeared to be a Hotel Street Saturday night like any other, but of course it was not. For some men, a

Swanky Franky would be their last meal, a beer at the Pantheon tavern their last drink, throwing a baseball at three milk cans their last fun, and a taxi dancer the last woman they would touch. In wartime, men understand this. But the tragedy of December 6 is that because it seemed an evening like any other, these lonely men did not drink more, screw more, or throw more baseballs.

There were some who argued that the tragedy of this night was that these servicemen drank or whored at all. Although Honolulu's civilians did little to entertain military men, some disapproved of their attempts to entertain themselves. At nine o'clock on the evening of December 6, Mr. Chris Benny, executive secretary of the Temperance League of Hawaii, and two other members of the league, Mr. Sanbourne and Mr. Castle, the head of one of Hawaii's wealthiest families and a director of Castle & Cooke, met at the Army and Navy YMCA, at the eastern end of Hotel Street, to investigate the alcoholic debauchery of a typical Saturday night. They walked down Hotel Street, up River Street to Beretania, over to Nuuanu, and back to the YMCA, past the most notorious dives. "We noticed a number of drunken Army and Navy men and a great many sitting at the tables in the taverns drinking beer and hard liquor," Mr. Benny said later. "We loitered on the streets, standing outside some of these places . . . to observe whether the men were going up and down to the entrances to houses of prostitution." His delegation never counted inebriated sailors, nor witnessed anyone being arrested, yet on January 3, he wrote a letter to the Roberts Commission charging the timing of the Japanese attack was "based on the well known but grim and awful fact that we have only half a Navy, half an Army, on Saturday night and Sunday morning." It was an exaggeration common to the stories circulated by temperance and prohibitionist organizations shortly after the attack, with one prohibitionist tract claiming that "the free flow of alcohol was a fifth column working for the Japanese" and that "prohibition *be-fore* Pearl Harbor might have saved us from the worst defeat our nation has ever undergone."

In truth, the military behaved rather well on December 6. About a tenth of the 100,000 sailors and soldiers stationed on Oahu visited downtown Honolulu. Yet the police arrested only four for public intoxication, and the military police and shore patrol removed only eighty from the streets. To slander servicemen for enjoying themselves on what for some would be their last night on earth, to blame Pearl Harbor on their attempts to entertain themselves, and to say Japan was victorious because Oahu's defenders woke with hangovers is as absurd as it is repellent. It would be comforting to dismiss it as peculiar to the Temperance League, or a nasty wartime phenomenon. Yet for years afterward, even to the present, other groups and individuals have exploited the dead of Pearl Harbor to further their agendas.

At midnight on December 6, as on every Saturday night on an island controlled by the descendants of missionaries who had banned the hula and dressed the natives in shapeless gingham dresses, bars closed and dances ended. Orchestras played the national anthem and men in uniform stood to attention. Sailors poured from bars and arcades, and Hotel Street again became a swollen river of white uniforms, now flowing east toward the YMCA, where buses waited to return sailors to Pearl Harbor. Back at the docks, they engaged in a Saturday-night ritual of fighting for places aboard the last liberty ships, falling into the water, laughing, and pulling in their buddies.

Tomorrow some would become heroes, diving into burning water to rescue shipmates. But tonight, the only real heroes on Oahu were the defense workers who labored on the night shift at the Pearl Harbor dry dock, repairing the battleship *Pennsylvania* and several destroyers. They would emerge from tomorrow with their honor intact, blameless for the defeat, given the crucial job of rebuilding the fortifications the military had misused, and salvaging the ships they had lost.

These defense workers—soon to be called "war workers" —were the kind of confident, muscular young men idealized in newsreels for building the New Deal's public works. But in Hawaii they were scorned. It was said that "no one extended them much of an aloha," and their grimy clothes and grease-smeared faces were a reproach to Hawaii's languid workday. I read that Oriental girls "looked down their noses at them," and that they wore their aloha shirts "badly." Enlisted men resented them because they had more money. The Caucasian establishment worried that their ranks concealed agitators come to corrupt plantation workers. They were blamed for Honolulu's crowding, traffic, and crime, just as newcomers from the mainland are blamed today, and it was feared that they were another in that line of single white men—whalers, beachcombers, and traders—who leave Hawaii the worse for their presence.

While the boastful military exercises and parades that filled Honolulu's skies and streets before Pearl Harbor now appear as exercises in bombast, the 1941 Honolulu Labor Day parade still sounds stirring. Eight thousand defense workers turned out to march: ranks of lathers, plumbers, plasterers, and boiler-makers, painters, carpenters, ironworkers, and hod carriers, the men wearing white shirts and ties or matching coveralls, the women in gingham dresses. They rode floats showing riveters and machinists at work, and carrying banners such as, "Iron-workers 101% for defense—Are You?" The sight of them was so impressive that spectators fell silent and, according to one newspaper account, no wisecracks were heard from those witnessing the "men who will build the air and navy bases which must someday protect Hawaii from a foe that will strike without warning."

One defense worker, Ed Sheehan, who was in the Pearl Harbor dry dock on December 6, remembers putting new steel plates on the destroyer *Downes,* listening to "Moonlight Serenade" and "Moonglow" blasted from loudspeakers during the mealtime pause, and the contrast between the dry-dock lights and the darkness outside—"how the drydock looked like a dozing volcano, its rim sharp against the glow of lights deep inside," and how a "blue-white light sent great shadows dancing upon the dock's walls."

At 11:00 P.M. on December 6, shortly before five Japanese "mother ship" submarines launched the two-man midget submarines of the "Special Attack Unit" ten miles from Oahu, some of their crews saw Honolulu's lights twinkling in their periscopes. Perhaps they saw the neon lights of Waikiki and Hotel Street, the flashing lights of the Aloha Tower, the headlights of Gus Ahola's car, the aircraft warning lights on top of the Hickam water tower, or, burning brightest of all, the drydock spotlights illuminating the work of men who would eventually prove more dangerous than these slumbering battleships.

Earlier that evening, the Army had ordered a Honolulu radio station to broadcast all night in order to provide a beacon for a flight of unarmed B-17s expected tomorrow from the mainland. Japanese sailors and pilots also picked up the music, hearing "plantation melodies" and KGMB's "Swing Nocturne." It also provided them with a beacon, and reassured them their attack would be a surprise. There is a photograph showing Japanese flight crews in the briefing rooms of their carriers on the evening of December 6, laughing and performing crude hulas to this music, believing it proved America to be as unprepared and hedonistic as their propaganda had promised.

PART THREE

December 7, 1941

12

Hawaii Takes a Deep Breath

BETWEEN MIDNIGHT AND 0300 OF DECEMBER 7, JAPAN COM-
mitted its first, irrevocable act of war when the two-man
crews of the five midget submarines boarded their craft, carrying warm sweaters and bottles of sake and shouting "On to
Pearl Harbor!" Steel clamps fastening the midgets to mother
ships were released, and they motored toward Oahu. Their
orders were to lie on the bottom of Pearl Harbor, waiting
until morning before launching torpedoes at American battleships.

The first midget reached the harbor channel at about 0330.
A sliver of moon lit a sky that was calm and empty except for
scattered trade-wind clouds. Eighty-six combatant and service
ships of the Pacific Fleet were dark silhouettes, moored at
docks, anchored singly or in pairs, lit only by anchor lights.
Three quarters of their gun batteries were unmanned, their
ammunition locked in boxes. The only three warships under
steam were the minesweepers *Condor* and *Crossbill*, checking
the channel entrance for mines, and the *Ward*, patrolling offshore waters. She was an obsolete World War One destroyer,
led by a captain on his first day of command and staffed with

naval reservists from Minnesota whose only sea duty had been on Lake Superior.

At 0340, the *Condor* sighted the periscope of a midget submarine two miles from the Pearl Harbor entrance buoys. She alerted the *Ward,* which went to general quarters and mounted an unsuccessful search. The midget slipped into Pearl Harbor. Two hours later, the supply ship *Antares* sighted another midget attempting to follow in its wake as it entered the harbor. In the breaking dawn, the *Ward*'s watch officer spotted the periscope trailing the *Antares.* Captain William Outerbridge appeared on deck, wearing a kimono over his pajamas, and immediately ordered an attack. At 0645, the *Ward*'s number three gun scored a "square positive hit" at the junction of the midget's hull and conning tower, sinking it in twelve hundred feet of water, and winning the first engagement of the Pacific War.

At 0653, an hour and two minutes before Japanese planes launched their attack, Outerbridge radioed 14th Naval District headquarters in Pearl Harbor, "We have attacked, fired upon, and dropped depth charges upon submarine operating in defensive sea area. Stand by for further messages."

Instead of electrifying its recipients, causing sirens to sound, pilots to dash for planes, and warships to put to sea, this communication touched off a round of telephone calls between the watch officer who received it and Captain Earle, the staff officer to Admiral Bloch who commanded the 14th Naval District, then between Admiral Kimmel's duty officer, Admiral Bloch, and Admiral Kimmel himself, who had risen at seven for an early round of golf with General Short. Because of busy signals, and because Earle and Bloch discussed the implications of Outerbridge's message for almost ten minutes, a half hour passed before any decision was made. Earle believed it was "just another of those false reports." Kimmel concurred, deciding to "wait for verification." Meanwhile, Bloch failed to notify the Army that a hostile submarine had been sunk off Pearl Harbor, a call that might finally have put General Short on the alert. He decided instead to "wait further developments." Finally, at 0751, four minutes before the attack and an hour after Outerbridge's report, the destroyer *Monaghan* was sent from the harbor to join the *Ward,* search for "developments," and provide "verification." These mistakes cost the *Ward* the honor of becoming the most celebrated United States Naval vessel of the century. Instead, her decisive action became a footnote, her crewmen formed a little-known organization called the First Shot Naval Vets of St. Paul, Minnesota, and her number three gun, instead of being in the Smithsonian, is displayed on the grounds of the Minnesota state capitol.

The *Ward* incident was one among several missed last-minute chances to sound an alarm. The second came at 0706, when Privates Joseph Lockhard and George Elliott, the operators of the Opana mobile radar unit on Oahu's northern coast, picked up a blip 132 miles northeast of Oahu, which they correctly interpreted as a large incoming flight of planes.

The Opana station was one of six established along Oahu's coastline at the end of November. However, since General Short was unconvinced of the value of radar and did not understand it or think it necessary—and because it could not warn against sabotage—he used it, as he later admitted, "for training more than any idea that it [an attack] would be real." This explains why radar stations on Oahu operated only between 0400 and 0700 on Sundays, and sporadically during the week, why he failed to establish approach lanes enabling friendly aircraft to be separated from enemy ones, and why he placed the Hawaiian Department's fighters on a four-hour alert, meaning it would take that long to arm and scramble them, although the radar picked up aircraft only when they were less than an hour from Oahu.

Lockhard and Elliott saw the Japanese first wave by chance,

only because the truck sent to collect them at 0700 was late. Elliott immediately called the Fort Shafter Information Center and informed Private Joseph McDonald of a blip that was "very big . . . very noticeable" and "out of the ordinary." McDonald alerted the pursuit officer on duty, Lieutenant Kermit Tyler, saying it was the first time he had received such a report, and it looked "kind of strange." McDonald called the Opana station, and Lockhard described "an unusually large flight—in fact, the largest I [have] ever seen on the equipment—coming from almost due north at one hundred and thirty some miles." Tyler was a pursuit pilot who had drawn this duty only once before. He had no training in radar, but he knew a flight of B-17s was expected from the mainland early that morning and, assuming Lockard was seeing these planes, he said, "Well, don't worry about it."

"What do you think it is?" McDonald asked when he had hung up.

"It's nothing," Tyler replied.

In Washington, several opportunities were missed to send a final warning. On December 6, a fourteen-part Japanese ultimatum had been decoded, but an ominous "trigger" message, instructing Japanese diplomats to deliver it before 1:00 P.M. on December 7, then destroy their code machine, was only decoded by Magic early on the morning of December 7. The Chief of Naval Operations, Admiral Harold Stark, received it at 1030 Washington time, 0500 in Hawaii. He recognized 1:00 P.M. in Washington to be early in the morning in the Far East, and concluded the delivery of the Japanese ultimatum was timed to coincide with "operations in the Far East and possibly Hawaii." His director of naval intelligence, Captain Theodore Wilkinson, asked, "Why don't you pick up the telephone and call Kimmel?" He lifted the receiver, then shook his head, saying, "No, I think I will call the President." The moment had been lost. The White House switchboard was engaged, and

Stark, believing Kimmel had been adequately alerted by the "war warning" of November 27, decided to rely on the Army Chief of Staff, General George Marshall, transmitting an alert to General Short, with instructions to inform the Navy.

Marshall had been out riding most of the morning, and did not see the "trigger" message until 1125, two hours after its decoding. He agreed it indicated a Japanese attack on an American installation shortly after 1:00 P.M. Washington time. He drafted a warning in long-hand to the Army's Pacific bases, saying, "Japanese are presenting at 1:00 P.M. eastern standard time today what amounts to an ultimatum. Also they are under orders to destroy their code machine immediately. Just what significance the hour set may have we do not know but be on the alert accordingly. Inform naval authorities of this communication." Although Marshall ordered his message sent the "fastest safe means possible," it was delayed because War Department clerks needed several minutes to decipher his hasty scrawl, then delayed again by poor atmospheric conditions over the Pacific. Finally, at 1217 Washington time, 0647 Honolulu time, an officer at the War Department Signal Center decided to send it to Hawaii via commercial cable. It arrived at the RCA cable office in Honolulu at 0733. Five minutes later, RCA messenger Tadeo Fuchikami collected it from the Kahili pigeonhole, but because the envelope was not marked "urgent," he did not jump on his motorcycle and race to Fort Shafter.

These last, heartbreaking chances to put Oahu on alert have the slow-motion inevitability of a nightmare. The outcome is known, but still they fascinate. When I read about them, they send my heart beating faster, making me wish I had been there, telling Stark not to put down that telephone but to call Kimmel directly, warning Marshall not to trust the vagaries of his signal center, urging Fuchikami to race to Fort Shafter, persuading Tyler to believe Elliott's radar report, and arguing Kimmel out of dismissing the *Ward*'s encounter as a possible false alarm. How could it be, I want to shout, when Outerbridge has reported "firing on" a submarine, meaning he used his deck guns, meaning he had to have *seen* it!

There were other missed clues, such as Mrs. Edgers's ignored translation of the "lights" message, and the Japanese scout planes that flew undetected over Maui and Pearl Harbor an hour beforehand, too many to explain away as "bad luck," and so many they become conclusive evidence of the thick carapace of overconfidence that cloaked Washington and Honolulu. Even had they prompted a last-minute alert, this would not have guaranteed an American victory. The alarms from Outerbridge and Lockard would have given Oahu a half hour, not enough time to wheel every antiaircraft gun into place or untangle and arm all fifty fighters, but enough to man ships' batteries, break up the Japanese formations, and blunt the attack. The few American pilots who saw action on December 7 recorded an impressive ratio of kills, four each for Second Lieutenants Ken Taylor and George Welsh. The fact that the Japanese inflicted the most serious damage during the first twenty minutes and relatively little during the following hour and a half when they met considerable resistance indicates what might have happened if Oahu had had thirty minutes' warning. It would not have prevented war or changed its outcome. Warships would have been damaged, lives lost, and planes destroyed. But by enabling the United States to rescue some honor from the day, such a warning would have reduced the humiliation and anger. Pearl Harbor would still be remembered, but with less passion, and bitterness.

The blips seen by Lockard and Elliott were the forty torpedo bombers, forty-three Zeros, and one hundred dive-bombers and level bombers launched at 0600 that morning by a Japanese battle fleet 275 miles due north of the Opana station (the same spot where thirty years later the *Apollo 15* astronauts would splash down after their mission to the moon). This first wave of 183 planes crossed the north shore of Oahu at 0740, throwing fast-moving shadows across checkerboard fields of pineapples and sugarcane, flying undetected by military command centers, but heard and seen by numerous servicemen and civilians. So common were large flights over Oahu, and so certain its residents they were immune from air raids, that few of the fishermen, surfers, churchgoers, or golfers who saw them gave them more than a glance.

Years later, witnesses would remember this morning as memorably beautiful, yet infused with an eerie quiet. They would remember the green Koolaus standing out sharp against sheets of blue sky, lines of surf, Pearl Harbor calm as a millpond, and the normal sounds of morning—whistling kettles, clinking plates, and crying babies. They would remember wives or husbands across a breakfast table, a familiar pew in church, an unusual stillness in the air, and a formation of silver planes, shooting between puffy clouds. Then, at 0754, the wind dropped, clouds froze, and a spooky quiet descended, as if the earth had paused for a deep breath.

The best views of this last minute of peace were shared by sailors on duty in the Pearl Harbor signal tower, private pilots in the air over Oahu, and, of course, the Japanese. Every morning at 0755 a signalman in the Pearl Harbor tower raised a white-and-blue flag standing for the letter *P,* known in the international flag code as "Prep." It told color guards assembled on warships to raise the Stars and Stripes in precisely five minutes, ensuring the spectacle would occur in smart concert.

On December 7, the Pearl Harbor signalman could see color guards assembling on many of the eight battleships, eight cruisers, twenty-nine destroyers, and assorted submarines, minecraft, tenders, and auxiliaries of the Pacific Fleet. The battleship *Pennsylvania* was nearest the tower, resting in dry dock number one alongside destroyers *Cassin* and *Downes.* The destroyer

Shaw was in floating dry dock number two, and to the north, alongside the 1010 dock, were the light cruiser *Helena* and minelayer *Oglala*. Farther northeast, the yard berths held over a dozen cruisers and destroyers. North toward Ford Island, seven battleships were tied to mooring blocks. The *Tennessee* and *West Virginia* and the *Maryland* and *Oklahoma* were moored in pairs. The *Nevada* and the *California* each sat alone, and the *Arizona* was tied to the repair ship *Vestal*. Farther north still, beyond the runways, hangars, and fuel tanks of the Ford Island Naval Air Station, more warships sat anchored, moored to blocks, and tied together in groups of two to six. On smaller vessels, a single sailor and boatswain with whistle prepared to raise an ensign. Cruisers had turned out a bugler and four-man Marine honor guard, and on some battleships the entire ship's band was assembling.

The signalman raised the Prep flag on schedule at 0755, just seconds before other men in the tower detachment noticed a line of planes approaching from the southeast, and another from the northeast, then another coming out of the sun to the east, and another from the south. Soon the air vibrated with droning, buzzing planes. Then bombers dived for the hangars and parked seaplanes of Ford Island, and a string of torpedo bombers, flying fast and low, headed for Battleship Row. Color guards, ship's bands, and men gathered on decks for religious services scattered like quail. A petty officer in the signal tower grabbed a telephone and called Admiral Kimmel's headquarters, and on Ford Island, radiomen sent out the message "AIR RAID, PEARL HARBOR, THIS IS NOT DRILL."

The pilots of the five small private planes that happened to be flying over Oahu also had a spectacular view. Two groups of amateur Army pilots had rented two-seater Aeroncas and were two miles off the west coast of Oahu, heading for Kauai, when they were shot into the ocean by the Japanese. Flying instructor Cornelia Fort was giving a lesson to a local Japanese man, circling the John Rodgers civilian airport for a practice landing, when she saw a bomber she assumed to be American approaching from the ocean, heading for them at the same altitude. Cursing the reckless pilot, she grabbed the controls, jerking her single-engine plane upward at the last minute. Then she saw red circles on the bomber's wings, black smoke rising from Hickam, and sticks of glistening bombs tumbling into Pearl Harbor.

Seventeen-year-old Roy Viousek and his father were two thousand feet over Oahu, able to see the first Japanese bomb explode in a Ford Island hangar. Roy thought it was a hangar fire and a flight of American P-40s. But as they dove to take a closer look, his father shouted, "P-40s, hell, they're Japs!" Afraid to land, they circled above the attacking planes for thirty minutes, hanging like bats over the attack, seeing bombs flash like mirrors as they caught the sun, then exploding in flashes and flame and sending waterspouts bursting skyward.

Seen from high above Pearl Harbor, the attacking planes must have appeared as well rehearsed as circus horses, as deferential as the Japanese diplomats who at this same moment were sitting in the anteroom of Secretary State Cordell Hull's office in Washington. Zeros in V-formations patiently waited their turn at strafing. Dive-bombers flew in circles, peeling off to make an attack, screaming down and disappearing into billowing smoke, then rising to reform the circle. Japanese pilots wagged their wings in triumph, and wounded planes spun out of control, crashing in cane fields to start fire lines that marched toward highways. Seaplanes burned like torches, and bombers parked at Hickam blew up in sequence, like falling dominoes. Sheets of burning oil raced across the water, warships puffed fists of black smoke, and scarlet dots of fire flashed across downtown Honolulu.

Once the first wave of attackers began to depart, Vitousek's father threw their plane into a steep spiral and dove for the airport. The rear gunner of a torpedo bomber fired on them, then a Fort Shafter antiaircraft battery opened up, mistaking them for the Japanese control plane. They landed at John Rodgers as the Japanese were strafing hangars, hitting a civilian aircraft that was boarding passengers for Maui and killing Bob Tice, the popular manager of a local flying service. The Vitouseks jumped from their plane and dove for cover behind a bunker. When the strafing ended they taxied to the hangar area, meeting passengers and workers who, still believing this was an American exercise gone wrong, were outraged that, as one man said, "some goddam drunk American pilot killed Bob Tice."

13

The Maneuvers Are Realistic

THE ATTACK FOLLOWED A SCHEDULE ROUGHLY THE SAME FOR everyone, but the emotions of defenders and witnesses had more individual timetables, determined by temperament and proximity to the battle. Most experienced denial and shock, then panic, fear, and anger, in that order. Some had a flash of disbelief, then hours of fear and panic. For some, the period of denial was long, but the shock never-ending, while others experienced a second of panic and a lifetime of anger. Troops in other battles came under fire suddenly and without warning, and civilians elsewhere found themselves in a battle zone, but the surprise of Pearl Harbor produced emotions of exceptional intensity.

Because I had met Elwood Craddock just after arriving in Honolulu, I did not fully appreciate how remarkable his reaction to the attack had been. He had been twelve years old, the son of the manager of the Waipahu pineapple plantation, situated on Oahu's central plateau, a mile and a half from Wheeler Field. On December 7, he woke before sunrise, dressed in sneakers and khaki pants, ate a quick breakfast, and set to hunt pheasants and doves with his twenty-two-year-old cousin, Rufus Hough. They walked a mile through pineapple fields to a ridgeline, shooting a pheasant with Craddock's shotgun, then stopping to admire the view. The land here was red clay, dusty and arid, a semidesert. They stood on the highest point for several miles, less than half a mile from the end of the Wheeler runway, and with a fine view of its hangars and planes. Overhead, some warplanes circled tightly before breaking loose, one by one, to dive and drop bombs.

The moment a hangar burst into flames, Craddock shouted, "Japanese planes!"

"No, they're Navy planes. It's a drill," his cousin said.

"But look at them. We don't have planes like that!" He had grown up in the shadow of this base, watching maneuvers and building balsa models of warplanes. "They have red circles on their wings," he argued. "Our planes have a smooth surface, and the Japs' are corrugated, like these."

"The insignia were painted on to make the exercise realistic," Hough replied. "And those aren't real bombs, they're just blowing up sticks of dynamite to make it look real."

The Japanese reorganized into a bombing pattern two miles in circumference, positioning themselves five hundred feet above Craddock and Hough. One plane fired its guns, perhaps for the fun of it. Bullets kicked up dust fifty feet away, and at last, Craddock remembers, "Rufus was convinced the attack was real."

What makes Craddock so remarkable is that he was the only witness I met in Honolulu, or read about in the narratives filling the University of Hawaii's War Records Depository, who right away recognized the planes were Japanese. Everyone else was like his cousin, believing it so inconceivable for Asians to attack Caucasians, or for a Japanese fleet to sail to Hawaii undetected, that when they saw the aircraft, shell bursts and tumbling bombs, they thought themselves witnessing a drill.

So widespread was this denial of the truth, and so resistant to all evidence, that it bordered on a mass delusion, a result of the same misconception about the invincibility of American forces and the inferiority of Japanese ones that was to make the attack successful. It was shared by civilians and servicemen, by haoles, native Hawaiians, Chinese, Portuguese, and Japanese, by those distant from the battle and sailors under direct attack, by Tadeo Yoshikawa, who at first thought he was seeing a drill, by officers on General Short's staff, and by General Short himself, who thought that "the Navy was having some battle practice, either that they hadn't told me about or that I had forgotten they told me about." When first informed of the attack by Lieutenant Colonel Bicknell, Short termed his report "ridiculous."

During the first hour, the military experienced difficulty persuading its men to return to their stations, and an Army intelligence officer later reported, "They did not believe that they were being correctly informed. Such a thing simply could not happen." Bicknell himself admitted experiencing "a few seconds of absolute disbelief" as he watched the attack from the lanai of his house on Aiea Heights. He became convinced it was war only when he saw the terrific explosion on the *Arizona,* and a clearly marked Japanese plane drop bombs on Hickam, then meet a burst of machine gun fire and fall flaming into the harbor. He rushed to the telephone and called headquarters, but had difficulty persuading the officer of the day that Oahu was under attack.

Many civilians failed to take cover, standing in the open, staring skyward, and watching with what a witness described as "no more show of emotion than witnesses to a fireworks display on July Fourth." Honolulu's mayor, Lester Petrie, watched for thirty minutes, believing the smoke was a practice smokescreen and the explosions were mines detonated to simulate bombs. Mr. Yee Kam York of the Territorial Tax Office heard an explosion, saw Pearl Harbor burning, and watched through field glasses as planes were hit by antiaircraft fire, and still could not believe it was a real attack, telling his wife, "These Americans, when they have maneuvers, they certainly make it realistic." A World War One veteran in Manoa was called by friends living in downtown Honolulu, asking if they could send their children up to him for safety. He thought the explosions were naval gunnery practice, and dismissed their call as "some sort of a hoax."

In Manoa Valley, Ethelyn Meyhre thought the silvery planes were American bombers. When she heard the truth on the radio, she ran into her father's bedroom. He laughed at the news and rolled over to go back to sleep. She woke him again, in time to hear the announcer say, "All men report to your post! Calling all nurses! Proceed to Pearl Harbor!"

"It's only another practice attack," he insisted.

They heard, "Oahu is being attacked! The sign of the Rising Sun is to be seen on the wings of the attacking planes!"

"It's impossible," he said.

A woman near the university watched planes dogfighting, heard the calls for defense workers and physicians to report to Pearl Harbor, and concluded it was all part of a "skillfully prepared practice." Her husband worried, "If the real thing should happen people might think they were crying 'wolf' and not respond." When an announcer said planes with the Rising Sun on their wingtips were over Pearl Harbor, she wondered if "the 'enemy' group of our air corps painted those emblems on their planes to simulate Japan."

Dorothy Anthony's eleven-year-old son ran into her room, saying, "Mother, this doesn't sound like practice." She and her husband dashed downstairs in time to watch an antisubmarine net being stretched across the mouth of the harbor. Yet they still refused to believe their eyes and, thinking the net and explosions were all part of a drill, they enjoyed a relaxed breakfast on their terrace.

Explosions woke correspondent Joseph C. Harsch in his room at the Royal Hawaiian Hotel. He told his wife they were "a good imitation" of what a European air raid sounded like. They then took their morning swim, assuming like other guests that it was "another practice maneuver by the Navy."

After seeing bursts of antiaircraft shells from his Waikiki apartment, Admiral Pye told his wife, "It seems funny that the Army would be having target practice on Sunday morning." At Wheeler Field, General Davidson continued shaving, certain he was hearing "those damn Navy pilots jazzing the base."

To persuade J. Edgar Hoover the attack was real, Robert Shivers held his telephone receiver out the window of his office so his chief could hear gunfire and explosions.

Ruth Flynn was driven to the FBI office by Fred Tillman, the Bureau's local Japanese expert. She told him a civilian defense worker reported Hickam "all shot to hell," and although they could clearly see smoke and shell bursts overhead, he said, again and again, "Ah, this is all nonsense. It's just another maneuver."

At Hickam Field, Walter Dillingham, still wearing his rumpled tuxedo from the night before, was driving through the main gate when the attack began. He thought his friend and fellow pilot Jake Jenkins was dropping dummy bombs and firing machine gun bursts to scare the Hickam pilots. "Goddammit! I bet Jakie's doing it again," he said to himself, "except this time he's dropped a real bomb instead of a dummy." Just outside the gate, a plane strafed his car. "Christ, this time Jenkins has gone crazy," he thought, rolling down his window and shaking his fist at the plane. "You son of a bitch," he shouted, "that's too close!"

At the John Rodgers Airport, Dr. Homer Izuma and Dr. Harold Johnson saw a flight of warplanes wheeling and circling in a loop formation directly overhead. Izuma noticed red circles on their wings and remarked, "Gee, Harold, that looks like a

Japanese emblem." "Yeah, don't they get realistic nowadays," Johnson replied as he hoisted his son onto his shoulders to get a better look. Izuma's plane for Maui was announced. Its passengers had boarded and were waving goodbye to friends through its windows when Izuma saw a man running across the field, shouting something that immediately caused the farewell crowd to dash for their cars.

Eleven-year-old John Smythe, the son of an Army colonel, kept riding his bicycle through Schofield Barracks, because he thought the bullets and bombs falling on nearby Wheeler Field were "just more Army maneuvers," and the red disks on wings simply identified planes as being among the "red forces" of the exercise. Even the sight of an officer firing his sidearm in the air did not trouble him, because, he said thirty-five years later, he so believed in the invincibility of his father's army he could not imagine a nation being so foolhardy as to attack it.

Private Kazuma Oyama, a local Japanese teenager recently drafted into a quartermaster battalion at Schofield and on leave, was pruning his father's grape arbor when planes flew over their Waipahu home. Until a misfired naval shell almost killed his sister, he dismissed everything as a maneuver, mainly because his drill sergeant in basic training had convinced him no one would dare take on the American Army.

From Maunalani Heights, high above Diamond Head, former Governor Lawrence Judd heard fire engines and watched shells splashing off Waikiki. "These maneuvers are getting too realistic," he told his wife. "Someone's going to get hurt." As black smoke rose from Pearl Harbor, he asked, "Isn't it unusual to be burning cane on Sunday morning?"

Admiral Kimmel witnessed the initial moments from a lawn overlooking the base. He and a neighbor, Mrs. Earle, saw planes circling in figure eights before diving at battleships. Fierce fires were already burning, yet, Mrs. Earle said, she and Kimmel found the sight "unbelievable" and "impossible."

On board the minesweeper *Oglala* in Pearl Harbor, Robert Hudson stood on deck smoking a cigarette with the ship's cook. As planes fell on Ford Island and its hangars burst into flame, they laughed, thinking it was a drill gone wrong, and the Army Air Forces would be "in real trouble now." They heard an explosion and agreed it must be accidental. A plane headed at them from forty feet above the water, dropping a torpedo. Convinced it was a dummy, they shook their heads and laughed again. They decided the red flashes flickering under a plane's wing came from a red light on the camera placed there to record the drill. Even when bullets from this machine gun ricocheted off a bulkhead, hitting the cook in the mouth and killing him, Hudson still believed it was a tragic error.

Lieutenant Clarence Dickinson piloted one of the eighteen scout planes sent ahead by the carrier *Enterprise* to check the waters near Pearl Harbor. He was approaching Ford Island for a landing as the attack began. He thought the smoke must come from cane fires, and that a "rain of big shell splashes in the water, recklessly close to shore" were coast artillery batteries gone "stark mad." "Just wait!" he told his tail gunner. "Tomorrow the Army will certainly catch hell for that!"

Marine bugler Richard Fiske was standing on the bridge of the *West Virginia*. He believed the planes were from Wheeler Field and told his shipmate Stanley Bukowski, "I guess we're going to have an exercise." When bombers, with torpedoes visible beneath their wings, circled Ford Island, then peeled off to make a bombing run, he said, "Well, there goes the Army. We'd better get to our battle stations." "No, wait," Bukowski answered, "They're going to drop some dummy torpedoes. Let's go over to the port side and see them." So they remained on the bridge as four airplanes flew at them fifteen feet above the water, dropping torpedoes. One exploded, throwing up a wall of water that washed Fiske through a passageway to the starboard side. Yet, like Annapolis ensigns, twenty-year veterans, fighter pilots, and rear admirals, he still believed it was an exercise, only accepting the truth when a Marine sergeant yelled, "Goddammit, get to your battle stations, it's the Japs!"

Lieutenant Victor Dybdal was standing watch on the stern of the destroyer *Helm,* which had just left her anchorage near the mouth of West Loch and was steaming into the harbor to be demagnetized (a process to prevent her attracting magnetic mines). He thought the planes were American ones returning from the *Enterprise,* only changing his mind when one dropped a bomb. Dive-bombers strafed the *Helm.* Afterward, Dybdal says, their pilots smiled and waved and, for some inexplicable reason, perhaps because no one yet believed the attack was real, "We all waved back."

Rear Admiral Victor Dybdal (Ret.) suggested we visit Pearl Harbor on one of the cruise boats, since that was the best way to see the waters at the mouth of the harbor where the *Helm* had fought on December 7. Even had we not been among the few haoles boarding this boat at Kewalo Basin, I still would have spotted him. Like Gus Ahola, he had the mahogany tan and laconic manner I had come to recognize as the hallmarks of a retired military officer in Hawaii.

We sat at a table on the ship's upper deck, surrounded by Japanese tourists who had arrived in a convoy of buses. The men wore droopy white shirts and golf hats. Heavy cameras and telephoto lenses dangled from their necks, giving them a stooped walk. They were middle-aged or elderly, old enough to know about Pearl Harbor. A brochure placed on our seats showed a map of the harbor printed in Japanese, and there was something vaguely disturbing about seeing the names and locations of the Pearl Harbor warships written in this language. Admiral Dybdal demanded a map in English, and looking around at our fellow passengers, he said, "When I took my grandchildren on this cruise it wasn't, well, it wasn't this crowded."

At least I think he said that, because I was having trouble hearing him. The Japanese at our table were loud, the crew frequently interrupted to hawk drinks and souvenir booklets, and a nearby loudspeaker sounded a narration of the attack in Japanese and English. As we steamed past Honolulu Harbor, Sand Island, Honolulu International Airport, and Hickam Field, I heard his account of December 7 in fragments, interrupted by loud bursts of Japanese and by a departing Japan Airlines 747, which caused the Japanese to shout in excitement and lean across us to take photographs.

As Dybdal offered me his version of the attack, the English narration referred to it as "brilliantly conceived and executed," adding that "it would be a glorious victory for Japan."

"That's why they like to come here," he said without bitterness, "and why they like to take these tours and see the *Arizona*. For them this was a great victory, one of the greatest in their history."

The narrator described Japanese planes bombing Wheeler Field and Schofield Barracks and said, "It was an old Japanese custom to begin wars with a sneak attack," as if it were a quaint national trait. He said American economic sanctions had put Japanese "backs to the wall," but omitted mentioning Japanese militarism, or the atrocities against the Chinese, who really did have their backs put to the wall.

Dybdal looked pained. "Claiming we forced them into the war is a lot of crap," he said. "We didn't start the damned war, they did. And those Japanese militarists were as crazy as Hitler. They wanted to take over all those Asian countries." This narration reminded him of the documentary film shown visitors to the *Arizona*, a "damned movie that gives the impression it was all our fault." He insisted he was not upset at Japanese tourists for visiting Pearl Harbor—it was understandable that they wanted to see this battlefield. He told me, with a sigh, that when his friends from the mainland complained about Japanese at the memorial, "I tell 'em it's a free country."

But slanting the causes of Pearl Harbor to avoid offending Japanese sensibilities did upset him. It is something that has always irritated me as well. Arguing that the United States bore responsibility for the attack because of its embargo of oil and other raw materials to Japan implies the United States had a moral obligation to supply Japan with the raw materials necessary to attack China and further its expansionist policies, and that total warfare was a justifiable response to economic sanctions. The Japanese advanced similar arguments after the war, with the former chief of the Military Affairs Bureau claiming, "The only place where Japan could continue to get oil and other raw materials had to be from the United States. If this failed, Japan, as a nation, could not survive, especially the industries and the navy. . . . Japan felt the United States was under obligation to furnish oil and raw materials as it meant the future existence of Japan." As the war becomes more distant and Japanese tourism becomes important to Hawaii, such justifications for the attack have gained respectability, finding their way even into the documentary at the *Arizona* Memorial visitor center and the Pearl Harbor sightseeing cruises.

As we entered the harbor, passing near the *Helm*'s anchorage on December 7, Dybdal said the landscape had changed little. Cane fields still surrounded West Loch, and Hickam's water tower and hangars dominated views to the east. The main difference was the smell. A sweet, pungent odor of sugarcane had enveloped the harbor in 1941. Now you smelled jet fuel.

Pearl Harbor's shape has been likened to a fleur-de-lis, a three-fingered hand, or a flower. Its most important characteristics are a long, narrow entrance, calm waters, and three extensive bays, called lochs by the original Scottish surveyors. It is an unusual anchorage for the Pacific, and an ideal harbor for the peacetime Navy because of its size and the protection it offers. But its narrow entrance channel makes it treacherous in wartime. A single disabled ship there can trap the fleet for hours, and a sunken ship can bottle up the harbor for days.

We circled Ford Island clockwise, passing the wreck of the *Utah,* the lawn where dying sailors had been laid in rows, and the empty mooring blocks of the other December 7 battleships, marked by shell fragments, and still carrying their names in black letters, as if any moment there were expected to return. As we neared the *Arizona* Memorial, it was announced our captain would lead us in a "brief ceremony of remembrance," throwing a flower lei on this "altar of freedom." Taps was played over the loudspeakers, and Admiral Dybdal shot out of his chair, right hand over his heart, left hand holding his hat, his eyes watering. A few Japanese struggled to their feet. Those at our table whispered and looked confused. The announcer said, "We must all pray that this terrible sacrifice shall not have been in vain," and then, after a pause so brief it was easy to miss, and without changing his tone of voice, he recommended a souvenir booklet—"Makes an excellent gift . . . the only booklet of its kind printed in color" and, I saw later, printed in Japan.

As he sat down, Admiral Dybdal admitted never considering the possibility of a Japanese sneak attack. "I thought you had to declare war, that there'd be a big buildup. To attack a warship without notice seemed to me basically unfair, against the rules, like shooting a policeman on the beat."

The Japanese leaned across us again to photograph the *Arizona,* and Dybdal said the *Helm* was the first warship to sortie from Pearl Harbor, inflicting considerable damage on the enemy. Her guns sent a plane crashing into Hickam and shelled Ensign Sakamaki's midget sub, disabling its steering. Just outside the harbor, two Japanese bombs fell close enough to disable her electrics. For the rest of the day she zigzagged off Waikiki, hunting submarines and preparing to repel an invasion.

We too were now steaming in circles and zigzagging off Waikiki. "We're waiting for the photographs," a waiter said. They had been taken as we boarded, and a motorboat was rushing out the prints. When they arrived, pandemonium ensued as the crew of young haoles tried to match enormous wedding-portrait-sized photographs with the correct Japanese.

Admiral Dybdal turned his back and stared back at the harbor. "December 7 taught me you never know," he said. "You can never be sure something bad won't happen. When I was in the South Pacific during the war, dolphins used to be attracted to my ship. I'd see them and think it was a torpedo wake. All at once I'd wonder, What should I do? Turn the ship and head into it? Or what? For years after Pearl Harbor I never slept well. I felt as if someone had wound something up in the middle of my stomach that was taking years to unwind."

14

"The Warm Air of an Unending Summer Land"

OAHU'S SENSATIONAL BEAUTY MADE SOME JAPANESE PILOTS regret their mission and caused others to remember the battle as a poetic event. They saw "four bombs in perfect pattern" becoming "as small as poppy seeds" before disappearing, just as "tiny white flashes of smoke appeared on or near the ship," and as waterspouts splashed over a ship's smokestack, tumbling down "like an exhausted geyser."

They saw American planes, "the color of gold dust," in tidy rows, and "beautiful clouds colored by the rising sun." They saw a "splash in the water and a torpedo streaking for a battleship . . . just like a dragonfly laying an egg on the water," and "black bursts . . . spoiling the once beautiful sky." They saw a fleet looking "so beautiful . . . just like toys on a child's floor—something that should not be attacked at all," and the "calm and picturesque scenery of the green island."

One thought, "This island is too peaceful to attack!" Flying so low his plane rustled the sugarcane, another felt "the warm air of an unending summer land."

On Pearl Harbor's twenty-fifth anniversary, only fourteen of the 609 Japanese airmen remained alive. What is startling is not how few survived war, kamikaze recruitments, and death by natural causes, but how many of the few who did survive felt compelled to return to this "unending summer land."

The Japanese were also "wound up" by December 7. "That moment changed my life," said Zero pilot Yoshio Shiga on the fortieth anniversary. "It was forever burned in my memory." Just as Pearl Harbor cast a spell of horror on American survivors, leaving a compulsion to revisit Oahu, so too were the Japanese fascinated by the place where they had enjoyed such triumph.

After the war, the Japanese officer who planned the attack, Commander Minoru Genda, visited Hawaii and the mainland often. He became a member of the Japanese House of Councillors (Senate) and persuaded Japan to accept U.S. bases and visits by nuclear-powered submarines. Nevertheless, when he gave a lecture at Annapolis, his presence was protested by the Pearl Harbor Survivors Association and relatives of men killed on December 7. His speech was remarkable for its honesty. He admitted that if the Japanese had developed the atom bomb, they would have used it, and if he could do Pearl Harbor again, he would have invaded Hawaii.

Zero pilot Makato Bando attended the fortieth-anniversary ceremonies accompanied by a translator and a Japanese television crew. He hired a launch and was filmed posing around the harbor. He turned up at the *Arizona* Memorial and by chance met a Mr. Fred Garbuschewski, who had been tuning up his clarinet for the Sunday call to colors aboard the *California* and remembered a pilot coming so close he "could have hit him with a baseball bat." Mr. Bando, described as "robust and animated," said he had never imagined being here, chatting with American survivors.

Six other pilots came in a group with their wives to the forty-fifth anniversary. They included Eijiro Abe, who had bombed the *West Virginia* and *Tennessee,* Hideo Maki, who had bombed *the Arizona,* and Junchi Goto, who had sent a torpedo into the *Oklahoma.* When they identified themselves, *Arizona* Memorial officials persuaded them to be interviewed on a videotape that I watched in a darkened room at the memorial's visitor center. I saw a line of elderly men sitting along a conference table, wearing dark suits so alike they might be uniforms. They were ill at ease, and their bald foreheads glistened under the lights. The sound was so poor I only understood sentence fragments. Mr. Yamamato, attacker of the *Nevada,* said, "We were so close . . . so low to the ground." Mr. Goto made a planing motion with one hand, while an interpreter said, "His wish was that he not be hit until he released his bomb. *That* was the only thing he was praying for." I had to be satisfied for most of the tape with watching them swoop their hands like seagulls as they explained tactics, or throw their arms over their heads, depicting clouds of billowing smoke.

There was something unsettling about these airmen on an organized junket, so cheerfully visiting the city they once saw through a bombsight, visiting the memorials to people they had killed. I wondered if the British pilots who destroyed Dresden had returned there on a group holiday, bringing wives and followed by cameramen as they visited buildings built on the ruins and sought out survivors. Did the German pilots who destroyed Coventry or Warsaw return on package tours, announcing themselves to local authorities? For years, World War Two veterans' groups have been visiting one another's countries and meeting at battlefields. German and British pilots have traded stories about the Battle of Britain. Americans and Japanese have embraced on Pacific islands, and I have never thought it inappropriate. Airmen of the unit responsible for dropping the atomic bombs on Japan, returned to Hiroshima, but did not identify themselves to the survivors or glory in the action. What was striking about the Japanese was the youthful enthusiasm and complete absence of mature reflection with which they relived what was no ordinary, midwar battle, but a surprise raid, the *casus belli* that resulted in three and a half years of slaughter. In 1941 the Japanese Pearl Harbor pilots may have been just following orders, but I had expected them in 1986 to see the ambiguities.

The most notorious airman to return to Hawaii was Mitsuo Fuchida, commander of the attack. He had guided in the first wave, fired flares signaling the order of attack, ordered his radioman to give the famous signal *"To, to, to"* (the first syllable of *totsugekiseyo,* Japanese for "charge"), and led a bombing run on the battleship *Maryland,* claiming two hits. He remained overhead throughout the attack, flying over Hickam and Wheeler to assess damage and circling Pearl Harbor to take the photographs now illustrating so many books. Afterward, he had begged Admiral Nagumo to launch a third wave against the submarine base and fuel tanks, which, if successful, would have forced the American fleet back to California, prolonging the war.

During the war, Fuchida was shot down during the Battle of the Java Sea, crashing in Borneo and spending three days walking out of the jungle. Six days before the Battle of Midway, he suffered appendicitis aboard his carrier, and the man replacing him was killed. During Midway, a bomb blew him off the flight deck, breaking his legs and nearly drowning him. He volunteered for a kamikaze mission that was canceled at the last minute. He was in Hiroshima the day before the bomb was dropped and afterward visited with eleven other men to evaluate the effects of the bomb. He was the only one not to die of radiation poisoning. He became a farmer near Osaka, where, he said, "my days passed in loneliness. It was a far cry from the regimentation and glamour of my military life. I was like a star that had fallen. At one moment I was Captain Mitsuo Fuchida, and the next, I was nobody!"

Perhaps because he came to attach religious significance to his narrow escapes, he became a Christian in 1950. Like everything else in his life, his conversion was dramatic. He jumped into the speaker van of evangelical American missionaries preaching in Osaka, shouting through a microphone, "I am Mitsuo Fuchida, who led the air raid on Pearl Harbor. I have now surrendered my heart and my life to Jesus Christ." Headlines proclaimed, "FROM A SOLDIER OF FAME TO A SOLDIER OF LOVE," and he became a "general" in Sky Pilots International, an organization of former war pilots converted to evangelical Christianity. He visited the United States in 1953, traveling 35,000 miles on a cross-country speaking engagement and meeting Billy Graham—and soon thereafter described himself as a "small-scale Billy Graham." American missionaries accompanying him dismissed the war veterans who opposed his visit as "small-minded."

He stopped last in Honolulu, where he announced he would place a wreath on the *Arizona*. There were widespread protests. He and his American supporters claimed to be surprised. But in 1953, too many Hawaiians still considered Pearl Harbor to be a unique act of treachery, difficult to forgive.

Fuchida continued returning to Hawaii and the mainland. For several years he lived in Seattle, and he considered applying for American citizenship. His daughter became an interior designer in California, and his son an architect in Manhattan. He visited Oahu again in 1956, in 1958, and in 1966, for the twenty-fifth anniversary. A documentary of his life was being filmed, and according to a supporter the anniversary ceremonies would make "a good backdrop." During the first week of December 1966, he inserted himself into so many ceremonies his presence became the major event of the anniversary. The year's Pearl Harbor story on the front page of the *New York Times* was accompanied by a photograph of Mitsuo Fuchida, no longer a "star that had fallen," no longer a "nobody."

On the evening of December 6, he attended a dinner party at the home of Bud Smyser, editor of the *Honolulu Star Bulletin*. Among the guests were Colonel Kendall Fielder, chief of Army intelligence in Hawaii in 1941, and his former deputy, Lieutenant Colonel George Bicknell. I became interested in the occasion after reading an account of it in a Honolulu newspaper in which Fielder was unable to manage the "all is forgiven" statement that is the approved reaction to such encounters. Instead, he said, "You try to forgive and forget," and was then described as "pausing for a moment" before adding, "I lost a lot of friends that day."

Bud Smyser now remembers Fuchida standing in the middle of the room, with the other guests grouped in a circle. At first, he was nervous, and the conversation was stilted. But the atmosphere changed as soon as Smyser's six-year-old son asked, "How big were the bombs you dropped?" Smyser produced photographs of the attack taken by Japanese planes, perhaps taken by Fuchida himself. Suddenly, he remembers, Fuchida "lightened up" and moved a finger back and forth across the photographs, naming every ship. "It was obvious he was still proud of the success of the attack," Smyser says, "and proud he'd done his job well."

Fielder and Bicknell have since died, but Bicknell's widow lives on Oahu and remembers Fuchida's performance. "His eyes were glowing as he recounted the attack," she says. "And you could see he was still thrilled by it. He made zooming motions with his hands, and I thought, 'He's still up in the air, bombing Pearl Harbor. It was the high point of his life and he's still there.' "

On December 7, 1966, Fuchida and his camera crew traveled to the *Arizona* Memorial at sunrise, two hours before the official ceremony. They arrived at the same time as twelve survivors from the *Arizona*, returning for the first time since 1941. Considering it a lucky coincidence, this opportunity to pose the man who led the attack with the *Arizona*'s surviving crewmen, Fuchida's entourage urged Fuchida and the American veterans to stand together for photographs. But there were objections, and a Mr. Don Stratton refused, saying, "They just killed so many people who never had a chance." It had not occurred to Fuchida that *Arizona* survivors who had traveled thousands of miles to see the wreck of their battleship and the grave of their shipmates might find it upsetting to find there waiting for them the man who on this day twenty-five years earlier had been circling overhead, making bomb runs, and directing the attack that ended the lives of the men they had come to commemorate.

Afterward, the Navy confiscated Fuchida's film because of "security violations." He had neglected to get permission to film in the harbor, and a warship had been unloading nearby. He continued on to official memorial services at Punchbowl, and in one photograph can be seen making a point of consulting his watch at 7:55 A.M. Later he drove to Aiea Heights and, accompanied by the noted Hawaiian minister Abraham Akaka, posed for pictures while standing on a hill overlooking Pearl Harbor. Akaka was impressed with his memory, his ability to look across the harbor and name the warships there on December 7, describing their precise location.

I found that the more I learned about Fuchida, the less I liked him. There was too much dissembling, too much exploitation, surrounding his trips to Hawaii. In his 1952 pamphlet *From Pearl Harbor to Golgotha* he admitted, "My heart was ablaze with joy for my success in getting the whole main forces of the Pacific Fleet in hand." But in 1953, when he sought permission to lay a wreath on the *Arizona,* he told a reporter that "there was no real joy in my heart at the time of the attack."

I disliked the way he thrust himself into the twenty-fifth anniversary, and the ego it must have taken to imagine he would be welcome everywhere on that particular day. But I think his trip to Hawaii in 1967 was the most odious. For ten days, he spoke in churches and military bases, and during these sermons and lectures, the man who led the attack starting the Pacific War, and who said at the time of his conversion, "I believe no war could be righteous and pave the way for peace," now declared himself eager for Americans of my generation to die in Vietnam. He argued that "the spread of Communism must be stopped" and frequently "expressed his irritation with those protesting against the Vietnam War."

15

"A Voice from the Bottom of the Sea"

As Mitsuo Fuchida's planes pressed their bombing and strafing runs, the seaplane tender *Curtiss* sighted the periscope of a Japanese midget submarine that had entered the harbor. She attacked, firing artillery and machine guns. The submarine, now called Midget B by historians, shot a torpedo, which exploded harmlessly on shore. The destroyer *Monaghan* rammed her, dropping depth charges later found to have decapitated her captain. Two weeks after the attack, she was raised from the harbor and used as fill for a new pier being constructed at the submarine base. Before a crane dropped her into a hole, a military funeral was held, and broadcast live across the country as proof of America's respect for battlefield protocol. The midget is entombed there, near the submarine base officers' club, with her crewmen still inside.

The other midgets fared no better. A defective gyroscope forced Kazuo Sakamaki, captain of Midget C, to rise near the surface and navigate with his periscope. Destroyers spotted him at the harbor entrance and dropped depth charges. He was knocked unconscious, waking later to see smoke rising from Pearl Harbor. Realizing the attack was on, he raced for the harbor channel, pursued by two destroyers. Twice he hit a coral reef and extricated himself. He made a final attempt to enter the harbor, but found the repeated groundings had damaged his steering. His sub swung in circles, filling with fumes and battery gas. Overcome by fatigue and smoke, he and his crewman, Kiyoshi Inagaki, passed out again, and Midget C drifted around Oahu to the windward coast. When he regained consciousness and saw land, he assumed he had reached the rendezvous point with his mother sub off the Hawaiian island of Lanai. Before he could reach shore, his batteries died in a shower of sparks, and his midget slid onto another reef. He and Inagaki lit a fuse attached to a scuttling charge and began swimming ashore, but the charge failed to ignite, and Inagaki disappeared in heavy surf. He awoke on December 8, lying on Waimanalo beach, guarded by David Akui, a Japanese-American sergeant in the Hawaii Territorial Guard, and about to become America's first prisoner of the war, or at least its first official one.

His submarine was pulled off the reef, repaired, and outfitted with dummy batteries, a motor, and two mannequins dressed as Japanese sailors. It was mounted on a trailer and hauled across forty-one states as the featured attraction of seven war-bond drives, on one occasion stopping in a town near the Wisconsin POW camp where Sakamaki was imprisoned, causing him considerable anguish and embarrassment. After the war, it was sent to the United States Navy submarine base in Key West, Florida, then transferred to Key West's Lighthouse Museum.

After his capture, Sakamaki begged to be taken to a hill overlooking Pearl Harbor and shot. Instead, he was imprisoned on Honolulu's Sand Island in an open "bird cage" prison near the gate so guards could prevent him from committing suicide. He refused to answer questions and disfigured his face with cigarettes, methodically burning himself with an inverted triangle of scars to symbolize the disgrace of his capture. He was sent to POW camps on the mainland, where he at first punished himself by taking cold showers and wearing thin cotton pajamas in winter. After several months he had a change of heart and, impressed by the beauty of the American countryside and his humane treatment, gave up thoughts of suicide. As the jacket of his best-selling book put it, "Educated for a ruthless war, he was changed from a beastlike, inhuman creature to a real human being."

After the war, he was repatriated to Japan as "POW #1," becoming a celebrity. Men wrote demanding he commit hari-kiri to atone for his capture. Women sent mash notes. He married and took a job at Toyota, rising to become production chief of the export division, then Toyota president for Brazil, causing rumors to circulate among American Pearl Harbor survivors that because of the disgrace of his capture he had been forced to emigrate.

He returned to Hawaii for the first time in 1961, on the twentieth anniversary, asking reporters who met him at the airport, "What is the way to Kaneohe?" (a windward town not far from Waimanalo). He returned four years later, confessing to being "attacked with strange impressions" while taking a sightseeing cruise around Pearl Harbor. He may have come again during the 1970s, but his next documented visit occurred in 1981, on the fortieth anniversary. For a former POW to return to the battlefield where he was captured is understandable, but to do it at least three times in twenty years is extraordinary. The former curator of Pearl Harbor's Pacific Submarine Museum, Ray de Yarmin, said he came in 1981 hoping to find crewman Inagaki's burial place and make sure it was properly marked and maintained. De Yarmin spent several days with him, checking death certificates, visiting cemeteries, following the rumor of a headless torso washed ashore near Bellows Field, and interviewing elderly Japanese-Americans, on the theory that local Japanese had secretly buried Inagaki. Sakamaki still had a compulsion to justify his capture, explaining he had not drowned himself because he believed Japan would soon occupy Hawaii, and saying that "the only thing I ever wanted to do was return to the Japanese navy and fight."

Midgets D and E were believed sunk by the four American destroyers that reported firing on enemy submarines. Midget E has never been recovered. But in 1960, Navy divers practicing near the mouth of Pearl Harbor found Midget D. She was two thousand yards offshore and submerged in seventy-six feet of water, crusted with coral, and badly warped, indicating damage from a depth charge. She was raised, brought to Pearl Harbor, and inspected by Navy specialists. An officer entered her, finding bent piping, shattered glass, and a motor torn from its mounting. The fuse of a scuttling charge had been lit, but the charge had not detonated. He found no maps, charts, or human remains. According to the official report of her discovery, "The ship's doctor states that even if human remains had disintegrated through the years, the victim's teeth would have resisted the water's corrosive effects. No teeth or evidence of bodies were found."

An article in the *Naval Institute Proceedings* concluded, "Little doubt exists that her two-man crew left the submarine. Whether or not they survived remains a mystery. . . . If they were able to swim the mile to shore across placid Keehi Lagoon, they could have easily melted into the local populace of Hawaii with its many Orientals. . . . Their devotion to Japanese ideology would likely have caused them to reveal to no one, either during or after the war, that they had failed in their mission. Therefore, it is a remote possibility that one or both may be alive today."

I asked Mr. de Yarmin what he thought. He was cagey, saying it was "not impossible they're alive" and that "the dishonor of having survived would have kept them hidden." He believed that "the truth will never be known, and there are things people have overlooked."

In 1967, a Japanese man in suburban Baltimore claimed to be Okino Sasaki, one of the crewmen of Midget E. His story, "A Voice from the Bottom of the Sea," appeared with his photograph in the December 1967 issue of *Our Navy,* a monthly magazine (which has since ceased publication) published for retired and serving U.S. Navy personnel. The author, a former Navy officer named Ellsworth Boyd, claimed to have met Sasaki by chance at the Jade East Chinese restaurant in Towson, Maryland. The regular bartender had fallen ill, and Sasaki, who said he was the owner, had taken over at the last minute.

Boyd asked how he had started his restaurant, and Sasaki, described as a "small, cordial, slightly balding forty-three-year-old Japanese gentleman," told of being drafted into the Japanese navy at the age of seventeen in 1941, assigned to the submarine service, and chosen by lot to be a ballastman in one of the two-man midget submarines that attacked Pearl Harbor. He said he had been captured on December 8 and spent the war in a prisoner camp. In 1945, he found work on a tramp steamer. He met a Japanese-American girl during a call at Baltimore and married her, becoming an American citizen and settling there, working in her father's restaurant until he had saved enough to open the Jade East.

This is all the article revealed about Sasaki's life after Pearl Harbor. It did not name his prison camp, nor explain why the government had publicized the capture of Kazuo Sakamaki, yet kept Sasaki's capture a secret. It did not say if he was repatriated after the war, or why he suddenly decided to reveal his story to Boyd. Instead, most of it is Sasaki's own, uninterrupted first-person account of his experiences between December 6 and December 8, 1941.

He described climbing into the midget on December 6 with its commander, a lieutenant named Sakamoto. He remembered that "as we were readying to board the midget, one of the crew thrust a small duffle bag into my hands. This crewman had originally been assigned to the Kaiten command. [*Kaiten* means a "turn toward heaven," and the Kaiten command was the undersea equivalent of the kamikazes—human torpedoes, or "impact submarines," fitted with a tiny compartment in which the pilot rode on his one-way mission. Unlike the crew of a two-man midget, a Kaiten pilot had no chance of survival.] Anticipating the cold he knew I would confront in the little sub, he had wrapped a bottle of sake in one of his heavy woolen sweaters and stuffed it in the duffel bag."

He described how the midget had malfunctioned during the attack, finally sinking "in ninety feet of water at the harbor entrance, with no power and our torpedoes still intact." He and Lieutenant Sakamoto had sat in it for nine hours, listening to "faint thumping sounds" from the battle above, and feeling violent undersea explosions that "rocked the ship like a cradle." As soon as it was dark, Sakamoto lit a fuse attached to a scuttling charge. They flooded the conning tower and escaped through the hatch. "I don't know what happened to the lieutenant," Sasaki said. "When I reached the surface, I swam like hell for shore. Fires raged everywhere. People were scurrying as sirens wailed in the night. When I reached the beach I collapsed. That's all I remember. When I awoke I was in a prison camp."

His story is made credible by details such as the sake bottle wrapped in the sweater, his explanation of the midget's technical problems, and several small mistakes that kept it from duplicating already published accounts. It also matches what is known about the midget submarines, and the fate of Midget E. The crewman of one midget is recorded in Japanese archives as being a Naokichi Sasaki, and Okino is presumably a shortened form of this first name.

The official salvage report confirms his account of the attempt to scuttle the sub, saying, "Demolition experts removed an explosive charge from the submarine that was designed to blow it apart. The fuse of the charge had been lit but the charge had not detonated. This factor, coupled with the discovery that the conning tower hatch was unlocked from the inside, led us to believe that the two crewmen escaped." It also confirms his description of the duffel bag given him at the last minute: "Some shoes and a pair of unmarked coveralls were found in the sub along with a small canvas bag. The bag contained a full bottle of sake and a woolen sweater. The sweater had Japanese writing on it which has been translated as 'Kaiten.'"

If Sasaki's story is a hoax, perpetrated by himself or Boyd, it is a puzzling one. Why would Boyd concoct this story, only to sell it to an obscure magazine? And if Sasaki had gone to the trouble of obtaining the salvage report from Navy archives and making himself an expert on the midget subs, then why did he not seek national publicity? Yet, if Sasaki was a POW, as he claims, why did the military not report his capture? This aspect of his testimony is particularly troubling since the government immediately publicized the capture of Sakamaki as a great victory, and since there is no record of Sasaki being a POW. More likely, he was reluctant to tell Boyd the whole truth—that on December 8 he had swum across the Keehi Lagoon, come ashore, and hidden himself among Honolulu's large population of Japanese aliens. Keehi Lagoon is near densely populated Kalihi, which in 1941 contained many aliens who spoke only Japanese.

The Jade East restaurant closed in the early 1980s, but I tracked down a Mr. Jimmy Han, one of its previous owners, who said it had been the only restaurant of that name in the Baltimore area. He had never heard of Okino Sasaki, although after the *Our Navy* article, he had received inquires about him. So perhaps Boyd changed the restaurant's name to protect Sasaki, perhaps Sasaki was merely another customer, or perhaps the story *was* a hoax.

But we are still left with a 1967 photograph of Sasaki that bears a resemblance to the one of a young Sasaki on a Japanese mural of the midget crews. And we are left with his accurate, detailed account of December 7, and the sake bottle wrapped in that crewman's sweater. And I am left with the suspicion that one of the legacies of Pearl Harbor is a sixty-seven-year-old Japanese gentleman who swam ashore from Midget E, lived incognito in Honolulu throughout the war, then moved to the mainland and remained underground, except for one evening in 1967 when he recounted his story, and disappeared again.

16

The Arizona *Opens Like a Flower*

TRACE THE PATHS OF JAPANESE PLANES OVER A MAP OF OAHU and the island becomes an insect caught in a web of lines and arrows representing the fighters and bombers, giving you an idea how confusing the attack on Pearl Harbor was for its victims. At times, more than twenty ships were attacked at once by several types of enemy planes. The most chaotic phase of the attack was the first, lasting from 0755 until 0825. It was in this half hour that most naval losses and casualties occurred, the battleships *California, West Virginia, Oklahoma,* and *Arizona* sank in flames, and most of the 188 Army and Navy planes lost on December 7 were destroyed on the ground.

There was a lull from 0825 until 0840, with only sporadic strafing and bombing. Phase two began as a second wave of planes crossed Oahu's northern coast at 0840. Joined by high-level bombers from the first wave, they struck the burning harbor and airfields again between 0915 and 0945. Zeros engaged American fighters, also strafing civilian automobiles and residential areas. During this final phase, American resistance was stronger, and damage was reduced because the best targets were obscured by smoke.

Pearl Harbor memories are less ordered, seldom divided neatly into timetables, and reflect the chaos of that day. Although people are vague about precisely when certain ships were hit or planes destroyed and uncertain if they were victims of bombs or torpedoes, they remember well how those great ships, and their crews, looked in their death throes, and remember the event dominating so many memories, the sinking of the battleship *Arizona*.

At 0810, fifteen minutes into the attack, an eighteen-hundred-pound armor-piercing bomb struck the *Arizona* between its number two gun turret and bow, creating a hundred-foot-wide gap, penetrating the deck, and exploding in a fuel storage tank. A fire flared for seven seconds, then traveled through open hatches to the forward magazine, where it touched off 1.7 million pounds of explosives. A fountain of flame and black smoke shot skyward. The *Arizona* jumped from the water. Its foremast pitched forward, and its deck opened like a flower.

Flaming bodies and body parts were blown upward. Naked sailors, limbs, and letters from home landed on nearby ships, or were snagged by trees on Ford Island. Men burning like torches stumbled across the deck. "They had their helmets on, but their clothes were seared off . . . they walked out of the flames and just dropped dead," remembers a spectator. Burning men jumped into the harbor and were heard to "sizzle." The body of the *Arizona*'s captain, Franklin Van Valkenburgh, was never found, although when the ship cooled, a boarding party dug his Naval Academy ring from a pile of ashes.

On Ford Island, several thousand survivors of the *Arizona* and other wounded battleships wandered through clouds of smoke, naked and dripping oil, skin, and blood, screaming in agony, falling over dead. A survivor remembers them "just burned like lamb chops. The only thing I could see were their eyes, lips, and mouths. Their mouths were reddish; their eyes looked watery. Everything else was black."

Two hundred *Arizona* dead were lined up on the lawns of officers' bungalows. Their blood soaked the ground and blackened the grass. Survivors gathered dismembered arms and legs from roofs and trees. Many had been snagged by a banyan tree near the water, now known as the Hiroshima Banyan.

When I reviewed my own images of the attack, all the product of countless documentaries, histories, and movies, I discovered none were morbid. I watched *Tora! Tora! Tora!* once again, and noticed there was not a single corpse, wound, or drop of blood. No wonder when I thought of Pearl Harbor, I thought of bravery, treachery, tactics, and surprise, but not of a thousand men killed in several seconds, or 2,500 in under two hours. I saw American pilots battling swarms of Zeros, wounded ships puffing smoke, and Japanese diplomats arriving at the State Department minutes before the attack in baggy suits. When I imagined casualties, they were serene maritime deaths, an underwater movie of air bubbles as captains went down with ships. I had not known or had forgotten about men trapped in pockets of air in the *West Virginia,* living for two weeks and chalking off the days with X's on overturned cabin walls before finally dying, or the antipersonnel bomb making a direct hit on the mess hall where five hundred men were sitting down for breakfast, sending "sharp jagged masses of steel moving at high velocity," which resulted in the "common sight" of "men without one or both legs and an arm" and produced "tremendous casualties," according to Ralph Cloward, the neurosurgeon who treated them. I had not known about the corpses stacked up to the windowsills at the Hickam Field hospital, the men dying on lush Hawaiian lawns, under flowering trees, while waiting for hospital beds, the forty garbage cans filled with amputated limbs seen outside the Tripler Army Hospital, or the Tripler amputation saw used and sterilized so often it stayed "hot" all day, or just how those sailors on the *Arizona* had died.

The more I read about sailors becoming ashes and charcoaled flesh, the more I found myself thinking about Hiroshima. The *Arizona*'s sailors had been "cut down in a single searing blast." One had "vanished" inside the port antiaircraft battery, and "the only place he could have gone was through the narrow range-finder slot." The explosion sounded "like a powerful and heavy wind blowing through thick foliage" and was remembered as a "fireball" that "mushroomed" into the air. Captain Fuchida had seen "a column of dark red smoke" rising to a thousand feet, and felt his plane shudder from the shock wave as his heart filled "with joy and gratification." One man remembered talk of a "great mushroom cloud" rising over the *Arizona*, and Honolulu residents seeing newsreels of Hiroshima which "reminded them of Pearl Harbor."

Sixty times as many people died at Hiroshima, and almost all of them were civilians. But in 1941, when the country was at peace, to lose over a thousand sailors in seconds, on a single battleship and to a single bomb, was an unprecedented catastrophe. This was more sailors than were lost in action in the Spanish-American War and World War One combined, and the greatest number of people killed by a single explosion in the history of warfare, a record broken only at Hiroshima.

In a way, both bombings were "sneak attacks." Although Hiroshima occurred during a declared war in which civilians had become frequent victims, it had a sneak-attack quality, because for the first time the total destruction of a civilian city was the sole purpose of an air raid. And in the moment between explosion and annihilation, Hiroshima's inhabitants must have been as stunned as the *Arizona*'s sailors, who had only those seven seconds between the muffled thud of an explosion in her fuel tanks and the thundering explosion in the magazine to ponder their fate.

These similarities provide context for what might otherwise be dismissed as coincidences. The banyan tree facing the
Arizona is known as the Hiroshima Banyan presumably because its shape resembles a mushroom cloud, but it is no more
mushroom-shaped than any other banyan. Both Honolulu and
Hiroshima have built memorials around ruins that survived,
and each is the most visited memorial in its country. At Hiroshima, the memorial is constructed around the ruined dome
of the Industrial Promotion Hall, a structure marking the epi-
center of the explosion as the *Arizona* does the destruction at
Pearl Harbor. There is also an official "sister city" relationship
between Honolulu and Hiroshima, based on their similar climate, size, and positions as Pacific port cities, but nurtured by
similar experiences and populations. Many Hawaiian Japanese
came from Hiroshima prefecture and had relatives killed there.
There are Japanese-Americans in Hawaii who witnessed Pearl
Harbor, suffered its consequences, enlisted in the Army, were
posted to the occupation, and returned to Hiroshima in American uniforms to search for family members.

The poignant photographs of belowdecks on the U.S.S.
Arizona, a world of stainless-steel galleys, brass caldrons, and
lines of hammocks, remind me of the ghostly ones of prewar
Hiroshima with its busy train station, packed streets, and trolley cars. Both show an innocent but doomed population just
before the catastrophe. The immutable fact that the victims of
Hiroshima and the *Arizona* were so unsuspecting and that both
were killed by what was essentially a sneak attack reveals the
most powerful connection between them to be that at the time,
both were outside the bounds of traditional warfare, and both
are better described as mass murder.

During the war, the *Arizona*'s twisted superstructure was
dismantled for scrap and its heavy guns removed for use as
coastal weapons. The rest remained, an oval outline sitting in

thirty-eight feet of water, visible beneath the surface, rust-brown and crusted with coral, a metal corpse. The idea of building a memorial over the wreckage came to a Honolulu businessman Tucker Gratz on December 7, 1946, when he laid a wreath on *Arizona* to commemorate the fifth anniversary of the attack and found there, undisturbed, the wreath he had laid to commemorate the fourth. Five years later, the Navy erected a flagstaff, although reluctantly, because many of its officers agreed with Admiral Nimitz, who "regretted that we memorialize Pearl Harbor Day—which was a great defeat for us." Next came a wood platform, a commemorative plaque, and in 1956 the first permanent memorial, a ten-foot stone obelisk. It was not until Memorial Day 1962 that the Pacific War Memorial Commission, headed by the same Tucker Gratz, dedicated the *Arizona* Memorial, a stark white rectangular structure that spans the *Arizona*'s remains and appears to hover over the water. Besides being the most important World War Two memorial in the country, it is one defying the usual pattern of such places, that as wars become more distant, their visitors shrink to an elderly trickle. Instead, every year the *Arizona* Memorial attracts larger crowds, until now, with a visitor count exceeding a million and a half a year, it has become the second-most-popular cemetery on earth.

The *Arizona* is both memorial and cemetery because the bodies of 1,102 of her crewmen have never been recovered. (Two divers were killed by pockets of gas in 1942, and two more in 1947, and further operations were abandoned.) What this means, although you will not find it in literature provided by the National Park Service or sold in the souvenir stand at the memorial's shore-based visitor center, is that beyond the *Arizona*'s open hatches and unbroken glass portholes, behind her fourteen-inch armor plating curled like lettuce leaves by the explosion, beneath a deck strewn with firehoses and the poles that once anchored awnings, and mixed in among shards of crockery and silverware from the mess, are the human remains most likely to survive fifty years of submersion—1,102 sets of teeth.

The *Arizona* feels like a cemetery. There is a heavy silence, broken only by the chug of a tour boat or ferry, and calm water surrounds it, flat and green, like a graveyard lawn. The white mooring blocks that once anchored the doomed battleships resemble old tombstones. Nearby are other buried remains: the wreck of a midget submarine, "crash sites" of planes, and urns containing the ashes of *Arizona* veterans, lowered over the years onto the wreckage in a stainless-steel cylinder the Navy has built for this purpose. And there is the *Arizona*'s oil, a droplet escaping every nine seconds, floating along passage-ways, up ladders, and through a small crack in the deck, spreading a rainbowed film on the water, a process the park rangers describe as "bleeding," as if the ship were a carelessly embalmed cadaver.

My impression of the *Arizona* as cemetery was reinforced by Fred Kokunu, a native Hawaiian park ranger with the sunken face and dignified manner of a funeral director. He has worked at the memorial since 1965, becoming its unofficial historian. Until 1978, he gave fifteen-minute lectures to as many as twenty-five groups a day. Every December 6, he scatters ti leaves and sprinkles salt blessed by a Hawaiian native priest on the wreckage, a ceremony designed to placate the Hawaiian shark god said to inhabit Pearl Harbor, and to have caused the collapse of the first dry dock in 1913, the Japanese raid, and a 1944 munitions explosion.

Hawaiians are sentimental, and their emotions are deeply felt. Even so, Kokunu's attachment to the *Arizona* is extraordinary. His eyes teared as he said, "I've had the honor to spend much of my life on a one-hundred-and-fifty-four-by-twenty-foot piece of property that represents one of the greatest tragedies in naval history." And teared again as he said, "I like going out in the morning before visitors arrive. I stare at the leaking oil and imagine it's the tears of the men buried in the *Arizona*, crying for us to keep America alert and strong."

He always recognizes Pearl Harbor survivors and their relatives. They stand alone, break into deep sobs, and leave without talking. The brother of the Anderson twins, both December 7 casualties, visited in 1968, telling Kokunu, "You are my brothers' keeper." The widow of Chief Yeoman Malecki came often, and had her ashes scattered over the wreckage. A Japanese woman brought flowers in memory of her fiancé, a pilot killed on December 7, and Kokunu himself supervised the burial of Stanley J. Teslow, lowering the stainless-steel cylinder containing his ashes into the number four gun turret.

I asked his impression of the half million Japanese a year who visit the *Arizona*. If there is anywhere, aside from Hiroshima, where Americans and Japanese should tread carefully, it is here. Fewer than a third of the memorial's visitors are Japanese, but on mornings when their buses arrive at once they overwhelm the visitor center. They pack shuttle boats, laughing and shouting as they line up for photographs, dismissively waving their hands at Americans who wander into their viewfinders. What did Fred Kokunu, who said the memorial was his whole life and a "sacred tomb," think of them?

The question made him uncomfortable. Instead of a direct answer, he made oblique comments, saying, "Until a few years ago the visitor center bookstore was forbidden from selling anything made in Japan. Now even our color commemorative book is printed there." He said Americans sometimes asked, "How can you let these goddam Japs come here?" But they were often pointing out a party of elderly Chinese. He said, "There was once a Japanese gentleman in his mid-forties who said, 'Sir, I am so sorry for Pearl Harbor.'" He paused, and this time his eyes were dry. "And that is the only Japanese visitor in my twenty years ever to say anything like that, ever."

The position of the National Park Service is that of course everyone is welcome at the memorial, and if you ask, the rangers at the *Arizona* will say for the record that the Japanese behave no differently from other nationalities. Nonetheless, I saw posted on a bulletin board in the park rangers' lounge a newspaper clipping headlined "JAPANESE TOURISTS FROLIC IN VATICAN." It described how the behavior of young Japanese in St. Peter's Basilica had enraged the Italians. They were accused of playing peek-a-boo behind statues of the saints, and eating pizza and laughing during mass. The presence of this clipping suggested some Japanese behaved the same way here.

But I thought if anything, the Japanese behaved better at the *Arizona* than most nationalities do when visiting sightseeing attractions in large groups. The problem was the nature of the attraction. Because they had come to the grave of men killed by a Japanese generation still alive, actions that at Disneyland or the Grand Canyon would seem harmless, or even commendable, became irritating or sinister. Their tendency to march closely behind a guide carrying a fluttering flag struck me as unnecessarily martial. Their fondness for buying models of the *Arizona* at the gift shop seemed perverse. I was annoyed by their custom of pitching small-denomination Japanese coins onto the *Arizona*'s submerged decks, and upset by their habit of gathering around the scale model in a tight knot—so tight there was no room for me—while their guide pointed with a flagpole to where the bomb had struck. They paid too much attention to this lengthy briefing. There were too many murmurs of agreement and nodding of heads, an interest unseemly in its intensity, and one feeding my suspicion some had come to celebrate a victory.

The other place to see Japanese visitors in great numbers is the National Memorial Cemetery of the Pacific, where many Pearl Harbor casualties are buried. It sits inside a volcanic crater rising above downtown Honolulu and known as Punchbowl, because of its distinctive shape. Standing among its flat grave markers, you see emerald lawns and flowering trees, the jungly slopes of the Koolaus, and rainbows. Gentle showers fall from a clear sky, misting the face like tears, and high-rise Honolulu is blocked by the crater's walls. It would resemble the heaven promised to Muslims and Sunday-school children were it not for the procession of tour buses, minivans, and limousines, coughing exhaust and shifting gears as they climb to a lookout on the crater's rim.

If you include the passengers in these vans and buses, then Punchbowl is a more popular cemetery than the *Arizona* Memorial. When I first went there, on a Friday morning, I counted twelve parked tour buses, and all but one had brought Japanese groups. They gathered to be photographed before a tablet saying, "In these gardens are recorded the names of Americans who gave their lives in the service of their country and whose earthly resting place is known only to God." A woman posed under an umbrella-shaped kukui tree, standing on a grave, with her arms spread open in the manner of a hostess offering an impressive buffet. In the memorial chapel, I surprised Japanese honeymooners who were kneeling, hands clasped in mock prayer, while a friend took their photograph. As they boarded their buses, on which smoking was prohibited, they could not help standing, and crushing out cigarettes, on the flat grave markers nearest the curb, on Private First Class Acie E. Culpepper of Mississippi and the 13th Engineer Battalion of the 7th Infantry Division (February 12, 1921–January 19, 1944), on Private Benjamin F. Davis of Oklahoma and the 2d Marine Division (March 18, 1924–November 23, 1943), and on Gunner's Mate Andrew Michael Marze of Pennsylvania (May 8, 1912–December 7, 1941).

I asked the Japanese at Punchbowl and the *Arizona* Memorial why they had come. They said: "Because it is a historical site," "Because we must learn from history," and, the most common answer by far, "Because it is on our tour." But *why* was it on the tour? Who thought they wanted to visit the remains of a thousand sailors killed by a single Japanese bomb? Or that Japanese honeymooners should begin married life at a place in the business of memorializing an act of Japanese treachery, or at the burial site of 31,000 Americans killed by Japanese forces?

These questions were answered when I returned the next day to Punchbowl and noticed a line of twenty Japanese gentlemen at the lavatory. Their clothes were rumpled and smelled of jet fuel. They wore cheap airport leis, squinted into the Hawaiian sunshine, and carried flight bags. Some clutched toilet kits. Back at the *Arizona* Memorial, Fred Kokunu confirmed my suspicions, saying many Japanese visitors had arrived the same morning on overnight flights from Tokyo. Their hotel rooms would not be ready until noon, so tour companies drove them straight from the airport to the *Arizona* and Punchbowl. Because they were free and had good toilet facilities, they were convenient places to dump them. Most of these Japanese had not come to celebrate their half-century-old victory, or to irritate touchy people like me, but simply to pass the time, brush their teeth, and piss.

Once I knew this, I had to pity them. Here they were, in the United States less than a day, and the first place they are taken is the site of what some Americans consider a Japanese atrocity. Then it's on to the graves of Americans killed by Japanese bullets.

I had been in Hawaii less than a week when I discovered this, and I wondered if I too was not the victim of my thirteen-hour flight and change in climate. For days I had felt fuzzy and light-headed, but once my jet lag faded, I noticed the Americans who visited the *Arizona*. While most Japanese wore sober suits, modest skirts, or polo shirts, Americans came in tank tops, tube

socks, and sweatshirts, in cutoff blue jeans, jogging shorts, and
bathing shorts. They wore plastic visors that turned their faces
green, and novelty T-shirts with four-letter words. I watched
them pick up tickets for the shuttle boat, and saw looks of
amazement and disgust on those turned away for failing to
meet the minimal requirement of "shirts, shorts, and foot-
wear." One man had set an example to his children by coming
bare-chested, another wore a T-shirt asking, "Wanna Get Laid?
Crawl up a Chicken's Asshole!"

The more I compared the Japanese to the American visitors, the better the Japanese looked, and the more obvious it
became that if anyone was desecrating this place, it was us.
After all, many of the buses and limousines dumping weary
Japanese travelers here were driven and owned by Americans.
The prominent signs at Punchbowl prohibiting "Skateboard-
ing, Rollerskating, Picnicking, Pets, Driver Education Activities, Drinking Alcoholic Beverages" gave you an idea of how
Americans behaved. The people asking the ignorant questions
about "dolphin shows" that found their way into the rangers'
"blooper book" were Americans. (Although I did read of a poll
showing 80 percent of all Japanese men and women in their
twenties could not connect Pearl Harbor with World War Two,
but many did identify it as a popular place for a honeymoon.)
It was an American who had written in a February 1988 edition of *This Week: Oahu,* "In the misty morning hours of
December 7, 1941, the Japanese dropped the atomic bomb on
Pearl Harbor and the U.S.S. *Arizona* became a tomb for 1,102
sleeping soldiers, many of whom are there still." The shuttle
boats taking visitors out to the memorial were piloted by American sailors who described the sinking of the *Arizona* in the
bored monotone of a flight attendant, adding, as they docked,
"Have a nice day." (Ask yourself, if you were leaving a group
at a cemetery, would you tell them to have a "nice day"?) The
Arizona was an American battlefield, on American soil, and

had Americans wanted, they could have posted the kind of austere signs the French have erected at Verdun: "You Are Entering the Actual Battlefield. This Earth Has Been Drenched with the Blood of Thousands Of Heroes. They Demand the Homage of Your Silence."

Americans were also behind the Infamy Flight. "RELIVE! The Morning of December 7, 1941," said the advertisement. "Thrill to being in the cockpit of this WW II airplane as you recreate the attack route of December 7, 1941. Feel the excitement and adventure from the copilot's seat of this restored warbird. Truly a sensational alternative to the traditional boat and bus ride!! The ultimate vacation experience."

I called the Adventure Store at 943-4FUN and was told that for $175 I could spend thirty minutes flying in the cockpit of a restored, fully instrumented 1942 Navy fighter, following the general route used by the Japanese planes that attacked Pearl Harbor. True, the plane was American rather than Japanese. The company had wanted to use a real Japanese Zero, but there were only two left flying in the world. And true, this plane was built a year after the attack, but it *had* been featured in the television miniseries *War and Remembrance*. I would be loaned vintage goggles and flight suit, and given a souvenir chart detailing the Japanese route. The plane's owner and pilot, a Mr. Peter Crown, would be at the controls, treating me to a "fabulous marriage of adventure and history."

If you think this enterprise sounds in dubious taste, you should know the original plan called for painting a Rising Sun on one side of the fuselage and mounting three dummy .30 caliber machine guns. The Infamy plane would take off from Dillingham Field in northern Oahu (named for Gaylord Dillingham, who was shot down over Japan), dive to a strafing altitude for a run across pineapple fields to Schofield Barracks and Wheeler Field, then fly along the Waianaes to Pearl Harbor, where, with the *Arizona* Memorial in the cross hairs of his dummy machine guns, Mr. Crown would make a pass at Battleship Row and, for an extra charge, execute a touch-and-go landing on the Ford Island airstrip in the middle of the harbor.

The inaugural Infamy Flight was announced for the morning of December 7, 1987, the forth-sixth anniversary of the attack, when politicians, dignitaries, and Pearl Harbor survivors would be gathered at the memorial to raise flags, play taps, present wreaths, observe a minute of silence, and deliver speeches honoring men killed by planes looking somewhat like this one. When asked about her Infamy Flight, a Ms. Kim Koogle of the Adventure Store had said, "We didn't want to stir up any bad memories, but we wanted a unique adventure."

The members of the Aloha Chapter of the Pearl Harbor Survivors Association (PHSA) are a fairly easygoing club of veterans, but even they thought this was too much. Like anyone living in Hawaii in the 1980s, they knew exactly which tourists could afford $175 for this brief amusement. They alerted the national chairman of the PHSA, who contacted the Adventure Store and reported back that the store staff "cannot understand what our complaints are or why we insist on making waves." They complained to their congressmen and the Pentagon, and at the last minute the Federal Aviation Administration found a regulation forbidding sightseeing planes from flying within eight miles of an active military base.

By going too far, the Adventure Store had at least proved it was possible, although flying over memorial services for men killed at Pearl Harbor in a plane marked with enemy insignia must mark the outer perimeter of any limits. As do the used-car advertisements of the Krumpholz Chevrolet-Buick dealership of West Chicago, which for several years showed a photographic montage of smoking and sunken U.S. battleships. Bold lettering across the page proclaimed, "December 7, 1941," and "In Remembrance of Pearl Harbor We Are Having a Gigantic Sale on American Cars Built by Americans!!" And of course,

"Save!" "Sporty!" "Make an Offer!" and "Priced to Sell!" When questioned about the taste of these advertisements, one of the owners said he and his brother were "just all-American boys trying to sell all-American cars."

The *Arizona* Memorial's design may be somewhat to blame for the lack of respect shown by some American visitors. It is a striking structure, even a beautiful one, but it lacks the necessary morbidity, the power to move even the most ignorant to tears. It does not immediately tell you, as does the Vietnam Memorial, or those rows of crosses in Normandy, that the ground has been "drenched by the blood of heroes." It was designed by Alfred Preis, an Austrian refugee who fled Hitler's Vienna as a young man and arrived in Honolulu with his wife in 1939. When I called him he said he had a guard dog who "didn't stop," and suggested we meet at a Burger King near the University of Hawaii. I thought it was a strange choice for such a sensitive and talented architect, but I had not been in Honolulu long enough to understand that real estate is too expensive in many neighborhoods to support outdoor cafés or casual restaurants. So, as we sat at a Formica table drinking iced tea from plastic cups, Preis told me his original design for the *Arizona* Memorial had called for it to echo the jewel-encrusted crypts of the Hapsburg emperors. From his boyhood in Vienna he remembered how these made death close and imminent. The wreckage of the *Arizona* reminded him of them, although its hull was encrusted with barnacles instead of jewels.

He first proposed an underwater chamber next to the *Arizona*, which he hoped would make a powerful antiwar statement. It would be open to the sky and be entered down a flight of stairs from a boat landing. Visitors would face the ship, viewing it through portholes cut in a wall, and standing opposite the remains of the crew. They would be reminded of the horror of being trapped underwater. But the Navy and his partners rejected this plan as "too morbid," the same charge later made against the Vietnam Memorial, and one reflecting an understandable military discomfort with memorials that too closely make the connection between war and death.

Similar thinking may be behind the flat markers at many national cemeteries that avoid the depressing impact of a lawn filled with rows of crosses. They make the cemeteries look like parks and golf courses rather than graveyards, and leave their grass easy to mow. Until 1951, temporary white crosses marked the Punchbowl graves, and the dazzling sight of row upon row of them was so moving that newspapers and veterans' groups protested when the Army replaced them. Had the crosses remained, it is difficult imagining anyone considering Punchbowl a good place to picnic, put out a cigarette, or park jet-lagged tourists.

After his first concept was rejected, Preis reconsidered the Navy's original suggestion for an open bridge over the wreckage and turned it into the soaring white rectangle now spanning the *Arizona*. The floor and ceiling sag in the center, reflecting the despair of December 7, then rise at both ends to symbolize victory. Stained-glass windows light a "shrine room," and the effect is reminiscent of Coventry Cathedral and other European churches rebuilt after the war. Preis describes it as a "serene and friendly" space. Although it does not make the antiwar statement he intended, he hopes visitors will consider it a place to daydream, "contemplate personal responses," and imagine the attack. This might have been possible in 1962, when an average of three hundred people a day visited the memorial. It might have been possible in 1973, when the average was fifteen hundred. But it certainly is not possible now, when more than four thousand a day arrive in batches of 150 every fifteen minutes.

I saw little evidence of contemplation or imagining. Instead, I saw many people becoming bored, wandering aimlessly, then lining up early for the boat. I saw them close their eyes, squinch their faces into wish-making expressions, and toss coins onto the sunken hull. "What are you wishing for?" I asked. They answered, "For nothing, I'm just doing it." "For peace." "For a safe journey home." I doubted this place would have become a wishing well, or just another stop on the Honolulu tourist agenda, if Preis's Hapsburg-tomb design had been accepted. Then, instead of standing in this "serene and peaceful" place with its fine views of Oahu's mountains, visitors would have had to descend into the *Arizona* and face the wreckage of an explosion that in a few seconds killed more than a thousand sailors, and perhaps catch a glimpse of those teeth.

Although the *Arizona* Memorial is a smoothly run operation and its Park Service employees have a fine sense of mission, there are other aspects of it that might trouble anyone who thinks it is simply a cemetery and memorial to the men who perished here in 1941.

There is the matter of the twenty-minute documentary seen by visitors before boarding the shuttle boats. It is a confusing film, which makes it appear as if the Japanese capture of Singapore and Hong Kong and the smashing of American air power in the Philippines all preceded Pearl Harbor, and it panders to Japanese sensibilities in stating that because of the American decision in August 1941 to freeze Japanese funds and embargo oil and other exports, Japan felt it had no choice but to go to war. The most charitable explanation for the *Arizona* documentary's slant is that it arises from an eagerness to promote reconciliation. Yet a reconciliation based on half-truths and misinterpretations is bound to fail, as this one has by angering some of the veterans who see it. Whether or not one approves, the *Arizona* Memorial is an integral part of Hawaii's "visitor industry," one heavily dependent on Japanese tourists, who account for a fifth of all visitors and spend three times as

fast as the average American. This fact is so much part of
Hawaii's atmosphere that it can put an unconscious spin on
transactions and decisions—the filmmakers need not have set
out to pander to the Japanese for that to be their effect.

There is also the matter of how, between 1957 and 1962,
funds were raised and Congressional approval sought to build
the memorial. It was not enough to present it as a tribute to the
dead of December 7, or as a cemetery for sailors still entombed
on the *Arizona*. Other angles had to be explored and other
agendas satisfied. At times, it was promoted as a monument to
the necessity for defense spending. And so Senator Carl Hayden
of Arizona, speaking to support the Congressional bill that
would enable the Navy to build it with funds raised by the
Pacific War Memorial Commission (PWMC) said, "It is im-
perative that we be prepared either to win a war against Godless communism or to prevent such a war by being so strong
that the dictators in Moscow will be afraid to drop the first
bomb. It is, therefore, appropriate that, through this memorial,
we focus our attention on our most striking example of unpre-
paredness, so that we may be perpetually reminded of the security that is found in strength."

At other times, the memorial was promoted as a device to
lure visitors to Hawaii, with the Hawaii legislature appropri-
ating $100,000 only after PWMC commissioners lobbied its
members with descriptions of the memorial's projected ability
to stimulate "tourist interest."

And at others, it was described as a bargain-rate cemetery,
with Congressman Mendel Rivers of South Carolina arguing
that the $150,000 needed to complete its construction was
much less than the total military burial allowances for the entombed sailors.

Ninety-five thousand dollars in public donations came after the senior surviving officer on the *Arizona,* Admiral Samuel
Fuqua, appeared on a national telecast of Ralph Edwards's

This Is Your Life. According to *Remembering Pearl Harbor: The Story of the U.S.S. "Arizona" Memorial*, a history of the memorial published by the *Arizona* Memorial Museum Association, "Appeals for contributions to the memorial fund were a prominent part of the program. Fuqua maintained a controlled military demeanor throughout the show, but clearly it was a time of high emotion." It sounds as though America narrowly escaped seeing Admiral Fuqua break down while begging for donations to memorialize his dead shipmates. In 1961, still short of funds, the PWMC accepted Elvis Presley's offer to perform in a benefit concert. (He was in Hawaii anyway, filming *Blue Hawaii*.) He appeared in a gold lamé coat, singing to the accompaniment of what a *Honolulu Star-Bulletin* reporter called "sub-navel quaking and shaking." A line, however, had to be drawn somewhere, and a proposal to raise money by trailering a gigantic piggy bank across the country was rejected.

There is also the matter of the anniversary speeches given at the Punchbowl or *Arizona* Memorial describing the "lessons" of Pearl Harbor. During the Cold War, the lesson was vigilance against Senator Hayden's "Godless communism." During the Vietnam era, the lesson was the danger of appeasing an Asian foe. During the Reagan presidency, it was the importance of military strength to deter aggression—at least according to Admiral Isaac C. Kidd, Jr. (Ret.), son of the Admiral Kidd who had perished on the *Arizona*, who during an October 10, 1980, speech dedicating the visitor center declared, "Pearl Harbor could have been avoided had we but been strong enough in the years preceding to deter the attack."

Bringing this lesson further up to date was Vice Admiral E. P. Aurand (Ret.), who on December 7, 1986, said, "The men who died there [Pearl Harbor] bought with their lives a lesson for Americans that should last forever. You cannot entrust the peace to the promises of men who rule countries where free elections and free speech do not exist." He went on to compare the outcry over President Reagan's alleged involvement in the Iran arms scandal to 1941 Congressional accusations that President Roosevelt was acting illegally by giving Britain fifty destroyers and conducting an undeclared war against German submarines. Aurand argued that although there had been truth to charges Roosevelt acted unconstitutionally, he persisted nevertheless, and "his actions, constitutional or not, probably saved Britain from an early defeat and the world from a victory by Hitler. For our country's sake, let us hope that things turn out as well for today's beleaguered President."

Few such lessons connect with what happened at Pearl Harbor, while the real lessons, the ones bearing a certain uncomfortable relevance to the present, are rarely mentioned, perhaps because they are too controversial, too depressing, or simply too terrifying. These are the lessons of how obsession with internal subversion may leave you vulnerable to your genuine enemies, the lesson of how a catastrophe described as impossible or unthinkable, such as Pearl Harbor—or an oil spill, nuclear plant disaster, or accidental nuclear war—can sometimes happen, and the lesson about over-reliance on technology, such as the belief that Magic's ability to decipher Japanese codes made a sneak attack impossible. And most of all, there is the lesson of how racism and national pride can lead to a false sense of security, or as Colonel William J. Flood, commander of Wheeler Field on December 7, put it, "To think that this bunch of little yellow bastards could do this to us when we all knew that the United States was superior to Japan!"

17

The "Little Yellow Bastards" Destroy the Army Air Force

GUS AHOLA WAS LYING IN BED IN HIS QUARTERS AT WHEELER Field, debating between golf and washing his car, when he heard the whine of a plane he assumed was having engine trouble. It kept coming, louder and louder, lower and lower, until he began saying to himself, "Jesus, pull out of it, pull out of it!" There was an explosion, and he thought, "Oh hell, oh hell, that poor fellow's bought the farm." The building shook. He spread open a crack in the venetian blinds and, shielding his eyes, looked for a parachute. Instead, he saw plumes of smoke rising from the far end of the field. His roommate woke, and despite weeks of headlines about a possible war with Japan, constant alerts, and training missions, neither thought these planes might be Japanese. Perhaps it was the "damned Navy," Ahola suggested, staging another mock raid and dropping sacks of flour. He rolled to the edge of his bed again and peered through the blinds, this time seeing a line of bombers, each painted with the distinctive Japanese meatball. "Navy, hell!" he shouted. "Those are the goddam Nips!" And then, remembering how the squadron was parked, he thought, "Boy, they're going to clobber us!" He pulled his uniform over his pajamas, jamming shoes over his bare feet. On the way, his car hit a Coke bottle, puncturing a tire and forcing him to get out and run.

He reached the flight line as the first bombing run ended. The hangars, enlisted men's barracks, and post exchange were in flames. Over a hundred aircraft, still in their tight antisabotage formations, had been lost to bombs, bullets that ignited fuel tanks, and a river of burning gas running across the tarmac. Having expended their bombs, a circle of Japanese warplanes formed overhead. One by one they peeled off, diving for a strafing run, coming so low they found telephone wires wrapped around their landing gear, so slow the Wheeler commander saw their pilots "lean out of their planes and smile as they zoomed by," even noticing the "gold in their teeth."

There were no antiaircraft batteries at Wheeler, because such defenses were thought useless against the expected saboteurs. Little small-arms or rifle fire was heard at first, because to prevent ammunition being stolen by fifth columnists, it had been locked in a hangar that was now in flames. Instead of fighting back, the unarmed airmen died in their beds and washrooms, in the open, while running for safety or trying to disentangle their planes, or huddled for cover in hangars and behind bunkers, because no air raid shelters had been built. Thirty-nine were killed and fifty-nine wounded, with the heaviest casualties among those sleeping in barracks or tents alongside the runway.

To avoid damaging morale, newsreels and photographs avoided showing the dead of Wheeler Field (and of other Oahu bases), picturing instead the injured recovering in a hospital, and making it seem wounds were clean and deaths painless. The earliest eyewitness accounts reinforced this impression. Private Charles Legshock from Monroe, Louisiana, said, "The men, most of them kids like myself, were really something to see while under fire. They all reacted well, and many died with smiles on their faces." One of Legshock's fellow airmen had "looked around him, examined his own injuries, and then died, a smile lighting his face." Compare this to the postwar testimony of a Wheeler Field lieutenant who could at last admit the airmen had been so terrified that "some [of the dead] had attempted to escape the strafing by digging through the wooden tent floors with their bare hands. Hands and fingernails were lacerated, and in many instances fingernails torn out."

When I visited Wheeler Field with Gus Ahola, I was surprised how much it resembled its 1941 photographs. Here were the same barracks, louvered windows, and art deco street lamps, the same runway, hangars, and views west to pineapple fields and the Waianaes. The hangars were decorated by the blue star insignia of the old Army Air Corps, and their steel beams were scarred by Japanese bullets. The officers' club was the same handsome stucco hacienda. The biggest change, Ahola said, was that palms, bougainvillea, and mangoes had grown taller, providing more shade and privacy, and so many mangoes the officers could not give them away.

In 1941, Wheeler, Hickam, and Pearl Harbor had been busy little military cities, surrounded by deserted beaches and cane and pineapple fields, impossible to miss from the ground or air. They had been constructed in a style popular in America's empire, a Southwestern mission architecture of thick walls, deep verandas, and high ceilings. Since its inauguration in 1922, Wheeler in particular had been important in aviation history; it was used for the first nonstop flight from California to Hawaii, the first flight from America to Australia, and Amelia Earhart's first solo flight from Hawaii to the mainland. By 1941, it had become a symbol of American aviation prowess and was the largest Army Air Corps fighter base in the Pacific, with more than 150 planes, including many P-40 Tomahawks, considered Hawaii's best defense against an air raid.

Bases like Wheeler are still impossible to miss now because

they are oases of space and calm amid a sprawl of condominium villages and strip developments. Simply by not having
changed in fifty years, they have become the most attractive
and unspoiled communities on Oahu. Outside their gates are
flimsy houses on an eighth of an acre, meadows of asphalt, and
scrubby transplanted palms; within are plantation mansions
and adobe ranch houses set in parklands of mature palms and
flowering trees.

Wheeler was quiet the day Ahola and I went there. Its
bungalows were occupied and its offices filled with communications and engineering units, but because its short runways are
unsuited to modern warplanes, its hangars held only army helicopters. We visited the bachelor officers' quarters where he
had lived on December 7. He looked down silent streets to the
empty runway, then west to the Waianaes. Today's weather
was the same, he said. Trades from the northeast, scattered
clouds, and brief showers. (Wheeler's weather is often different
from Pearl Harbor's.) We drove to the runway following the
route he had taken on December 7, then walked to an over-
grown bunker where he had taken cover. He began describing
the attack, pausing longer between sentences, and sometimes
flicking his eyes to the horizon. He said that as the first Japanese planes departed, he had run down the flight line and
jumped into an apparently airworthy plane, taxiing it away
from the others. Its tail section was burned out, its controls
damaged, and its guns had no ammunition, but he hoped to
ram an enemy aircraft, cutting off its tail with his propeller
(and thereby becoming America's first kamikaze). Instead, it
spun into a huge ground loop, refusing to take off.

"God, what a disappointment," he said. "There we were,
the best, fully trained, gung ho, with the best planes, and we
never had a chance to fight. If only we'd had twenty minutes
warning, only twenty minutes, some of us could have been up
there, and there wouldn't have been such devastation at Pearl

Harbor, although a lot of us probably would have been killed."

"Including you," I said.

He shrugged. "Perhaps."

I had no doubt if he could change history, he would want that warning, preferring to exchange the certainty of fifty years of life for the chance to duel with a Zero on December 7.

We had attracted attention by standing on the empty apron, gesturing toward the sky and hangars, making planing motions with our hands. One of the Army engineers tending the helicopters—Sergeant Thompson, his name tag said—came over to check us out. When Ahola identified himself as a Pearl Harbor survivor, his manner became more friendly. This was no ordinary senior citizen trespassing on the base. He insisted on shaking Ahola's hand and showing him where Japanese bullet holes still pockmarked a hangar. He wanted to know which direction the Japanese had attacked and asked about the yellow bumps on the apron. Ahola explained them as part of the old refueling system. As we left, Thompson stiffened, as if to attention, and said, "Honored to have met you, sir. Yeah, that sure was something . . . December 7, 1944 [sic]."

Ahola gave a pained smile, and we started back in silence. As Pearl Harbor came into sight, he said, "You know, by mid-afternoon we had some planes in service and I was able to fly two missions. Fighter command told us to fly as high and fast as we could. Five of us took off, but only three made it up to twenty-six thousand feet. The city was blacked out, but fires still burned in Pearl Harbor. Our flight commander, Charlie McDonald, asked what we were supposed to be going after. Fighter command said a bogey had been reported over Diamond Head. We kept climbing to thirty thousand feet and saw nothing. Finally Charlie radioed back, 'Doesn't anyone there have an astronomy table? Don't you know that Venus is bright this time of year?' There was a long embarrassed pause, then someone in control said, 'Okay. Come in and land.'"

At Hickam Field too, the Japanese attacked without being challenged by fighters or antiaircraft fire. They bombed hangars, ammunition storehouses, and the Hale Makai barracks, where a direct hit killed thirty-five men eating breakfast. They destroyed or damaged most of Hickam's sixty-four bombers, which had been parked on the aprons with their wingtips just ten feet apart, guarded by soldiers armed with revolvers to repel saboteurs. The only warplane to become airborne was the one blown through the roof of its hangar.

Hickam also looks the same as in 1941. A Moorish water tower is its most prominent feature, lawns border four-lane parkways, and its wing operations building is a modest art deco structure. When it opened in 1939, it was the most modern and self-contained of any overseas American base, described by the Army as "laid out like an exclusive residential park. . . . Streets wind and curve in an easy, carefree manner, and with a leisurely Hawaiian indifference to the Euclidean maxim." Its Hale Makai barracks was the largest in the world, an octopus of a building, with ten wings sleeping three thousand soldiers, and a mess hall feeding 3,500 at two sittings. The *Honolulu Star-Bulletin* compared it to "the heart of Palm Beach or any of the resort centers of the southland."

The Hale Makai barracks has since become offices for the headquarters of the U.S. Air Force in the Pacific, but its exterior remains untouched. Lines of bullet holes run up walls, stopping at windows, and bomb fragments scar its courtyards. One base commander ordered the holes filled, but veterans protested, he relented, and the building is now a National Historic Monument.

Relics are on display in the lobby. There is a rusty part from a P-40, a bullet taken from a hangar door, the Protestant chaplain's communion set, and the flag that flew on December 7, later the centerpiece for the most famous Pearl Harbor photograph. It shows this flag, flying from a tower over the three-story barracks. Machine gun fire has ripped its middle and shredded its end, but it continues flying straight out. A line of palm trees are bent backward in the wind, and a thick column of smoke pours from Hale Makai, drifting across a parking lot of beetle-backed cars and making it seem the explosion has just occurred. The uncanny way it illustrated the lyrics of the national anthem led to captions such as " . . . The Flag Was Still There," and it came to symbolize American defiance, becoming the war's most famous flag photograph until replaced by one of Marines raising the Stars and Stripes over Iwo Jima.

Just west of Wheeler Field, at Schofield Army Barracks, Private Bob Kinzler awoke to what he thought was a mess-hall oven exploding. He looked outside to see a plane circling the roof of the headquarters building. Its fuselage was marked by a red circle, its canopy was black, and its landing gear was fixed open. Two men sat in its cockpit. He noticed their helmets were lined with fur. An attack by Japan was so inconceivable he continued believing the explosion was accidental and these strange planes belonged to the Navy. He went down to breakfast, and it was not until buglers trumpeted an alert that he and the men in the mess hall ran into the quadrangle, while others grabbed rifles and fired from rooftops at planes attacking Wheeler.

At 0930, with the second wave still overhead, men of Kinzler's company climbed into a truck to be driven to positions from which to repel a Japanese invasion. As they came over a rise in the Kamehameha Highway, they saw ships burning in Pearl Harbor. "Our average age was nineteen," Kinzler remembers, "and we thought we were going to die. We wore World War One pie-plate hats, and were lightly armed. I had a .45 caliber pistol I later discovered was defective." The only conversation he recalls verbatim came when his buddies, upon seeing the devastated harbor, speculated on how much it would hurt to be hit by a Japanese bullet. One boy said, "Hey, I've heard the Japs only have .25 caliber ammo. Do you think that would hurt as much as being hit by a .30 caliber?" Another scared boy agreed it would have to hurt less. But how much less?

Kinzler served throughout the war, becoming an officer and afterward moving back to Hawaii to manage the sugar mill still operating at the foot of Aiea Heights, where he has lived for thirty-five years. In 1941, there were cane fields here up to 650 feet, and above that, houses scattered through forests of bamboo. Since building here in 1954, he has watched construction crews creep up the hill, crisscrossing it with curving streets and suburban homes. Today, his once spectacular view of Pearl Harbor is partially blocked by a neighbor's roof, although from an angle he can see the *Arizona* Memorial, floating in the harbor like a sugar cube.

I had always thought of the attack on Schofield as being dramatic and terrifying, and was troubled because Kinzler could not remember any casualties, nor any bombing or strafing, although he said others had told him this had happened. A popular book of Pearl Harbor photographs, published in 1981 and reprinted fourteen times since, says, "Schofield was attacked as well. Building 1492 on the west end of the barracks was one of the first structures hit. Quad C, one of the main barracks, was strafed, as well as the post library." In the movie *From Here to Eternity,* Japanese planes swoop low over the barracks while soldiers scatter across a quadrangle, some pitching forward dead. The book on which it was based was a novel, but I always believed that since its author, James Jones, had witnessed the attack, his portrayal of events at Schofield was factual. He described three planes coming from the southeast "firing full blast," a strafing attack continuing fitfully for over an hour, a boy being killed ("The red-haired boy lay sprawled out floppy-haired, wild-eyed and silent, in the middle of the pavement"), and a Japanese pilot flying so low that soldiers saw "the helmeted head with the square goggles over the slant eyes and the long scarf rippling behind it and the grin on the face as he waved."

I should have been suspicious that although hundreds of official photographs show attacks on Oahu's other bases, the only one I could find of Schofield Barracks on December 7 was captioned "C Quad at Schofield Barracks under mock attack. This photo depicts a dramatization of the attack done for the movie *From Here to Eternity*."

At Schofield Barracks I met Herb Garcia, a retired Army colonel who is curator of the base museum. He is convinced the Japanese never attacked Schofield, because he can find no mention of any casualties or enemy action in its official military police reports, nor in its duty rosters, nor in the journal of the 25th Infantry Regiment. He showed me this last document, an impressively detailed, minute-by-minute account of that day. It described the attack on Wheeler, and rumors of paratroopers and saboteurs, but never a single bomb or bullet falling on Schofield itself. Garcia had also checked the Army engineers' reports of home repairs for December 1941, believing that if the post suffered damage it would be mentioned there. But he read only of clogged toilets and broken screens. He checked the journal of the base hospital chaplain, which showed him attending only to casualties from Wheeler Field. The fact that troops such as Kinzler's company could have moved out as early as 0930 was more proof no attack had occurred.

He concedes a dud naval shell from Pearl Harbor fell into a barrel of flour in the kitchen, that a Japanese pilot may have squeezed off rounds while heading for Wheeler, and that empty casings may have fallen into Schofield's quadrangles and been mistaken for live ammunition. "Remember, the soldiers who witnessed this were not trained observers," he said, "just excitable Depression-era kids. Then rumors got bigger in the telling and were reinforced by erroneous scenes from the *From Here to Eternity* movie. Now, ninety percent of the veterans who return say, 'Yeah, I was bombed, I was strafed.' If I argue, they say, 'Look, buddy, I was here and you weren't.' "

Garcia almost admitted he wished he *had* been here. "Those guys in the Schofield battalions lived together for several years in the peacetime Army, making a miserable twenty-one dollars a month," he said. "When the war came they fought together, surviving terrible combat for four years as their numbers dwindled. As they got fewer and fewer, they became closer." He, on the other hand, had commanded a battalion in Vietnam, where, he said, officers quickly revolved through commands, a tour of duty was a year, and troops seldom experienced the intense bonding common in World War Two.

Garcia was short and energetic, a man of great enthusiasms, but I thought he may have delighted too much in deflating the earlier generation's war stories. When I mentioned the shell hole in the base library, described by Kinzler as evidence that Schofield came under attack, he just laughed and said, "Three holes, more likely made by a drill than a bullet. See for yourself." On the north wall of the stone building that housed his office and museum, someone had painted a red bull's-eye around three holes. They were smooth, low, and sloped upward at an impossible angle, and they were the wrong size for the Japanese .50 caliber shells.

"To make these, a Japanese pilot would have had to be flying four feet above the ground," he said.

But had someone drilled them on purpose? I wondered. Were they left by some forgotten workman, then labeled a Pearl Harbor relic by an officer upset because the Japanese had not considered Schofield an important target, and angry the Army Air Force and Navy had hogged the "glory"? And make no mistake, as the expanding membership rolls of the Pearl Harbor Survivors Association prove, there is glory.

I thought these bullet holes proved how Pearl Harbor fact and myth have become braided, even in the memory of living witnesses. On my way to Schofield, I had paused at Wheeler Field again, to examine the P-40 sitting on a pedestal inside its main gate. The guard said it was a December 7 survivor, but then I walked closer and read a plaque identifying it as a replica, built in 1966 and used in *Tora! Tora! Tora!*

At a reunion of the 25th Infantry Association, Herb Garcia had met a Mr. Welden, who was the model for James Jones's Sergeant Warden, and a Robert E. Lee Stuart, who like the Robert E. Lee Prewitt in *From Here to Eternity* came from West Virginia and was a bugler and a boxer who had once blinded an opponent. Stuart had printed business cards identifying him as "Prewitt," and, according to Garcia, "He blew taps at the drop of a hat, and preferred being called 'Prew' to Stu, his real Army nickname." Garcia considered this evidence of how closely Jones modeled his characters on real people, but I thought it also showed how people will adjust their real lives to conform to fictional ones, and how easily fictional and factual memories of historical events can become fused. This happened to Jones himself when he returned to Schofield in 1973 and tried reimagining the time when he had been ordered to march to the Kolekole Pass carrying a full pack. "I had used the incident on Prewitt in the novel, and it had been reproduced in the film version," he wrote. "Now I no longer knew whether Prewitt had done it, or I had."

I asked Garcia to point out the Kolekole Pass, through which, according to so many books, Japanese planes had flown on their way to attack Wheeler Field.

"Another myth!" he said, delighted I had mentioned it. "Not a single plane ever flew through that pass."

But *Tora! Tora! Tora!*—which purported to be a meticulously accurate recreation of Pearl Harbor—showed planes flying through Kolekole, and I had read in magazines and newspapers about Japanese pilots "barreling" or "screaming" though it. In *Day of Infamy,* Walter Lord reported a staff sergeant seeing "a line of six to ten planes come through the Kolekole Pass to the west." One of my books of December 7 photographs contained a picture captioned "Kolekole Pass looking east out into the Leilehua Plain. This was the view the Japanese pilots had as they came out of the pass. Wheeler Field and Schofield Barracks were dead ahead."

Garcia explained that although from Schofield and Wheeler the pass appears to be a clear gap in the Waianae Range, from the air you can see a mountain rising in its middle on the western side, making it impossible to fly through. The Japanese had actually come along the eastern side of the Waianaes, turning near Kolekole to attack Wheeler. Seen there for the first time, silhouetted against an open sky, they appeared to have flown through the pass. I checked the official Japanese and American maps and saw he was right—not one showed planes flying through Kolekole.

He drove me up there on a military highway. A plaque read, "It was through the Kolikoli [sic] Pass and through this valley that some Japanese aircraft flew on their way to Pearl Harbor on December 7, 1941." But just beyond, as Garcia claimed, was a small hill filling its center. Considering all the evidence to the contrary, the real mystery of the Kolekole Pass is not whether the Japanese used it—they clearly did not—but why the fable enjoys such longevity.

I returned on my own the next day, stopping again at Wheeler, walking through Schofield, and staring up at the mountains. The Kolekole Pass story was appealing, I decided, because it supported the impression that Japanese planes had not appeared in plain sight until seconds before attacking, thus making the failure to detect them somehow excusable. It also confirmed the treacherous nature of the Japanese. For Americans, there has always been something despicable about lying

hidden behind a ridge, then swooping down on an unsuspecting enemy, a technique usually ascribed to the Indians. Except
for the pineapple fields, the landscape here resembled the American Southwest. The Waianaes were stark and red, like the
ridge of hills concealing an Indian ambush in a Hollywood
western. The United States has fought only two enemies it considered subhuman, the Indians and the Japanese, and it was
only natural for the second of these to assume some of the
alleged characteristics of the first. The Indians too were seen as
treacherous and sneaky, having no regard for human life or the
"rules" of war. They too lay in wait behind pink desert ridges,
ready to ambush white men. The connection between them was
easy to make in this arid landscape, and in military posts whose
architecture echoed the American Southwest. Perhaps this par-
allel explains not only the Kolekole Pass myth, but also why the
expression "The only good Injun is a dead Injun" so quickly
became "The only good Jap is a dead Jap."

As the attack on the Kaneohe Naval Air Station began,
Lieutenant Cy Gillette was taking a shower at his home on
nearby Kailua beach. His wife shouted that the duty officer was
calling, ordering him back to base at once. Gillette dismissed
this as "more war game emergencies" and decided to shave
first. It took another call, reporting that planes were on fire, to
send him racing to Kaneohe in his convertible.

He found the air station in chaos. Hangars were burning.
Sailors ran across the runway chased by Japanese bullets, pa-
jama legs poking from underneath their uniforms. Most of the
flying boats were already in flames. When the attack began,
only three of Kaneohe's thirty-six PBY seaplanes had been on
patrol; the rest were riding at anchor, sitting in hangars, or
parked in antisabotage formations on the apron, their guns
unloaded. Kaneohe had no fixed gun emplacements, and the
mobile Army antiaircraft guns assigned to protect it had been

rolled away for the weekend. Even its Springfield and automatic rifles, pistols, and .50-caliber machine guns, weapons for
defending against the saboteurs predicted by Commander Martin on December 6, were locked away in the armory.

Sailors smashed the armory open with rifle butts and axes
and passed out weapons. Gillette grabbed a Thompson subma-
chine gun and ran across the runway, chased by strafing bullets.
The ensign next to him fell over dead, and Gillette still describes this event as if he cannot yet believe it: "One moment
we were running next to each other, and the next, suddenly, he
was down on the tarmac."

At 0915, a second wave of bombers attacked. This time
Kaneohe's defenders fired back with rifles, pistols, and machine
guns. The bombers retreated and Zeros descended, flying at
rooftop level, strafing. Duels became personal. A sailor remembers a pilot laughing at him, "seeing his teeth and the motion of
his lips quite distinctly."

One pilot crashed into the ocean. A second lagged behind
as others reformed to return to the carriers. Its pilot, Lieutenant
Fusata Iida, turned back, deciding to make a last strafing run.
He came in low and alone, guiding his crippled plane toward
the armory, and becoming a target for every gun on the base.
His plane was hit several times and slammed into a hillside
above the airfield. His mangled body was pulled from the
wreckage, still wearing its "belt of a thousand stitches," a good-
luck charm sewn by his fiancée. His head had been mangled
and his feet amputated, making it easy for someone to steal his
flight boots. Nine years later, they were mailed to his mother
with an apology.

His corpse was stuffed into a galvanized garbage can because, it was later claimed, there was no suitable receptacle at
hand. It was left on a sidewalk in front of the sick bay. The next
day, it was buried on the base with full military honors, near
the American casualties.

A second ceremony was held at Kaneohe forty years later, on December 6, 1981. It was attended by several of the sailors who claimed to have killed Iida, and by the woman who had once sewn the thousand-stitch belt for the man she now called "my eternal sweetheart." Through coincidences and a correspondence too complicated to recount here, Iida's fiancée had contacted one of these sailors, a Mr. Conrad Frienze of Seattle, arranging to have herself invited to ceremonies at Kaneohe marking the fortieth anniversary. Mr. Frienze claimed to have fed bullets into the weapon that his brother Richard fired to bring down Iida. Yet also present at these ceremonies was John Finn, who had won the Medal of Honor for heroism at Kaneohe, and who said Iida's Zero was in his machine gun sights as he fired off some rounds seconds before it crashed. Although another Kaneohe sailor, Guy Avery, credited an aviation ordnanceman named Sands with the kill, saying that he "emptied the rifle at the roaring Zero which was coming in on a constantly decreasing line of flight as though the pilot intended to crash at the fighting sailor's feet."

In truth, all three probably contributed to Iida's death, and the first two, anyway, felt badly about it. Finn was reported "nearly overcome with emotion" as he visited a monument marking where Iida's plane crashed. He told journalists he respected Iida, and had learned he was "real cheerful, a jolly little guy who was much liked." Meanwhile, Frienze said Iida had "died like a samurai," adding, "I'm sure he was down there because he intended to draw as much fire as possible so the other Japanese planes would have a better chance to get away. He served his nation and his emperor as well as any man could and I'm proud that I've got to 'know' him." (This is a generous interpretation of Iida's last strafing run. All other accounts indicate his plane was already badly damaged, and that before taking off he had told comrades he would "make a crash dive into an enemy target rather than an emergency landing.")

Frienze and others attending the ceremonies at Kaneohe came to "know" Iida through his fiancée, Kikuyo Iida, who had acquired his surname by marrying his cousin. She came carrying diaries, letters, photographs, and an essay—"Commander Iida Has Been My Eternal Sweetheart," describing the years she had worked, as she put it, "to serve the commander's grave," and concluding, "Yes, he was my first lover, and I believed him to be the most respectable man in the world." She bought a cache of Lieutenant Iida memorabilia she planned giving out as "souvenirs" to the Kaneohe veterans, and she brought Yaeko Munakata, Iida's former landlady, and a repository of syrupy stories about his fondness for children. She too was coming, according to her English-speaking friend Hisao, "to worship [the] commander's monument."

The monument is an ambiguous one, a small pile of lava rocks bonded together with concrete and topped with a stone marker proclaiming in capitals, "JAPANESE AIRCRAFT IMPACT SITE," and then in smaller letters, "Pilot—Lieutenant Iida, I. J.N. Cmdr. Third Air Control Group." It is arguable whether it is the sort of historical marker found on battlefields or, as Mrs. Iida chooses to believe, a memorial to Iida. On the afternoon of December 6, 1981, she and Mrs. Munakata decorated the memorial with a photograph of Iida, burned incense, and anointed it with sake. She wrote later to the base commander, Colonel C. D. Robinson, saying, "It was a very emotional moment to face Lieutenant Iida's memorial, for I have been dreaming [of] it during the past forty years. . . . I can see the monument in the night when I close my eyes," and adding she hoped to return in July. I was told by the Kaneohe public affairs officer she had indeed come back numerous times, "making a nuisance of herself."

Over the years, veterans have protested Iida's marker, and I was shown a letter from a Mr. Joseph Nemish, sent to Colonel Robinson just after the 1981 anniversary, saying, "As an American citizen, I take extreme offense to that marker being on property of the Government of the United States of America. With your permission I will at my own expense remove that marker and plant grass. . . . Yours in comradeship.''

Robinson replied, "There seems to be a slight misunderstanding regarding the marker. It is not a monument to Lieutenant Iida, but merely a historical marker. . . ." But I thought the misunderstanding was more than slight, and concerned more than this marker. The authorities at Kaneohe had probably imagined a small ceremony of Japanese-American reconciliation taking place at their monument, with Mrs. Iida embracing and exchanging reminiscences with the men who claimed the honor of killing her fiancé. How could they know that, still obsessed by her loss, she would treat this marker like a grave? Or that her visit would monopolize press coverage of the anniversary at Kaneohe? Or that the attention paid Iida might prompt a backlash? I know I left the base wondering why his death site had received such attention, while the seven American dead were listed on a small plaque fixed to the backside of a hangar and so neglected that, until I pointed it out, the sergeant from the public affairs office had not known it existed.

After the war, Cy Gillette settled in windward Oahu, living on the beach at Kailua. From his house he could look across to Mokapu Point and the air station and, he says, "still imagine it was the same." He now lives in a condominium development overlooking Kaneohe Bay. From his lanai he pointed out where the seaplanes had taxied and turned around, and where they were moored. He struck me as an intelligent man, but not a particularly emotional one, and I wondered how much it affected him, living within sight of the battlefield where he had almost been killed. He said he rarely thought about it, and had chosen Kaneohe because of its excellent sailing.

But before I left, he took me outside again for a better view of Mokapu Point. "After the Japanese left," he said, "we heard rumors of paratroopers landing on Barbers Point. We moved cars and trucks onto the runway to prevent their planes from landing, then took machine guns, blankets, and water to a hill overlooking the base. We were ready to make a last-ditch stand against a Japanese invasion." They had stayed there throughout the afternoon and evening, listening to the panicky firing of Army units along the coast, imagining that an invasion had begun and that tomorrow they would either be dead or seeing the Rising Sun flying over Kaneohe. "Instead, at eight the next morning, we saw the Stars and Stripes raised over the base," he said. "Immediately, we broke down and cried because . . ." He stopped to wipe his eyes, tried to continue, then broke into deep sobs. Tears ran down his cheeks. "Because it looked like those words from the Star Spangled Banner—'our flag was still there'—and we were so proud, so emotional . . . and, I suppose, so glad to be alive."

"Once a Japanese, Always a Japanese"

DELUSIONS ABOUT THE INFERIORITY OF THE JAPANESE MILI-
tary did not vanish with the sinking battleships and charred
airplanes, and new ones arose within minutes of the first bombs,
attempting to explain how Americans could be humiliated by
Asian flyers. It was said Oahu's defenders had been befuddled
by alcohol and stabbed in the back by local saboteurs, that
President Roosevelt had known the Japanese plans but failed to
alert Hawaii, and that the attack had been masterminded and
executed by another Caucasian people, the Germans.

The German-pilot rumor began with sailors claiming to
see swastikas painted on planes flown by blond pilots. Civilians
on the heights above Pearl Harbor also identified "German"
planes, and among the "Rumors and Facts as Jotted Down by
Mrs. Robert Thompson Immediately after December 7, 1941"
was: "German shot down in Wahiawa, flying Japanese plane.
. . . H.K., who lives on Alewa Heights, saw the actual coming
in of the enemy planes from the sea; swears that those planes
were German Stukas."

From the hill behind his Alewa Heights home, Mr. Harold
Kay had such a superb view of the attack that Army intelligence

asked him to summarize his observations. He wrote, "The observer and his family gained the immediate conviction that the great majority of planes observed were German. . . . The planes considered to be German were black and dark grey in appearance, without any insignia. . . . The more experienced pilots, German in the observer's opinion, were assigned to the major objectives which were all stationary." He said he knew this because the aircraft matched the pictures of German planes recently appearing in news magazines and commented, "The planes appeared to be operated with the skill and experience exceeding that attributable to the Japanese in general, leading to the conclusion that the attack was led by German pilots."

On December 8, the *Chicago Tribune* reported that many congressmen believed German pilots had carried out "the damaging blitzkrieg . . . in planes marked with swastikas." On December 9, the *Honolulu Star-Bulletin* ran a story headlined "TALL AVIATOR OF ENEMY DOWNED; WAS HE GERMAN?" and describing "the body of an aviator more than six feet tall . . . found in the wreckage of a Japanese plane," adding that "reports from Hongkong quoted eye witnesses as saying a German was the pilot of one of the twenty-seven planes which raided Kowloon."

The Japanese were also considered incapable of planning such a successful operation, and the December 15 edition of *Newsweek* carried an article by retired Admiral William Pratt titled "Jap Onslaught: A Blend of Treachery and Skill," asserting, "Undoubtedly it [the attack] had its birth in Berlin, for it bears all the earmarks of the Nazi method of operation."

Even the Japanese consul general in Honolulu, Nagao Kita, discounted the abilities of Japan's military. When interviewed after the war by American intelligence, he said that at first he had not thought the attacking planes were Japanese because he did not think "the Japanese navy was strong enough to get that close to Hawaii." Instead, he believed a bizarre rumor circulating through the consulate that the planes were piloted by Frenchmen from the Vichy air force in Vietnam, sent into battle as part of a deal between Japan and Nazi Germany. He was so convinced the planes were not Japanese that he delayed burning ciphers and correspondence.

In 1951, a small Chicago newspaper, *Women's Voice,* published an editorial stating the pilots attacking Pearl Harbor were really American and British, ordered into battle by Roosevelt and Churchill as part of a plot to drag the United States into the war. It asserted that on the evening of December 6, sailors returning to the harbor from Honolulu were prevented from boarding their ships by "officers with drawn revolvers," that planes were defueled by the Army itself "to make absolutely sure that no plane could be gotten into the air," and that one staff sergeant who did take off reported seeing "planes manned by white men, men whom I knew—British and Americans. There seemed to be a few Japs, but the shooting was done by white men. . . ."

This is an extreme example of the revisionist theory that Pearl Harbor was the fault of a Washington conspiracy headed by Roosevelt. The most common version of this theory claims that Roosevelt, because of his campaign promise not to fight unless attacked, wanted the Japanese to strike the first blow, and provoked them with his oil embargo and inflexible demands to cease aggression in China. When he learned the Japanese task force was sailing on Pearl Harbor, he kept Kimmel and Short from receiving the decoded Magic material that would have alerted them. He then held them responsible for the defeat and oversaw a massive cover-up of his conspiracy.

As popular delusions go, this one ranks with Lyndon Johnson's planning the Kennedy assassination and Elvis Presley's faking his death. It enjoyed the greatest popularity in the decade following the war, touching off a pamphlet war between FDR's enemies and admirers. It has been embraced by former isolationists needing a rationale to explain their own misjudgments, by implacable Roosevelt-haters, and, for obvious reasons, by retired Army and Navy officers. Its propagandists have ranged from scoundrels, such as the author of the *Women's Voice* editorial, to respected historians like John Toland, who considered it the most rational explanation for the failures of Washington to share intelligence with the Hawaiian commanders.

It is difficult arguing facts or logic with anyone who believes the conspiracy theory. You can point out that the dynamics of large organizations are such that just because it became known on the morning of December 7, at some levels in the Washington hierarchy, that Japan was likely to attack some American base at 1:00 P.M. Washington time, it does not follow that this information was automatically available to Roosevelt. You can point out that although Roosevelt may have needed Japan to strike first, there was no reason for this strike to result in an American catastrophe. Kimmel and Short could easily have been alerted the day before and inflicted serious casualties on the Japanese. You can argue the Japanese would not have turned back if sighted, that Admiral Nagumo had orders to press the attack if American forces discovered his fleet within the final twenty-four hours, and that Yamamoto had told Nagumo he might have to battle his way to Oahu.

You could argue that a Japanese task force's coming so close to Hawaii would have been *casus belli* enough for most Americans, and that even Rear Admiral Edwin Layton (Ret.), Kimmel's former fleet intelligence officer, who is sympathetic to Kimmel and scathing of the Navy bureaucracy in Washington, concludes that because of Magic, "beyond any reasonable doubt . . . our leaders in Washington *knew* by the evening of 6 December that Japan would launch into war in a matter of hours rather than days. Not a shred of evidence has been uncovered from all the declassified intelligence files to suggest that anyone suspected that Pearl Harbor would be the target."

You can point all this out, as I did to survivors who still cling to the Roosevelt conspiracy theory, and none of it matters, because underneath this theory, and underneath the other December 7 delusions, is a stubborn, immutable racial and military pride, and a desperate need to explain what happened at Pearl Harbor without conceding victory to Japanese arms or defeat to American errors and overconfidence.

On December 7, Admiral Kimmel appeared to blame himself for the debacle. As he stood at the windows of fleet headquarters, watching the destruction, a spent .50-caliber machine gun bullet flew into the room, striking him on the chest and leaving a dark splotch on his white uniform. He picked it up, saying softly, "It would have been merciful had it killed me." Later, according to one aide, "he reached up and with both hands tore the four-star boards off his shoulders. He went into his office and came back wearing his two-star boards. He knew that was his swan song."

But Kimmel soon came to change his mind about his responsibility. From the end of the war until his death in 1966, he waged a campaign to prove himself blameless, laying responsibility for the defeat on Washington and President Roosevelt. In an interview given to mark the twenty-fifth anniversary he said, "My principal occupation—what's kept me alive—is to expose the entire Pearl Harbor affair." He charged "they" had made him a scapegoat, by this meaning "President Roosevelt and General George Marshall and others in the Washington high command." He said, "FDR was the architect of the whole business. He gave orders—and I can't prove this categorically— that no word about Japanese fleet movements was to be sent to Pearl Harbor except by Marshall, and then he told Marshall not to send anything." In another interview, published in *Newsweek* on December 12, 1966, he charged, "FDR and the top brass deliberately betrayed the American forces at Pearl Harbor." After Kimmel's death, his sons unsuccessfully petitioned Congress to restore their father to the highest rank he held before his resignation shortly after the attack.

Almost as long-lived and pervasive as the Roosevelt delusion is the one claiming Japan was assisted by fifth columnists in Hawaii. Rumors to this effect began during the attack and spread quickly throughout Honolulu. Japanese were accused of cutting phone lines, signaling with blinker lights to offshore submarines, drawing a large Oriental character with a bulldozer across bare ground on Sand Island, and cutting arrows in cane fields to direct Japanese aviators to Pearl Harbor, although why this was necessary when it was clearly visible from the air was never explained.

Japanese drivers were accused of driving slowly and breaking down on the narrow two-lane roads leading to Pearl Harbor, blocking traffic and preventing reinforcements and ambulances from reaching the base. It was said ammunition caches had been found on Japanese property, and Kewalo Basin sampans had picked up downed flyers at sea and provisioned Japanese submarines with fresh food, explaining why a loaf of Love's bread was purportedly found on board Ensign Sakamaki's submarine, which itself, the story went, had been manufactured somewhere in Hawaii by Japanese-Americans and fueled from a secret depot on Kauai's remote north shore.

Japanese residents were blamed for spreading these slanderous rumors themselves in order to cause panic, and for using ham sets to interfere with Army broadcasts. Some dead Japanese fliers were said to be local boys who wore Honolulu high school letter sweaters under their flight jackets and had pockets filled with American money and Honolulu Rapid Transit tokens. Among Mrs. Robert Thompson's "Rumors and Facts" is the "almost proven fact," received secondhand from an Army colonel, that "some of the aviators who attacked that Sunday were island boys. He saw the McKinley [High School] ring himself on one of them. The belief is that Kurusu [the special Japanese envoy to Washington who stopped overnight in Honolulu in the month preceding the attack] went thru Honolulu, these boys contacted him and received their orders and instructions from him as to the zero hour. They went by sampan to meet the carrier . . . boarded it and flew the planes back the next morning."

The most vicious stories described sniper attacks by local Japanese. Saboteurs were accused of driving down the flight line at Wheeler and disabling fighters by smashing their tail sections. As late as 1943, *Collier's* magazine was reporting, "Fifteen minutes before the first bombs fell . . . a Jap dairy truck entered Hickam Field to deliver milk. After it had reached a point in front of the barracks, the driver stopped and pretended to fix his engine. As our pilots rushed out to man their planes, the sides of the truck fell off and six Japs hiding in it with machine guns were able to kill eight Americans before they themselves were shot."

Some of the rumors had a factual basis. The genesis of the dairy-truck story may have been the two Japanese teenage defense workers who burned their hands while feeding ammunition into a machine gun so a sailor could fire it. (After helping shoot down a plane, they ripped the insignia off the uniforms of the dead crew and brought them to the naval intelligence office at Pearl Harbor, saying they had come "off the damned Jap fliers.") Traffic on the Pearl Harbor road was congested in the morning by service personnel rushing to bases and civilians evacuating military areas, and congested again after sunset as confused motorists drove home in the blackout without headlights. An experimental cane field in Ewa had recently been harvested, leaving a bare spot, of which one diagonal could be seen as an arrow pointing to Pearl Harbor. The rumor of poisoned drinking water may have originated with a woman who suffered an epileptic fit at a downtown drinking fountain. The Japanese voices jamming emergency and military radio frequencies came from a commercial Japanese-language station in Argentina whose beam to Japan intersected Oahu. Reports of "hidden caches" of ammunition began when stolen small-caliber ammunition and shotgun shells were dug up from an Oahu junkyard. Fires set to signal to Japanese submarines were cane fires ignited by antiaircraft shells and a downed power line. The "signal lights" were caused by loose window shades, open doors, and the reflection of the moon on skylights. The rumor local Japanese were among the pilots can be traced to the mysterious disappearance of two young nisei boys from Honolulu in the spring of 1941, one of whom was an amateur pilot. It turned out they had been recruited by U.S. Army intelligence and sent to the Philippines to infiltrate the alien Japanese community in Manila.

Although the rumors now appear preposterous and illogical, they had the effect of placing every Japanese resident under suspicion. For days afterward, police and military switchboards received calls about the sinister activities of local Japanese, about "a Japanese man who does not understand English," Japanese women seen "filling bags with dirt," Japanese families owning carrier pigeons, "a suspicious Japanese boy dressed in leather jacket and black shoes . . . carrying a package under his arm," and "Japanese holding a meeting," who turned out to be a family purchasing groceries. Colonel Bicknell reported, "In the minds of many people every local Japanese became an enemy agent or saboteur. . . . Desire for revenge upon any and all individuals of Japanese blood was frequently expressed . . . from wishing to shoot each Jap on sight to devising the most lingering form of death. These false stories created a fear of the local Japanese that became greater than the fear of the armed forces of Japan."

The rumors encouraged discrimination and attacks on Japanese residents. A nisei maid overheard speaking Japanese on the telephone on the morning of December 8 was immediately dismissed by a Caucasian employer, who explained, "I won't have any Jap plotting against me and my country within my own home." And on December 9, a sailor from the battleship *California*, riding as a passenger on a military truck, watched helplessly as his driver swerved to the shoulder, trying to run down a middle-aged Japanese laborer, while other passengers cried, "Kill Him! Kill the dirty Jap!" The next day a Filipino drove a panel truck to Pearl Harbor, telling Marine Lieutenant Cornelius Smith, Jr., "Got four Japs in truck, no good man, I kill them!" Smith went outside and found them, "dead as mackerel, throats slashed from ear to ear." The Filipino boasted of six more buried under his house at Wahiawa, and Smith headed the party that exhumed their remains.

The rumors of Japanese sabotage were also believed by senior officials. When Governor Poindexter spoke by telephone with President Roosevelt at 1240 on December 7, he claimed local Japanese now posed the main danger to the Islands. Minutes later, General Short met with Poindexter, declaring Japanese landing parties to be en route. At 1258, Poindexter talked with FBI agent Shivers "re: impounding Japs."

The first Hawaiian Department wartime intelligence bulletin, published on December 8, states, "Fifth column activities are generally developing throughout the whole island of Oahu. . . . Blinker lights were observed from many positions on the islands. . . . On Ewa plain, a cane field was found with a wide swath cut in the form of an arrow pointing directly to Pearl Harbor."

On December 11, Lieutenant Smith, who had spent several days in Aiea Heights confiscating Japanese ham radios, concluded, "One thing is shaping up; there was fifth column working attending this raid—probably a lot of it." Navy Secretary Knox arrived on Oahu the same day. He spent two hours with

General Short, who, having based his defense of the island on the presumption of sabotage, now had to convince Washington it had occurred. He described alleged Japanese fifth column activities in detail, causing Knox to report to Roosevelt, "The activities of Japanese fifth columnists immediately following the attack, took the form of spreading on the air by radio dozens of confusing and contradictory rumors concerning the direction in which the attacking planes had departed. . . ." When Knox made his report public on December 15, General Short's desperate hand could be seen in its conclusion that "the most effective 'fifth column' work of the entire war was done in Hawaii, with the possible exception of Norway." And in a letter dated December 12, Admiral Kimmel wrote, "Fifth column activities added great confusion . . . [making it] most difficult to evaluate reports received [on December7]."

Ten days after the attack, however, the official position had changed, with the *Honolulu Star-Bulletin,* the FBI, and the military governor of Hawaii declaring there had not been a single proved case of espionage or sabotage by the Japanese residents. An editorial in the *Star-Bulletin* of December 16 attacked the "weird, amazing, and damaging untruths" that had been circulated by recent evacuees from Hawaii (mostly military dependents) and printed in mainland newspapers. On December 17, General Delos Emmons, in his first broadcast as the new military governor of Hawaii (Short had been relieved of his command), said no act of sabotage had been committed during or after the attack. In the following months, and years, variations on this statement were repeatedly made by persons of authority, in speeches, press releases, and testimony to Pearl Harbor investigating bodies. In April 1942, FBI Director J. Edgar Hoover declared there had been no sabotage committed before, during, or after the attack. In May 1942, Secretary of War Henry Stimson announced, "The War Department has received no information of sabotage committed by Japanese during the attack on Pearl Harbor, and no evidence of sabotage in Hawaii." And a year later, Colonel Kendall Fielder, still in charge of military intelligence in Hawaii, stated he was "surprised to learn that some of the many Island rumors about the Hawaiian Islands during the first few days of the war are still prevalent on the mainland. They have been repeatedly denied by all authorities."

On Hawaii, such statements were widely believed, but on the mainland, stories of Japanese sabotage continued to circulate. "Do not forget that once a Japanese, always a Japanese," Representative Rankin of Mississippi told Congressional colleagues. "I say it is of vital importance to get rid of every Japanese whether in Hawaii or on the mainland. They violate every sacred promise, every canon of honor and decency." He said the internment of all Japanese was justifiable because "the Japs who had been there [in Hawaii] for generations were making signs, if you please, guiding the Japanese planes to their objects of iniquity."

Sabotage stories were taken up by editorial writers and columnists like Westbrook Pegler and Walter Lippmann, and repeated in the *Time* magazine issue of December 15, 1941, which mentioned "Japanese spies that teemed in Honolulu," and in the January 5, 1942, issue, which said, "In the 159,905 Japanese in the Hawaiian Islands (more than one-third of the population), Tokyo had plenty of talent. . . . Last week Honolulu was fluttering with stories of fifth-column activity. One story was that a display advertisement in a newspaper, ostensibly pushing bargain sales of silks, was actually coded instructions to spies. Another was that a Jap saloon-keeper was shot beside his shortwave transmitter during the Pearl Harbor raid. . . . Fed on tolerance, watered by complacency, the Jap fifth column had done its job fiendishly well and had not been stamped out."

Two weeks later, *Time* was reporting, "In the minds of

many of Hawaii's 105,000 haoles (whites) invasion loomed as a very real threat. What would the Islands' Japanese do then? Islanders who remembered that Jap high-school boys from Hawaii had helped pilot the planes that attacked Pearl Harbor looked uneasily at Hawaii's thousands going freely, imperturbably about their business. What about the houseboy, the cop on the corner, the farmer down the road? What about the Japs [in the Hawaii Territorial Guard] set to guard the Islands?"

The Roberts Committee's official report was issued on January 24, 1942, and although it contained no accusation or proof of sabotage, the fact that it did not specifically deny it came to be seen as proof of its existence. Afterward, the *Washington Post* rebuked Hawaii's delegate to Congress, Sam King, for absolving Hawaii's civilians of sabotage charges, adding that the Army's tolerant attitude toward Hawaii's Japanese, and presumably its failure to intern the lot, was "a blunder worse than a crime."

The espionage and sabotage rumor contributed to the imposition of martial law on Hawaii. According to notes made on December 7 by the Secretary of Hawaii, Charles M. Hite, General Short had appeared at Governor Poindexter's offices in the Iolani Palace at about 1245 "obviously under great strain" and "requested and urged martial law, saying for all he knew landing parties [were] en route. Apprehensive about local Japs."

Short could not declare martial law on his own. He persuaded Poindexter to sign the proclamation by arguing it was necessary to prevent espionage and sabotage and essential to Hawaii's defense, and by promising that "if it developed this was a raid only, and not the prelude to a landing, martial law could be lifted within a reasonably short time."

After signing the declaration, Poindexter told Hite he had "never hated doing anything so much in all his life." A month later he testified to the Roberts Commission he had agreed only because the Army had advanced the argument that "the large

Japanese population we have in Hawaii ... could be better handled through martial law than by civil authorities," although being a civilian, he "was not very keen about having martial law." Had he known a Japanese invasion was not imminent or that Hawaii had not suffered any civilian disorder, misconduct, or disloyalty, it is doubtful he would have surrendered power so easily.

Martial law gave the military governor a monopoly on legislative, judicial, and executive power, and did not bind him by the laws of the Territory of Hawaii, the United States, or the Constitution (although the United States Supreme Court eventually ruled the imposition of martial law on Hawaii to be illegal). The very term "military governor" revealed something of the character of the regime. The term had no basis in federal or territorial law, and was customarily applied in a conquered nation, or an area of territory in rebellion against the central government. Press censorship was total, military trials rarely resulted in anything but a guilty verdict, and even trivial offenders of curfew and blackout regulations were ordered to buy war bonds or donate blood. Wages and employment were frozen, and absenteeism became an imprisonable offense. Military regulations as harsh as this were never imposed in Britain, even during the worst months of the London Blitz, when civilians were nightly coming under enemy attack and Germany was preparing a cross-Channel invasion.

Hawaii's military government was a peculiarly American institution, the final fruit of the United States' obsession with internal security and subversion. One cannot help suspecting prejudice against Hawaii's largely Japanese population was behind its nasty, absolutist character, and behind the fact that, contrary to assurances given Poindexter on December 7, 1941, it was not lifted until October 1944. Espionage and sabotage were certainly the principal justifications offered by the Army for keeping martial law long after June 1942, when the American victory at Midway made a Japanese invasion of the Islands impossible. Although Army intelligence had found no evidence of sabotage or espionage on December 7, some officers asserted the very absence of these crimes proved the Japanese of Hawaii to be possessed of sinister cunning, a view summarized in 1944 by the Army Pearl Harbor Board: "It is obvious that the reason why the Japanese aliens did not commit sabotage was that they did not want to stimulate American activity to stop their espionage and intern them. . . ."

Rumors of sabotage at Pearl Harbor also increased anti-Japanese hysteria on the mainland, providing a rationale for Californians agitating for the mass internment of their Japanese. In February 1942, President Roosevelt yielded to these pressures, signing an Executive Order authorizing military commanders to remove Japanese residents from the West Coast. The internment program began in March. Weeks later, prominent Hawaiians, hoping to avoid internment in Hawaii, swore out affidavits denouncing the sabotage rumors and attesting to the loyalty of Hawaii's Japanese. The reasons for these affidavits were not entirely simple or praiseworthy. There was, of course, a desire to tell the truth and defend friends and employees, but there were also economic and political motivations. Business interests feared catastrophic labor shortages if the Japanese were interned, and worried the rumors would become an argument against Hawaiian statehood.

Chief of Police William Gabrielson swore that "no authenticated case of sabotage of any kind whatsoever or evidence of fifth column activities on the part of alien Japanese or citizens of Japanese ancestry on the island of Oahu has been found." John Burns, the police lieutenant in charge of espionage investigations and a future governor of Hawaii, stated that in the ten days before the attack, "no evidence of any kind was found indicating that any residents of Japanese ancestry were engaged in any activity or had any knowledge relating to an impending attack." John Midkiff of the Wa-ialua sugar plantation testified finding no evidence of arrows cut in the cane fields and did not see any Japanese drivers "park vehicles across the roads or do any act which might lead to confusion or place others in danger."

But the need to have sabotage explain Japan's victory and excuse the internment of Japanese-Americans was so powerful the rumors continued to be believed. The 1943 article in *Collier's* about the treacherous Japanese milk truck prompted the *Honolulu Advertiser* to comment, "The 'Jap dairy truck story' has bobbed up many times in mainland newspapers and magazines and some books. It has been repeatedly exposed as just another of the countless Pearl Harbor yarns, rumors and canards that took to the air on and after December, 1941. But the story still keeps bobbing up like an uneasy ghost, and some people in Honolulu still repeat it and apparently believe it. . . ."

A 1942 Hollywood film, *Air Force*, depicted Japanese residents of Maui firing at a fictional American plane after it made an emergency landing there on December 7, and one of its characters asserted that during the attack on Oahu, trucks driven by Japanese vegetable farmers had driven along a runway, smashing the tails off a line of fighter planes. Military authorities in Hawaii censored the film, cutting out these scenes before it was shown in the Islands.

In her 1950 book *Hawaii's War Years,* author Gwenfread Allen reported, "Many islanders discount official denials and still believe such stories as the one about the prominent Honolulu Japanese who, kimono-clad, waved a Japanese flag to the attacking planes, and the equally fantastic tale about the owner of a uniform of 'the Japanese military governor of the Islands,' who was prepared on December 7 to assume control under direction of Hirohito."

I encountered similar stories, still fervently believed, and said to "prove" Japanese disloyalty and sabotage. A Navy survivor was convinced Japanese workers at KGMB had played music throughout the night of December 6 to provide a radio beacon for Japanese pilots. Another survivor said the owner of a tavern near Schofield Barracks had been a commander in the Japanese navy, using a shortwave radio to "beam the Japanese pilots to Pearl Harbor." A haole civilian who witnessed the attack as a boy insisted there had been sabotage on December 7, saying, "The loyalty of the Japanese is bullshit. The Japanese who enlisted and fought in Europe during the war just thought it was great opportunity to go and kill haoles."At Kaneohe Naval Air Station I attended a briefing for a bus tour of World War Two veterans. One asked, "How did the Japanese know all these ships and planes were here?" The young briefing officer answered, "There is ample documentation that Hawaii's Japanese worked with the Japanese, passing them information." Even witnesses who denounced the sabotage stories as lies mentioned shortwave radios in Japanese homes, or Japanese maids and gardeners failing to appear for work on December 7—even they were seemingly unable to abandon the comforting delusion that treachery by Hawaii's Japanese had ensured Japan's victory.

Sailors at Ford Island Naval Air Station watch the burning U.S. battleships.
BELOW: Planes and hangars burning at Wheeler Field as seen from a
Japanese plane   OFFICIAL U.S. NAVY PHOTOGRAPHS

Destruction in downtown Honolulu caused by misfired U.S. Navy shells   NATIONAL ARCHIVES

Mr. John Adams, his father, and another passenger were killed while driving to their jobs in Pearl Harbor.   NATIONAL ARCHIVES

USS *Arizona* resting in Pearl Harbor three days after the attack

The USS *Arizona* Memorial

The day after the attack, fifteen servicemen killed at Kaneohe Naval Air Station are buried. BELOW: Oil painting on silk by an unknown Japanese artist of nine of the ten Japanese sailors who participated in the midget submarine attack against Pearl Harbor. Missing is Ensign Kazuo Sakamaki, who was presumably excluded because he permitted himself to be taken prisoner.

In March 1943 the Japanese-American volunteers who became the core of the much-decorated 442d Infantry Battalion assemble on the grounds of the Iolani Palace in Honolulu prior to their departure for training on the mainland.   HAWAII STATE ARCHIVES

Wymo Takaki in 1944
COURTESY OF WYMO TAKAKI

View of Bishop Street taken in the
late 1980s
HAWAII VISITORS BUREAU

The view up Bishop Street in 1940   RAY JEROME BAKER, BISHOP MUSEUM

Sailors on liberty at the corner of Bethel and
Hotel streets during the war   RAY JEROME BAKER, BISHOP MUSEUM

Aerial view of Waikiki in the late 1930s, showing the Royal Hawaiian and
Moana hotels

Aerial view of Waikiki today

19

"A Deep Shock Wave" Is Felt

"SURPRISE IS AN INEFFECTUAL WORD TO DESCRIBE OUR FEEL-ings," one witness wrote twenty years later. "It was a kind of surprise so tremendous that it was like a deep shock wave going through us." Navy wife Peggy Ryan remembers that within minutes of the attack, "a small crowd of young Navy wives and small children, still in nightclothes, had gathered in our lane looking wonderingly at the sky and at each other. Probably we were in a state of shock." This word, "shock," is used by almost everyone to describe the instant of realization that the attack was not an exercise but, as KGMB announcer Webley Edwards put it, "the real McCoy."

The shock was magnified by the attack's unexpectedness. Most Hawaiians did not expect a Japanese raid any more than the average Californian did, and only seconds before, they had been immersed in their usual Sunday-morning routines, listening to the radio, sleeping off hangovers, taking showers, praying in church, or dressing their children, one moment seeing an ocean and sky that had never offered a surprise, the next moment swimming through burning oil, diving for cover, or saying a hurried goodbye to husbands who might soon be dead.

The shock of Pearl Harbor was perhaps greatest, and most traumatic, for the military wives who found themselves in this heartbreaking situation, one that was unique in United States history. There are some parallels between their position and the first Battle of Bull Run, when civilians drove out in carriages from Washington to watch the battle. But if there were military wives among those spectators, they had said more leisurely goodbyes, and gone by choice. If they were shocked, it was by the defeat, not by the suddenness of the battle.

On the morning of December 7, wives on Oahu had seconds, minutes at most, to embrace and exchange last words with men hurrying to join a battle in progress. They had no warning, and no preparation for this agonizing parting. Many could see the attack from their homes, and knew their husbands could be killed by an explosion or exchange of fire they themselves might witness. That afternoon, many were evacuated into the valleys, and gathered in impromptu shelters. The curfew and blackout restricted their movements, and for days they had no idea whether their husbands had survived. No wonder some were described as "hysterical," and succumbed to spreading outrageous rumors about the local Japanese.

Journalist Joseph C. Harsch encountered one such distraught wife at the Royal Hawaiian Hotel. His belief the attack was simply a drill had been confirmed by the scene in the dining room. Navy officers and their wives sat eating their breakfast, while through the windows a ship could be seen on the near horizon, zigzagging and dodging bomb splashes. Suddenly, a woman "in a semi-hysterical condition" ran into the most elegant dining room in Honolulu shouting, "The battleships are burning! I saw red balls under their wings! They were shooting at our car! I was taking my husband down to his ship!"

In their quarters at Wheeler Field, Mary Ellen and Wells Lawrence woke when low-flying Japanese planes rattled their venetian blinds. They dashed next door to the home of his flight leader. At first, the two couples were "frozen with shock," uncertain what to do next. As they stood in the living room, a bullet flew through the ceiling, nicking the floor between their feet and throwing sparks at their legs. This convinced Wells "we were dumb to stay there." The men told their wives to get behind the fireplace wall and started for the door. Mary Ellen grabbed her husband back, embraced him a last time, and said simply, "Come back." She was right to be concerned. Many of his squadron's P-36s had been spared, camouflaged by the smoke of the burning P-40s. He readied one with ammunition, but as he was requesting orders from his squadron commander, another pilot jumped into it, took off, and was immediately killed in a dogfight.

Navy Lieutenant Bernard Clarey had been eating breakfast with his wife and fifteen-month-old son in their house on Moanalua Heights. His first thought was that a terrible accident had occurred and the exploding shells came from an ammunition dump in Ewa. When a spectacular explosion at Hickam launched a bomber through the roof of a hangar, he decided an Ewa shell must have landed there. As the explosions continued, he became uneasy, deciding his wife should drive him down to Pearl Harbor early to report to his submarine. "We took our son in the back of the roadster," he remembers, "something we never would have done if we'd really thought there was any danger."

A block from home he heard the news on the car radio and saw lines of civilian cars coming fast in the other direction, fleeing Pearl Harbor, loaded with toys and clothes, some with baby buggies strapped on top, reminding him of the refugee caravans shown in newsreels of the European war. Turning onto the Kamehameha Highway, he saw the extent of the damage—the *Arizona* in flames, the *Oklahoma* capsized. He told his wife it was too dangerous to continue. She should leave him and return home. They both realized in an instant he would be going into combat once his submarine was fueled. Their conversation turned serious, their tone of voice changed, and the atmosphere became so charged with emotion that, sensing it at once, their son began crying hysterically.

The "deep shock wave" triggered by Pearl Harbor probably explains the flashbacks that still haunt survivors. Bernard Clarey became a rear admiral, commanding the Pacific Fleet submarine force, and in 1963 he was given the job of welcoming a Japanese submarine to Pearl Harbor for training. "To have to greet them as friends and train them . . . well, let's just say I had mixed emotions about it," he said. When he saw the submarine's Rising Sun flag coming into the harbor, "that suddenly brought back all the events of December 7."

Ensign Ike Sutton spent the attack racing across the harbor in Admiral Bloch's personal launch, pulling wounded and dying sailors from the water, and in such shock that the sequence of events is a blur in his memory, just "two hours of chaos." But he does remember being strafed by Japanese planes, even though he says it was obvious he was on a mission of mercy. He also remembers sailors wearing dress whites because they had been attending religious services, his own life vest smeared with blood, grabbing burned men only to have their skin come away in his hands, and most of all, the faces of those who died because he decided to save the greatest number by waiting until the boat was full before racing to Hospital Point. It is the shock and guilt over not being able to save those men that still cause him to wake screaming in the night.

A private from Hickam Field was evacuated from Hawaii "crying and combative, hallucinating Pearl Harbor again and again." Twenty-five years after the attack, he was still a patient at a Veterans Authority psychiatric hospital, under constant sedation, and responding to the mention of Pearl Harbor by saying, "Noises, noises, noises. Just another day. Leave me alone."

*   *   *

I met Richard Fiske at the *Arizona* Memorial. We sat on a
bench in the visitor center, facing Ford Island and the mooring
quay that had anchored his battleship. Because he worked here
as a volunteer guide several days a week, I had assumed it
would be easy for him to sit with me, surrounded by the usual
swirl of Japanese tourists, watching propeller planes circle Ford
Island for their practice touch-and-go landings, and describing
December 7, all the while staring at where it had happened.
Instead, just looking at this familiar landscape with his photograph album open to its 1941 pages caused his voice to break
and his eyes to water. "My first day here as a volunteer was
awful," he said. "I kept reliving the attack. I would try to talk
to people, but I would just break down. When I moved back to
Hawaii and came out here, I had no idea it would be such an
emotional experience."

He had brought a scrapbook of fading black-and-white
photographs to refresh his memory. He showed me a picture
of Ford Island, taken from this shoreline and showing much
the same view as today. "Yes, except for the palm trees being
taller it's the same," he said, flicking his eyes between album
and island, between 1941 and 1988. "Sometimes I can look
out there and . . . honest to Pete, I can *see* those airplanes
coming in.

"I was a Marine bugler on the *West Virginia,* and I stood
all my watches on the bridge. There was a small office on the
quarterdeck with a microphone, and we would blow our bugles
into it. We blew calls to mail, taps, reveille, assembly, chow
call, away all boats, officers' call, and inspection. In all, there
were a hundred and four bugle calls in the Navy, and I knew
them all." To prove it, he puffed his cheeks, cupped his mouth
with both hands, and turning toward where the *West Virginia*
had been moored, performed "number two motorboat" and
"admiral's barge," although most of this second was drowned

out by an announcement in Japanese over the visitor center's public address system.

I pointed to a tinted portrait of three men taken in a photo studio. It was Fiske posed with his father, who had been a chief petty officer, and older brother, a private at Schofield. His father had been in China in 1937, aboard the gunboat *Panay* when it was attacked by Japanese planes. When he returned to California, he urged his sons to enlist, begging them to join the Navy because the other services "would be doing the heavy fighting."

"But I thought that would be glorious," Fiske said. "So I joined the Marines with my best friends from high school, Finley and Jones. We all put in for sea school and battleships together. I got the *West Virginia,* they got the *Arizona*, and they . . ." His voice cracked and he stared at the Memorial. "And they're still out there." When he recovered he said formally, "They were Charles Jones and William W. Finley."

He remembered the shock of watching the path of the slow-moving bomb that had killed them, first thinking it would hit the *West Virginia,* then watching it draw closer, change direction, and fall into the *Arizona*. As in many Pearl Harbor accounts, his had a sense of the attack unfolding in slow motion, of torpedoes moving so slowly sailors had time to comment on their progress, of bombs taking forever to tumble to the ground, of witnesses watching transfixed as bullets stitched holes in pavements and cars, and of planes appearing suspended in midair, giving people time to study pilots' faces and expressions, to notice their scarfs and goggles, make eye contact, and exchange waves and obscene gestures.

From the *West Virginia*'s bridge, he saw the *Arizona* transformed into a ball of fire, and men thrown high in the air. The shock wave blew him back against the bridge, and the battleship's captain, who was standing next to him, was mortally wounded by shrapnel. An hour and a half later, after the *West*

Virginia had herself been hit by seven torpedoes and settled upright on the shallow bottom with its decks awash, and after he had grabbed a fire hose and sprayed water on shipmates as they staggered from belowdecks in flames, he jumped off the bow and swam to Ford Island through burning oil. Now, on weekends, he goes flying there with his Japanese-American son-in-law, practicing landings on Ford Island, and seeing it from the same vantage point as the Japanese pilots. Could he, could anyone, have imagined this? Or imagined that his only grand-daughter would be half Japanese—"a little doll," he says, "who I just love to pieces." Or that he would spend his retirement guiding Japanese tourists through a memorial to Pearl Harbor built within sight of that patch of burning water, and of Jones and Finley's grave?

His scrapbook contains photographs illustrating these iro-nies. One showed him with his arm draped around a shriveled Japanese gentleman wearing a white ski cap. The man had been a dive-bomber pilot on December 7. They had been introduced by a Japanese tour leader shortly after Fiske began volunteering as a guide, at a time he admitted to having "so much hate in my heart I probably could have strangled him."

He asked the Japanese pilot if he had known war had not been formally declared when he released his bombs. The pilot said he had not. The answer satisfied Fiske, who, like many survivors, still feels failure to play by the rules of war was the greatest of Japanese crimes. He asked if the *West Virginia* had been among this pilot's targets. The man said no again, and although Fiske realized he might be reluctant to admit this to someone already identified as a veteran of that ship, the answer made it possible for them to pose together, arm in arm.

Other Japanese visitors also sought him out. He had been one of six out of his thirty-four-man platoon to survive over a month of combat on Iwo Jima without injury, and one day at the *Arizona* he was introduced to a Mrs. Sugawara, who had lost three brothers there. She had thrown her arms around him, uttered a long wail, and handed him an envelope containing a ten-dollar bill, a gift that still puzzles and unsettles him.

A Chinese woman had approached him, her face contorted with hate. "Mr. Fiske, how can you allow the dirty Japs to come aboard this ship?" she asked. He described his experiences at Pearl Harbor and Iwo Jima, saying that after so many years at the memorial, and seeing so many Japanese, he had come to forgive them. She shook her head, explaining that her parents and grandparents had been murdered by Japanese soldiers. "No, after all that, you should hate them as I do."

"If you have all this hate in your heart, then there's no room for love," he said. But it was obvious she disagreed. Unarmed civilians who suffered atrocities are slower to forgive than soldiers with the advantage of a more level field.

The December 7 "deep shock wave" may also explain the phenomenon of the Pearl Harbor Survivors Association (PHSA), to which Fiske belongs. I had met several members at the *Arizona* Memorial, where they work as volunteers, answering questions and introducing the documentary. When they invited me to attend the monthly meeting of the Aloha Chapter, I imagined their association as a smaller version of the VFW, and larger than the fraternal World War Two groups that are organized around warships, flight wings, or combat divisions.

When I was in Hawaii, it seemed everyone over sixty-five belonged to some veterans' club and was about to attend a reunion. There were ones for the Kaneohe Klippers, who had served at Kaneohe Naval Air Station between 1935 and 1950, for the American survivors of Wake Island, for the Army radar unit that detected the first Japanese planes over Oahu, for members of Motor Torpedo Squadron 1 of the Pearl Harbor submarine station, and for the crew of the *Helm*, who had their first reunion thirty-eight years after she was scrapped in 1947. Forty women had traveled from the mainland for the fortieth anniversary of the Women's Air Raid Defense (WARD) unit that plotted aircraft on a grid board in Fort Shafter, and eight survivors of the successful mission to shoot down Admiral Ya-mamoto had met for a 1989 reunion symposium in Fredericks-burg, Texas, hometown of Admiral Chester Nimitz. Japanese Zero pilots who survived the Battle of Midway had gathered in Pensacola, Florida, and the Japanese-Americans interned in Crystal City, Texas, were holding a convention in San Diego, with an excursion to Disneyland.

The PHSA is different from these fraternal clubs, since it has a political agenda and a mission. The Aloha Chapter's meeting was a Sunday brunch at the Pearl Harbor officers' club. Seventeen survivors came wearing smart green aloha shirts, overseas caps, and white trousers, bringing wives, children, and grandchildren, several of whom were Japanese-American. They were as attractive and relaxed a group of elderly men as you can imagine, and quite heterogeneous, including a private from Schofield barracks, a pilot, a Marine Corps bugler, an artillery corporal, and a rear admiral. None had known any of the others on December 7. Some had almost been killed, others had been miles from the fighting.

I could understand why men sharing months of combat might travel thousands of miles to meet and reminisce, or why men sharing a military triumph might later memorialize it. But the Pearl Harbor Survivors shared only a two-hour military defeat, and on that alone they had built the most active, pow-erful veterans' organization in the nation. They held five-year reunions in Hawaii, biennial national reunions, yearly district and state reunions, and local chapter meetings every month. They sponsored a golf tournament and a ham radio network. They sold PHSA hats, decals, belt buckles, coffee mugs, official rings—ten-karat gold with a blue zircon setting in a "fireburst pattern"—and "My Grandfather Is a Member of the PHSA" T-shirts. Their quarterly magazine, the *Pearl Harbor–Gram,* had grown from twelve pages in 1960 to forty in 1989. They had a membership of 10,648 in 1989, 10 percent of the military personnel present on Oahu on December 7, twice as many members as in the early seventies, and 318 more than the year before. In other words, an organization whose membership pool was over the age of sixty-five was recruiting more new members than it lost through death.

At the Aloha Chapter's brunch we sang "Happy Birthday Dear Survivor" and "Happy Anniversary Dear Survivor." We learned the Memphis Convention for the Sons and Daughters of Pearl Harbor Survivors had been a success with many new members enlisted in the cause. We decided the Aloha Chapter should be listed in the telephone book, so that visiting mainland survivors could make contact. We discussed the PHSA license plate bill that was moving slowly through the Hawaii legislature. The meeting closed with a survivor saying, "We must remember the reason we exist is to better keep America alert—so if anyone has any ideas how we can do this better, well just let me know."

My impression that the PHSA had to work to fill its frequent meetings with content (perhaps because it was an organization of former strangers) was confirmed by back issues of the *Gram*. On the mainland, survivors had seized upon Hawaii as common ground, no matter that most had probably hated it as servicemen, and wore aloha shirts to reunions, which usually featured a luau. They had adopted a political agenda in keeping with their motto, "Remember Pearl Harbor—Keep America Alert," petitioning Congress to declare December 7 a "National Remembrance Day" and to establish a medal for all veterans present on Oahu during the attack. They lobbied state legislatures to strike license plates identifying the driver as "Pearl Harbor Survivor." They greeted each Secretary of the Navy with letters demanding a warship be named the U.S.S. *Pearl Harbor*, usually receiving polite replies to the effect that "while this name indeed signifies the selfless bravery and heroism of many Americans, it must be said that it does not represent a significant victory in the sense normally memorialized in the assignment of a ship name." (This was an argument guaranteed to anger the survivors, and in a letter to the *Gram*, one replied, "So our government officials won't name a ship in the Navy after Pearl Harbor because it wasn't considered a significant victory. Pearl Harbor was our greatest victory since the Revolutionary War and World War One . . . once we realized what was happening we got our guns going, our ships moving, our shipyard facilities into action. . . . Take a look at any picture during that attack and you will see the sky covered with antiaircraft flak.") But the most extraordinary thing about all the Survivors' campaigns was that they did not begin until years after the attack, so that California and Alaska, for example, had not started issuing their Survivor license plates until 1988.

Their "Keep America Alert" motto led Survivors to argue for a strong defense, to oppose cuts in military spending, and to be strongly anti-Communist. They were also quick to argue with anyone who argued that dropping the atomic bomb was unnecessary. They kept a competitive eye on Hiroshima Day, August 8, with one *Gram* editorial complaining, "We find more concern in America over Hiroshima's anniversary than over Pearl Harbor Day." They showed an interest in Japanese veterans and peace activists, and the *Gram* had a long article about a Japanese delegation that had visited the Richland, Washington, high school to object to its symbol, a mushroom cloud celebrating the town's role in the production of nuclear arms, including the plutonium that destroyed Nagasaki. The school's principal had walked out of a meeting with the Japanese activists, after reminding them "we did not start that war." The *Gram* subtitled this story "High School Principal Takes a Stand on His Own Principles. . . ."

In 1986, the Survivors passed a resolution praising Short and Kimmel, mentioned their "sincere and dedicated performance of duty and for carrying until their deaths, and thereafter, the unfortunate stigma associated with the catastrophe at Pearl Harbor." They struck special commemorative medals celebrating their former discredited commanders, announcing that funds from voluntary contributions over and above the price of these medals would be used to establish, of all things, "an educational scholarship fund for deserving descendants of Admiral Kimmel and General Short." They then invited these descendants to receive these medals during a special ceremony to be held in Hawaii on the forty-fifth anniversary of the attack. There is not a reputable history that does not attach some measure of blame to these men, who were, after all, in command of the ships sunk at their moorings and the planes destroyed on the ground. Yet Pearl Harbor memories have undergone such gyrations that here, forty-five years later, were their descendants accepting posthumous medals and college scholarships from the very men who suffered the most from their mistakes of judgment and leadership, and whose own parents had probably once joined the legion of politicians and editorial writers demanding they suffer punishments ranging from court-martial to execution.

Despite efforts to give their organization historical and political content, the "business" at a recent meeting of the PHSA executive board revolved around such questions as "Should the PHSA handbook be put in a master ring binder?" "Should the 6th district be permitted to transfer the PHSA emblem onto hats to be worn at the district convention?" And "Should the Olympic Peninsula Chapter of Bremerton, Washington, be allowed to put the PHSA emblem on a recreational vehicle flag?" One cause célèbre was commercial calendars that failed to identify December 7 as Pearl Harbor Day. And at the Saturday night banquet of the 1989 California state convention, held at the Westin Hotel in Costa Mesa, the featured "guest speaker" was Mr. Dick Wilson, described as "Mr. Whipple of the 'Please Don't Squeeze the Charmin' commercial."

If you stripped away the "guest speakers," luaus, and souvenirs, you were left with what brought the Pearl Harbor Survivors together and accounted for their growing membership—the conviction that they had witnessed the most important event in twentieth-century American history, and that nothing since had equaled the "deep shock wave" of December 7, 1941. No one was demanding Iwo Jima, D-Day, or Midway Survivor license plates, because these battles had not so abruptly shaken the foundations of anyone's world. The shock of one minute believing in American military might and the next finding yourself surrounded by ruined battleships and the bodies of your friends was unique. It still haunted these men, sometimes with flashbacks appearing as suddenly and unexpectedly as the Japanese planes, illuminating their memories with the harsh, nervous light of an electrical storm.

20

"How Could They Do This to Me?"

WHAT THE JAPANESE OF HAWAII FEARED MOST HAD FINALLY happened, leaving them threatened by an enemy invasion, suspicious neighbors, hysterical soldiers, and the FBI. They were more shocked than anyone, deeply hurt by haoles who now questioned their loyalty, and furious at Japan for putting them in this precarious position.

Some maids ran home during the attack to remove their kimonos, returning in haole clothes, or, too embarrassed to face their employers again, never returning. One told her employer, "I am so ashamed, I wish I could change my face." Kathy Cooper remembers, "My mother's little Japanese maid simply never came back again." Novelist Margaret MacKay, a longtime Honolulu resident, described her friend's maid, Sumi, as "a good, neat little person" who was "content to dress in the disciplined way required by the old Honolulu families—trim and subtle in kimono, sash and sandals." During the attack, she stood "very, very still at the window, looking out toward the harbor and the planes and the smoke." She refused to speak, but the next morning appeared in a crisp white linen dress to serve breakfast. "I'm very sorry, madam," she said. "If you please, I not wear kimono anymore. I am American."

A few Japanese made the mistake of succumbing to the Oriental habit of concealing embarrassment with smiles and laughter, and rumors circulated of giggling Japanese. William Diem drove his family up the Kamehameha Highway, away from the attack. They stopped where the road reached its highest point, affording a spectacular view of the harbor (the same place from which Bob Kinzler had first seen the burning ships). Among the other spectators here, Diem later described "an elderly Jap with a grin on his face from ear to ear," and after seeing this, he said, "We were so disgusted we turned back."

Japanese defense workers were expelled from Pearl Harbor at bayonet point, and Japanese medical attendants, like Kazuma Oyama's sister, were removed from hospital wards so their hands would not touch servicemen wounded by Japanese bullets. Curses were hurled at Japanese pedestrians, several were punched, and Filipino cane cutters were said to be sharpening their machetes.

There was some evidence of Japanese joy. An inebriated man on Kauai exulted in the attack; some rural grammar school children shouted "Banzai!"; two Japanese men on the isolated Hawaiian island of Niihau assisted a downed Japanese flier in terrorizing the native Hawaiian populace. Such incidents received attention because they were so rare. More common were the Japanese who recall "fear, embarrassment, and anger at Japan for bombing our country," or "telling my folks that the Japanese were rats for attacking us when Japan and the United States were in the midst of peace negotiations," or who wondered, "Where were our planes?"—using "our" without imagining anyone could doubt they meant America.

Ted Tsukiyama, then a junior at the University of Hawaii, was sleeping at his parents' house in Kaimuki when he woke to thunderous explosions. He says when he heard the truth on the radio, "I kinda turned numb, wondering, 'Am I really hearing this? How could they be so stupid? They're crazy! They're attacking the USA! Who the hell do they think they are?'" When it was announced the governor had placed the University of Hawaii ROTC under the Territorial Guard, he threw on his uniform and hurried to the Manoa campus. "I had no second thoughts, not one, about putting on that uniform," he told me. "The enemy was attacking. Our outfit was about eighty percent Japanese, and on December 7 no one was thinking, 'Hey, we can't trust you because you're Japanese.'"

He arrived to see his instructors putting firing pins in the cadets' Springfield rifles. His company deployed in the bushes along Manoa Stream, ordered to defend the city from Japanese paratroopers believed approaching from St. Louis Heights. Years later he told the *Honolulu Star-Bulletin,* "As we thought of the sneak attack, a wave of fury and anger swept over us. There was no doubt or indecision as we advanced, it was going to be either 'them or us.'" And he told me, "We were scared shitless, but we felt proud to be defending our country. You know, I wanted to punch and kick the first damned Japanese I saw." Fearing he had not put this strongly enough, Ted Tsukiyama, graduate of Yale Law School and a polished, successful Honolulu attorney, raised his voice and pounded his desk, saying, "I was so *angry* at Japan and the Japanese that I promised myself, 'The first Jap I see, I'm going to kick him in the balls!'"

Another ROTC cadet, Ralph Yempuku, was the only one of five brothers who elected not to return to Japan with his parents when they left Hawaii in 1934 because of his father's poor health. By 1941 he had become the intramural sports director at the university, and he was at the Moana Hotel on December 7 to escort the visiting Willamette football team on a sightseeing excursion. He realized the attack was real when two Navy pilots ran down the steps of the Moana buttoning their shirts and shouting for someone to drive them to Pearl Harbor. Yempuku took them, stopping at a pharmacy to buy Bromo-Seltzer for their hangovers, then stopping again at the Pearl Harbor gate, where he remembers "dead bodies piled like sardines in trucks." Afterward, he reported to his ROTC unit, joining Ted Tsukiyama. During this time, he says, he never once thought of himself as anything but an American with the misfortune to resemble the enemy. "There's no way I can change it," he told fellow ROTC cadets. "Until the day I die I'm going to look like a Jap!" He felt no loyalty to Japan, only fear of being killed by a Japanese bomb or a revenge-seeking haole. Most of all, he remembers, "I was *angry* at the Japanese! Not just because they had attacked Hawaii but because the raid was so embarrassing for me. I kept thinking, 'How can they do this to me?' "

While Japanese planes were still overhead, future U.S. Senator Daniel Inouye, a senior at McKinley High School, sped on his bicycle to the first-aid station at Lunalilo School to help the wounded. As he passed groups of frightened Japanese civilians, he thought, "They had worked so hard. They had wanted so desperately to be accepted, to be good Americans. And now, in a few cataclysmic minutes, it was all undone." Then he realized he might face trouble too, because his eyes were "shaped just like those of that poor old man in the street." He looked up into the sky and shouted, "You dirty Japs!"

"Spud" Ishimoto was at Pearl Harbor, fixing a tractor's steering mechanism, when the attack began. He had a good job as a mechanic, and good relations with his haole coworkers. He worried the Japanese would ruin it all. He dived behind a pile of lumber, angry at them for "coming down here and disturbing us Japanese." After the attack, he and other nisei workers rescued sailors, and repaired engines, beginning the job of salvage. He returned home to find his father making plans to surrender the family's most prized possession, a ceremonial sword recently brought back from Japan.

George Akita, the young, prize-winning Japanese orator, wrote of hearing "the rat-tat-tat of a machine gun from a swooping plane." Only then did he "begin to realize that this was the real McCoy!" He still went to the Honolulu Bible Training for his Sunday-school class, narrowly escaping a bomb exploding near the Schumann Carriage Company. At school he joined the other students, most of them Japanese, in singing, "Are we downhearted? No! No! No! Are we downhearted? No! No! No!" He arrived for services at the Nuuanu Congregational Church just as an antiaircraft shell burst across the street, killing two young Japanese. That afternoon, he wrote in his diary, "We have to be brave. This crisis will test out our guts and gumption."

As Nancy Sato ran home, terrified of Japanese strafing, she heard people cursing the "damned Japs." But who did they mean? she wondered. The Japanese pilots? Herself? Both? For her the worst part was "knowing they wouldn't accept me for what I really was—an American; knowing no matter what I did, I'd always be a 'Jap.'" She arrived home feeling "so ashamed to be Japanese" that she immediately made a bonfire of her Japanese-language books.

More vividly than the attack itself, Wallace Fujiyama remembers the slights and taunts of "Jap" that followed it. He saw the first wave while driving over the Pali Highway to Kahuku, accompanying a Japanese-league baseball team owned by his father. Several months later, he became a Honolulu policeman, and almost fifty years after that he becomes angry when remembering the Navy officer whom he arrested and who taunted him, saying, "You're a Jap, aren't you? Well, I was sent here to kill guys like you."

Sue Isonaga was spending the weekend of December 7 with FBI agent Robert Shivers and his wife, Corinne, at their home in Diamond Head. She had met the Shiverses in 1939, and while a student at McKinley High School had worked for them as a live-in housekeeper. At first, Mrs. Shivers had been reluctant to hire her. She and her husband had just arrived, and had little contact with Orientals. But within months, they had become close. The Shiverses were unable to have children, Isonaga's father had died, and soon they were introducing her as "our child" and treating her like a daughter. She left their employment in 1941 to work as a teacher, but continued returning on weekends. As Shivers ran out the door on December 7, his last words to his wife were "Don't let Sue out of your sight." He was worried about reprisals.

Isonaga had burst into tears upon hearing the radio bulletin, and now she joined Mrs. Shivers on the lawn, staring in disbelief at the planes' Japanese markings. Diamond Head was a military installation and a potential target, so an FBI agent evacuated them both to a house in Manoa Valley, where hysterical haole women filled the rooms and a man passed out revolvers, shouting, "At the sight of a Jap, don't ask questions, shoot to kill!"

"I have never forgotten that moment," she told me. She also remembers the time she worked at the Kahuku emergency feeding station and a haole woman accused her of wanting to poison everyone, the time she and a girlfriend were waiting to buy movie tickets and overheard a Portuguese girl say, "If it wasn't for these damn Japs we wouldn't have to stand in line," and the time a Filipino man ran after her, cursing, and shouting, "Because of you Japs Bataan fell." She had shouted back, "I had nothing to do with the fall of Bataan, and if you keep going on, I'll report you to the FBI. I was raised here and I'm an American citizen."

Private Tom Tsubota was strafed by Japanese planes while standing guard at Waimanalo Beach, and wondered if he knew the pilot. Six months earlier, he had returned to Honolulu on the next-to-last Japanese liner. He had left Japan after his instructor at Tokyo University explained that unless he joined the military he would never pass his examinations. "I felt American," he says, "and I knew I would rather die for the USA than Japan."

Richard Ishimoto had a weekend pass from the Army and was staying at his parents' home in downtown Honolulu. He told me he "never dreamed" Japan would bomb America, and thought it "had to be an exercise." He jumped on a bus heading for Schofield Barracks, but outside Hickam, a hysterical MP boarded the bus, jabbed him with a rifle, and screamed he should shoot him because "the Japs blew up my buddy!" Ishimoto believes his life was saved because three weeks earlier he had been drafted and could produce a military identification card.

Edwin Kawahara was walking back from the latrine at his tent encampment at Schofield Barracks when the Japanese attacked nearby Wheeler Field. He was an intelligence corporal, one of the thirteen hundred nisei draftees and volunteers under arms in Hawaii on December 7, most of them in two Hawaii Territorial Guard regiments called to active duty fifteen months earlier. He was proud to be a soldier, considering it "part of my duty as an American citizen." Like all niseis born before 1926, he had been registered at birth at the Japanese consulate, giving him dual citizenship. But unlike many, he had renounced his Japanese citizenship at eighteen, because "I knew my life was here, not in Japan."

As the attack continued, he hurried to company headquarters to alert his commanding officers. The only one he could find was the deputy company commander, Lieutenant Robert Louis Stevenson. When Kawahara told him, "You are the senior officer present, sir," Stevenson immediately opened the office safe, removed the cipher and division field codes, and handed them to him. "Edwin, guard these with your life," he said. Kawahara still treasures this moment. "It was absolutely magnificent to be the recipient of such total trust," he says. "I knew then that my love for the USA had been right all along."

Stevenson had no recollection of this incident, one so important to Kawahara. Since it never occurred to him *not* to trust Kawahara, the exchange did not strike him as extraordinary enough to remember. Stevenson is a third-generation kamaaina whose mother's family were great admirers of author Robert Louis Stevenson ("My son, incidentally," he told me, "is named John") and who had absorbed Hawaii's traditional racial attitudes, which were far more tolerant than those of mainland soldiers. His company, formerly in the Hawaii Territorial Guard, was about 60 percent Japanese. The rest was a mixture of Hawaii's other races. There were no racial tensions, he says, and the only racial incident he recalls from before the war involved the refusal of Regular Army officers to admit non-Caucasian Territorial Guard officers to their club. This so angered the guard's commander, Colonel Wilhelm Andersen, that he boycotted the club and built a multiracial one for his officers.

Stevenson does remember a Private Nakamura, who on December 7 already had a broken arm encased in a cast stretching from wrist to shoulder. He nonetheless climbed onto the truck taking the company to windward Oahu to repel an expected invasion. Stevenson ordered him off, and then left for several minutes to organize food for his men. By the time he returned, Nakamura had ripped the cast off his arm and climbed back on the truck. "And now he had a twisted wrist because of that," Stevenson said. A year later, Stevenson overheard a Caucasian woman telling Nakamura, who was then guarding the waterfront from a machine gun emplacement, "You dirty Jap! You should be behind barbed wire."

Larry Nakatsuka, author of the "Mr. Sato" columns in the *Honolulu Star-Bulletin,* slept through the first bombs and was waked only by a telephone call from editor Riley Allen, who wanted a report from the Japanese consulate for an extra edition and had decided on Nakatsuka (even though, he later admitted, he feared for the young reporter's life) because he knew the consular staff, and because in a city that was half Japanese, he was the *Bulletin*'s only Japanese reporter.

In the confusion, neither military intelligence nor the FBI had thought of throwing a guard around the consulate or entering it to seize its papers. Nakatsuka found Consul General Kita standing on the front steps of the residence in his pajamas. "Don't you know there's a war on?" he asked. The impassive Kita dismissed it as an elaborate American exercise, refusing to make a statement. Nakatsuka remembers that even when told of the casualties, Kita "seemed unconvinced that any bombing by Japanese planes had taken place. Likewise, Otojiro Okuda, vice-consul, expressed surprise and disbelief when told that 'this bombing is serious.' "

Nakatsuka hurried back to his office for a copy of the first extra edition, hoping it would convince the skeptical diplomats. Returning at noon, he thrust it at Kita and persuaded him to grant an interview. As they spoke, two police detectives ran up the consulate steps, announcing they were putting the building under guard. They hurried inside, forcing their way into a back room in time to catch Tadeo Yoshikawa burning codes and intelligence documents in a washtub. Of this whole episode, Nakatuska says, "There was never any doubt in my mind that I was anything but an American. For me, they were the enemy who had attacked us, and I had no other thought than that it was my job to get what I could out of the senior representative of the enemy in Honolulu." Unlike Riley Allen, he was unconcerned about vigilantes roaming the streets. "I was naive, and in my naiveté, since I knew I was loyal, it never occurred to me I might be seen by anyone as the enemy." Instead, he feared Japan, worrying that if it occupied Hawaii he would be among the first "lined up and shot."

Although Seiyei Wakukawa feared a Japanese-American war and had recently led a Japanese delegation to the post office to make a public show of purchasing defense bonds, he told me he "never for a moment" imagined the Japanese "would be so stupid as to attack America directly." He had written a thesis about the liberation movements in Japan's colonies of Taiwan, Korea, and Manchuria that was strongly critical of Japanese aggression, and had visited Japan several times, researching this thesis and writing articles for the Japanese-language newspaper *Nippu Jiji*. He was a Japanese citizen only because of America's restrictive immigration laws and considered himself "one hundred percent Americanized."

When Japan struck, he was "dumbfounded." Even when he saw Japanese markings on a plane he could not believe it. He had to drive to one of the heights overlooking Pearl Harbor to be convinced. "Then, more than anything," he says, "I feared a Japanese invasion. I thought I could prove my loyalty to the Americans [although as it turned out, he could not], but if the Japanese army landed, I knew I would be among the first to be shot."

The attack caught Tadeo Fuchikami in the RCA office, with General Marshall's last-minute warning from Washington still in his delivery pouch. He was an American citizen, with few ties to Japan, and he thought, "Hey! It can't be Japan. Those Jap warlords are all cuckoo, like Hitler, but they're not strong enough to beat the old USA!" Despite the exploding shells and a radio announcer shouting, "This is the real McCoy!" it never occurred to him not to deliver his messages ("Hey! It was my job"), nor that a young Japanese man riding a motorcycle and dressed in an RCA uniform might be in danger.

At first, the streets were almost empty. He passed spectators standing in front yards and on sidewalks, pointing to the sky and laughing, certain they were witnessing a fabulous exercise. Suddenly, roads filled with ambulances and delivery vans commandeered as ambulances, with fire trucks and taxis full of sailors returning to Pearl Harbor. Some civilians drove into the valleys to escape the military bases, others hurried in the opposite direction to witness the spectacle. A woman screamed, "Hey! You dirty Jap!" and Fuchikami wondered who she meant. Many of the military wives on his route were hysterical, and every time he delivered a message, he was given one for the mainland, assuring relatives the sender was safe. At the end of the day his pockets were stuffed with telegrams and money.

At one roadblock a soldier advised him to go home and forget about his cables. Japanese paratroopers wearing green overalls with a red shoulder patch had just landed in Kalihi Valley. The soldiers had almost shot Fuchikami because his uniform was dark green, and from a distance the red, circular RCA patch resembled a Rising Sun. It was later said this paratrooper rumor began circulating when an American Army mechanic wearing overalls was seen parachuting from a damaged aircraft over the north shore of Oahu. But Fuchikami thinks it started when he was seen racing down the sidewalk on his motorcycle, passing traffic jams of cars as he sped to deliver his cables.

He remembers that when he arrived at Fort Shafter, the clerks greeted him as if nothing unusual had happened. They stamped his chit and took the cable, and it was not until several days later when FBI agents accused him of intentionally delaying General Marshall's warning that he suspected its contents had been important.

Wymo Takaki was a machinist on a civilian dredging barge in Pearl Harbor, working so close to the battleships he knew the attack was real. "I was dumbfounded," he says. "The day that I had dreaded had happened." He was another son who had been left behind by a family that had chosen to return to Japan in the thirties. His father had believed, he says, "that my future was to stay in Hawaii and be a true American citizen." When he left in 1933 he told Takaki, "If there should ever be a war with Japan then your loyalty should be with the United States." Takaki attended high school in Honolulu, living with a haole family and training to become a machinist. He had American citizenship and considered himself totally American, but so feared a Japanese invasion and occupation that he secretly stocked a remote north shore cave with emergency provisions, planning to hide there until the island was recaptured by America.

As Japanese bullets ricocheted off his barge he dived for cover. The Norwegian captain ordered him to climb to the bridge to fetch binoculars. He remained there several minutes, mesmerized by the attack. Framed in the binoculars' circles were dive-bombers racing down the Halawa Valley, and a string of torpedo bombers attacking Battleship Row. He was on the western side of Ford Island, with a thicket of trees blocking his view of the battleships. He could see only their superstructures and masts rising above the trees, then falling over one by one and disappearing from view.

He saw green and yellow shell bursts as a destroyer fired on a midget submarine, and a parachute opening and carrying a pilot into the waters of Pearl Harbor, where he immediately sank from view. It is a sight that still intrigues him. Did this man hope to surrender? he wonders. To kill more Americans with his pistol? Or did he want to survive, but changed his mind and drowned himself?

He brought the binoculars down to the captain, and they watched a Japanese plane crash-land in the water two hundred yards away. This time, the pilot wore a life jacket and was treading water. The captain, chief mate, and Takaki jumped into the work boat and headed toward him, through water colored red by blood that Takaki would remember every time he cut himself shaving and saw blood tinting the water in the bathroom sink. He lay in the bow, prepared to pull the pilot on board. But as they approached, the man calmly removed his goggles, helmet, and life preserver and drowned himself, ending his life but beginning a story that would bring Takaki to Japan forty-five years later.

Takaki fished the man's possessions from the water. His crewmates on the dredger insisted he translate the writing on the life preserver. When he explained he could not read Japanese, these men, Hawaiians, mainland haoles, and Chinese who had been friendly twenty minutes earlier, turned on him. One grabbed him by the neck, shaking him and shouting, "You dirty Jap spy, read it to us! C'mon, read it!" Another began choking him. The captain drew a pistol to protect him, then put him ashore. Takaki is somewhat critical of this action now. "After I attended counterintelligence school," he says, "I realized that captain had made a gross mistake, releasing me on the backside of the harbor. After all, what if I really had been a Jap spy?" He is also quick to excuse his former friends, saying, "I guess under that kind of situation it's understandable for people to lose their heads."

He was strafed as he ran home along the Kamehameha Highway. "Bullets came rushing toward me, just like in the movies," he says, "and I dived into a drainage ditch. Ever since, whenever I hear people trying to excuse the Japanese by saying they never strafed civilians, I tell them it's a lie." Within a half hour, he had almost been killed twice—once by a Japanese plane, and once for being a Japanese spy. That evening, in a delayed reaction, he shook with fear, telling his Caucasian foster mother he was too scared to return. "If you don't," she said, "they'll be sure you're a Jap spy."

He went back on December 9, seeing lines of corpses covered with sheets, and working on salvage. But the next morning, a Marine guard pointed a gun at his chest, shouting he was a "fucking Jap" and forbidden to enter. Despite this, he says, "I never forgot that my enemy was Japan." Several days later, when he received a call telling him to collect his precious machinist's tools, he remembers "feeling really good," and thinking, "Only in America good things like this could happen. With those tools I can serve my country again."

21

The United States Navy Shells
Honolulu

THERE WERE MANY INSTANCES OF SELF-SACRIFICE AND HERO-
ism on December 7, of men exposing themselves to strafing to
pull shipmates from the harbor, or going belowdecks on burning ships to rescue crewmates. A black mess attendant on the
West Virginia, Doris Miller, grabbed an abandoned machine
gun and fired at dive-bombers, and was awarded the Navy
Cross for heroism. On the *California,* Machinist's Mate Robert
Scott insisted on remaining at his below-decks station despite a
torpedo that had holed his compartment, making his drowning
certain. On the *Nevada,* Machinist Donald Ross made two
perilous trips to the forward dynamo room to rescue shipmates
trapped there. In the port antiaircraft battery, Ensign T. H.
Taylor continued directing fire despite being wounded, burned,
and deafened by shattered eardrums that sent blood coursing
down his cheeks.

There was also fear and panic. A colonel remembered
"confusion plus, when the attack came," and men being "simply petrified and frightened stiff." Another recalled a senior
officer who "went all to pieces . . . and had to be sent back to
the States on a stretcher." Joseph C. Harsch was at Army in-

telligence at Fort Shafter, obtaining a war correspondent card, when, he said, "a typical Army sergeant's voice came on the intercom . . . announcing such things as 'paratroopers landing on Diamond Head . . . troop transports and cruisers approaching Kailua Beach . . . two battleships off Barbers Point.' " On hearing this, the colonel who was making out his card strapped on his holster and strode out the door, heading to meet the enemy.

At Pearl Harbor, Kathy Cooper was staying with her parents in a large house on "Admirals' Row," which was in the flight path of Japanese bombers. They came in so low her brother lay on the roof, taking photographs as they flew past. She watched from the patio, feeling a "little reverberation" in her chest from the "deafening noise," seeing a Japanese pilot wearing goggles, and thinking, "My God! If I had a ball I could hit him with it." She imagined herself killed and her husband marrying someone else, and became furious. There was a knock, and she opened the door to face a jittery young sailor, carrying a huge rifle and explaining his orders were to guard the women from the Japanese. "He said he had never fired a rifle in his life," she remembers, "and he was so scared we had to sit him down in the kitchen and give him a cup of coffee."

The panic resulted in casualties. American gunners shot down American warplanes hours after the Japanese had left, and American fighters strafed Japanese-American fishermen returning to Kewalo Basin in their sampans. The destroyer-minelayer *Gamble* opened fire on an American submarine. Machine gunners protecting Kaaawa Beach shot at stars, mistaking them for signaling lights. At Kaneohe, reservists manning antiaircraft batteries fought a night duel, then turned their guns on civilians coming to watch what they imagined to be a Japanese landing. Shore-based gun batteries and ships fired on American fighter planes from the carrier *Enterprise,* killing a crewman in the mess hall of the *Argonne* and hitting three aircraft, killing their pilots. A civilian was shot dead by a nervous sentry when he stuck his head and arm through a fence, trying to retrieve a hat blown off in the wind.

Panic was responsible for naval gunnery crews forgetting to use fuses, setting them improperly, or mistakenly firing shells that only exploded on contact. These shells fell on Honolulu's buildings, gardens, and homes, crashing into the yard of Thomas Fujimoto's home, going through the roof of Lewers & Cooke, destroying the Schumann Carriage Company, and cratering Kuhio Avenue in Waikiki. One burst on the grounds of the Iolani Palace, another in the driveway of Governor Poindexter's residence, sending splinters flying across the street to kill an elderly Chinese man. American ordnance also hit and killed a woman in upper Nuuanu Valley, two amateur boxers at the corner of Nuuanu and Kukui, four defense workers driving to Pearl Harbor in a green Packard, and eleven-year-old Matilda Faufata, who died in her mother's arms.

As Elwood Craddock and his cousin returned from their hunting trip, Navy shells fell on the Waipahu plantation. It was seventeen miles from Pearl Harbor, at precisely the point where they could no longer remain in the air. They exploded in fields behind his house, throwing up clouds of dirt and sending pineapples flying into the air. He assumed they were enemy bombs. Later he learned "they were shells our ships were firing broadside at the planes. The sailors just jammed in rounds without setting their fuses, they were so panicked."

Even though naval shells hit Honolulu long after the Japanese had left, civilians still believed they were Japanese. A month after the attack, Honolulu Mayor Lester Petrie would write, "And it must not be thought that the victims of the tragedy were slain in a military attack. The ruthless Japanese deliberately slew helpless civilians in areas where the death toll would be greatest. The city proper escaped only because it did not offer so easy a target for mass slaughter."

The shelling killed sixty-eight civilians and wounded

thirty-five. Most casualties were United States citizens, but police and newspapers reported them as "28 Americans, 15 Portuguese, 32 Japanese, 9 Hawaiians," and so on, thereby denying these "lesser races," even in death, the honor of full citizenship. A teacher writing about the attack explained, "Most of the casualties were Japanese, because there are few white people on the streets so early on a Sunday morning."

At the time it was considered an exquisite irony for the Japanese to have "killed members of their own race." Three years later, English teacher Herbert Coryell wrote an account of his experiences, describing a shell that exploded in the Lunalilo School and making the poisonous insinuation that it was "ironic" for Hawaii's Japanese to be killed by Japanese bombs because they had expected special treatment from the attackers. "Fortunately there were no children in the school at the time," he wrote. "If there had been they would have been chiefly of Japanese ancestry. One of the things that makes our island Japanese so bitter toward the Tokyo Japs is that the Tokyo Japs rained down their bombs on them and strafed them with machine gun bullets, quite disregarding their common racial extraction."

Throughout the war, the Navy never admitted the real source of the "slaughter" in Honolulu. But in 1943, during closed-door hearings of the Army Pearl Harbor Board, an Army ordnance officer who had investigated forty bomb sites testified, "We found what these things were. They were not Japanese; they were not Army ammunition. . . . They were antiaircraft ammunition of another service, sir, whose time fuses had failed to function in the air." And the commander of the coast artillery in Hawaii said, "A great deal of it [the ammunition] was defective and 'duds.' Unfortunately the 'duds' detonated on contact with the ground. . . . That 5-inch ammunition was falling all over the island. A great many people thought they were Japanese bombs, but only one [Japanese]

bomb hit the town of Honolulu and I think that was an accident. All the rest of them were Navy 5-inch shells. . . . I went
out and dug up the fragments and looked at the markings on
them. I know they were Navy shells; so does the Navy.''

This shelling increased the civilian panic. People pulled
furniture from houses, scattering it across lawns to protect it
from fire. They loaded cars and fled to the heights, just as
residents there were heading in the opposite direction to escape
enemy paratroopers. Those who were inside rushed outside,
fearing fire; those outside ran inside, fearing shrapnel. Plantation workers grabbed children and hid in cane fields. Water
mains broke, sending geysers fifty feet into the air. Fire engines
and ambulances mounted sidewalks to pass jammed intersections. Nothing moved at normal speed, and for hours Honolulu
resembled a silent movie in which everything is blurred, fast,
and jerky.

One of the few residents not panicked was Pat Morgan's
neighbor, the manager of the Honolulu branch of the Yokohama Specie Bank. His spacious house bordered her family's,
and although she had never met him, she had often seen him
play tennis on a backyard court. She saw him again on December 7, playing doubles even as the attack continued. The Japanese men wore whites and green eyeshades, and their women,
also dressed in white, watched from the sidelines. Morgan was
so upset she had a "sudden juvenile desire to shake my fist at
them and yell something." She still wonders about them. "Do
you think they knew they were going to be arrested, and decided to pass the time playing tennis?" she asked. "Of course,
it was a perfectly reasonable thing for them to do. Eventually
they just vanished."

Panic came later to civilians living on the heights. At first,
they had a detached, long-distance view of the action, as if
seeing it through the wrong end of a telescope. Don Woodrum
now remembers it as "seen at a distance, without the close-ups

we expect from television." Morgan, who lived on the heights above Punahou School, thought it was strangely beautiful, mentioning "orange flames within clouds of smoke, and the wakes of little boats cutting across the harbor, disappearing in and out of walls of smoke."

Soon the rumors of paratroopers, saboteurs, and poisoned water spread from military to civilian communities. Radio unwittingly spread the panic. An announcer suggested listeners remain calm, but his voice quivered. Governor Poindexter, who came on the air around noon, is remembered being "so nervous he could scarcely speak." Civilian radios received the police band, enabling everyone to overhear the terrifying rumors. These started among the military, were believed by civilians, then were reported to the police, who broadcast them to more soldiers and civilians. Twice on the evening of December 7, police bulletins announced another attack was underway, saying, "All cars turn off your lights! Pearl Harbor is being bombed again!" The panic was increased by civil defense announcements such as "Get your car off the street! Drive it on the lawn if necessary. . . . If an air raid should begin, do not go out of doors. . . . You may be seriously injured or instantly killed by shrapnel falling from antiaircraft shells."

At times, it was believed Japanese paratroopers had landed on the north shore, in Nuuanu Valley, and on St. Louis Heights, and that Japanese transports were landing assault troops off Barbers Point, off Lualualei, and off Nanakuli. Saboteurs were said to have poisoned the Aiea reservoir, or the water tower on St. Louis Heights. Teenage boys drove through plantation towns honking horns and shouting, "Poisoned water! Don't drink it!"

Someone identified a barking dog as an enemy agent taught to bark in code, although it was not specified if it was barking in English or Japanese. A man dropped a lighted flashlight that rolled down a steep hill, leading to reports of slowly oscillating signal flares. The hum of an electric pump was mistaken for a radio transmitter, and soldiers shelled a school of fish off Barbers Point, thinking it was an enemy submarine, then fired on clumps of seaweed they mistook for survivors swimming ashore.

Such was the panic that according to the Honolulu Police Department log, a man removing personal belongings from his own bomb-shattered home became a "suspected looter," a backyard luau tent was a tent for Japanese paratroopers, and a "haole man listening to mainland news" was a "fifth columnist transmitting intelligence via shortwave radio."

Such was the panic that a lineman became "man up a telegraph pole signaling Japs at sea," two men lighting cigarettes were "spies signaling with blinker lights," and San Jose College football players dressed in warm-up suits were taken for Japanese paratroopers. Kites snagged in a tree also became enemy paratroopers, and so did six children on a Sunday-school outing, the branches of a eucalyptus tree, and an American pilot bailing out over Barbers Point. Crowds attacked a Chinese-Japanese man for being a saboteur, and two air raid wardens beat to death a close friend, a sixty-year-old Chinese-Hawaiian warden they mistook for a Japanese parachutist in the dark. No wonder that on December 8, the *Honolulu Advertiser*'s headline read, "SABOTEURS LAND HERE," and the article underneath claimed that "the saboteurs were distinguished by red disks on their shoulders."

The most terrifying time for civilians came after sunset, on the first night of blackout and curfew. They listened to rumors of paratroopers and saboteurs on the police radio band, felt the ground shake from the passage of trucks trailering artillery pieces, and heard the rifle shots of nervous guards, the antiaircraft fire of panicky gunners, and the grinding gears of mortuary wagons bringing the dead to cemeteries in the Nuuanu Valley. Shells flashed like sheet lightning, burning battleships projected a dull red glow across the sky, and around midnight a rare and vivid lunar rainbow appeared, according to native Hawaiian tradition the symbol of approaching victory.

For fear and panic to follow a surprise raid on a civilian city was not unusual. But Hawaii's unusual population and geography magnified these emotions. For months the military had been scaring itself, its dependents, and civilians with warnings of how local Japanese would rise up once war began, staging massacres. Hawaii's isolation, before a source of comfort, also fed panic as people realized they were too distant for quick reinforcements and had nowhere to flee from invasion and occupation. When Pat Morgan heard Japanese paratroopers had landed behind St. Louis High School and were approaching her house, she and her brothers armed themselves, even though she admits that "we did not know which bullet went into what." She expected "to see the Japanese coming over the hills. . . . Our plan, such as it was, was to shoot from the veranda, and then if they kept coming to get in the car and rush out the back way, up the Tantalus Road, and then, if necessary, try to disappear into the mountains. . . . There was no [other] place for us to run to. We couldn't get into a car and drive to Arizona."

22

The A List Japanese Pack
Their Bags

YUKIKO AND FUMIKO FUKUDA REMEMBER LITTLE OF THE AT-
tack. "We heard loud noises.... Our parents thought it was
practice. Then our neighbors told us." But the moment that
same afternoon when policemen arrested their father is still
vivid, and no wonder, since it led to their repatriation to Japan,
near starvation in Hiroshima, and their small pensions from the
Hawaii State Department of Education.

"Our father was wearing a short-sleeved shirt and work
pants," one told me.

"He was weeding and hoeing our small garden," said another, "and he had a cold, but the FBI agent and policemen did
not allow him time for packing a bag. We watched him go from
the porch, and were scared."

He was among 370 Hawaiians of Japanese ancestry picked
up on December 7, all from the "A List" of Japanese suspects
compiled by Lieutenant Colonel Bicknell, FBI agent Shivers,
and Detective John Burns of the Honolulu Police Department.
They included Shinto and Buddhist priests, the teachers and
headmasters of Japanese-language schools, and all 242 of the
unpaid Japanese consular agents who assisted alien Japanese

residents in filing birth, death, and marriage certificates. Many expected arrest, and they stood on street corners, suitcases packed, dressed in suits and ties, waiting.

In the following days more Japanese were detained, 1,441 in all. Aside from consular agents and language teachers, the largest contingent was made up of "kibei," men born in Hawaii, educated in Japan, and holding dual citizenship. A third of all detainees were released within several months, leaving fewer than a thousand. A similar roundup of several thousand suspected Japanese sympathizers occurred on the West Coast just after the attack. But it was not until March 1942 that all of the West Coast's 110,000 Japanese were rounded up and interned.

It is easy to believe today that in 1941, every Japanese resident in Hawaii was a Wymo Takaki or Ted Tsukiyama, cursing Japan and praying for American victory. Few issei remain alive, and fewer still admit to loyalties either divided or pro-Japanese. The myth of total Japanese loyalty—of their "100 percent Americanism" and superpatriotism—is moving and compelling: it flatters haoles by depicting all Japanese as wanting only to imitate them, and in the foundation of Japanese-American economic and political power in Hawaii. But it is at odds with logic and fact. On December 7, forty thousand Japanese residents of Hawaii, almost 10 percent of its total population, held only Japanese citizenship. Most would have become American citizens if immigration laws had permitted it, but some suffered divided loyalties, and a few, although it is now heresy to say this, took secret pride in the attack, and might have assisted Japanese troops had they invaded. (Had they failed to do so, since they were Japanese citizens, Japanese military authorities could have executed them for treason.) The postwar Japanese "victory societies" like Hisso Kai prove the existence of pro-Japanese sentiments long after Pearl Harbor, and at a time when French, Dutch, Nor-

wegian, Belgian, Danish, Polish, and Russian citizens were helping the Nazis impose an occupation of their own countries, it
stretches credulity to imagine some Japanese aliens would not
have collaborated.

Some Japanese-Americans will now admit, or at least hint
at, the existence of pro-Japanese sentiments in Hawaii. Larry
and Minnie Nakatsuka wanted me to understand that, as Larry
said, "there is a tendency, particularly in a multiracial society
like Hawaii, to think racial communities share reactions to
events. Instead, the Japanese community in 1941 was hardly
monolithic. There were many splits, and summary conclusions
will always be wrong."

Nancy Sato admits, "During the war many of the old people were pro-Japanese, although they weren't much of a threat
to anyone." She describes a neighbor's son as "always very
pro-Japanese, even when he joined the Army. His family had a
shortwave radio and listened to the Japanese broadcasts
throughout the war, and he felt that the war in Europe was
completely different from the one against Japan." Her own
mother was an alien who could separate America's enemies,
saying, "I hope we win the war in Europe," because her own
son was fighting there. Yet, Sato thinks, "half of her was still
hoping that Japan would win." When President Roosevelt died,
her mother connected it to the invasion of Okinawa and
gloated, "See! That's what happens when he invades our country. That's why he died." Sato also remembers a Japanese-
language school teacher who "came back from serving in the
army in Japan and was always trying to get us to change our
thinking and have us worship the Emperor. But all us kids
knew we were Americans, so he didn't get very far. Later, when
I heard he had been interned in California, I thought to myself,
'Yeah, well, he should have been interned.' "

Seiyei Wakukawa believes, "If there had been an invasion,
many Japanese would have stood on the sidelines, waiting to

see how the wind blew. But once the Japanese army had established its primacy I think almost all would have collaborated. But I think many haoles would have done the same. So to say you couldn't trust the Japs is like saying that the French people couldn't trust themselves during an occupation, which turned out to be true!" He says few of his friends were pleased by the Japanese attack and "most were just worried about their personal safety, and whether or not they would be interned." But one man did burst into his house on December 7, crying, "They have finally done it!"

Wakukawa was visited by military intelligence officers, who distrusted him because of the portrait of Karl Marx hanging over his desk. He was also watched, he thinks, by the "Oahu Citizens Committee for Home Defense," a group of prominent Japanese recruited by FBI agent Shivers to promote loyalty within their community, and he noticed one prominent Japanese college professor sitting for hours in a car in front of his house. Shivers later confirmed that niseis assisted the FBI, saying "[they] have supplied us with quite valuable information . . . [and] with the names of alien Japanese who they say should be interned."

Wakukawa was picked up ten days after the attack and kept in solitary confinement at the U.S. immigration station. After interrogation by several hearings boards, he was sent to Sand Island and questioned by intelligence officers, who believed he knew something about the Mori telephone call. He was soon transferred to a camp in the New Mexico desert he remembers for its rudimentary barracks, mesquite, and heat. He wrote a letter of protest to President Roosevelt, which led to his parole on Lincoln's Birthday, 1943, although he was so angry over his imprisonment he refused a free government rail ticket. Forbidden to travel to Hawaii or the West Coast, he went to Chicago and taught Japanese. He moved to Columbia University to translate Japanese material for a Navy research project. Japanese academics were in demand, and soon Harvard had recruited him to write a paper about Japanese land systems that was to become the basis for the land reform program imposed on Japan during the occupation. Later, Wakukawa toured Japan at the invitation of the government and was disappointed to find his program of selling land to tenant farmers, instead of making them more liberal, had converted them into wealthy little capitalists.

Alfred Preis, the future architect of the *Arizona* Memorial, was also taken to the immigration station with his wife on December 8. He was a Jewish convert to Christianity and had fled Vienna in 1939 to escape the Nazis, but since he and his wife still carried Austrian passports, they were considered enemy aliens. Because of the blackout, the immigration station was dark. Dull lights glowed behind blue paper, and officials shone flashlights in prisoners' faces. One unseen guard separated Preis from his wife and ordered him to empty his pockets; another pointed a bayonet into his back and urged him up a flight of stairs. A steel door opened, and he stumbled into a room lit by burning cigarette ends and reeking with the fishy odor brought by the many Japanese fishermen under detention. He lay on the floor, kept awake all night by a German woman in an adjoining room protesting she was an American citizen and had left her baby at home alone. The next morning, he broke down when his wedding band was confiscated and he was ordered to scrub the latrines with his bare hands.

Yet, soon his ring was returned and he was moved to Sand Island, where he ate excellent meals prepared from canned food by detained German chefs. Here the European internees bickered, the Japanese lived in harmony, native Hawaiian guards napped in detainees' tents, and the only shot fired came when a guard fell asleep under a coconut tree, accidentally discharging his gun and bringing down a coconut. On orders of the camp's commander, Preis spent every day with Nazi spy Otto

Kuehn, listening to his unconvincing pleas of innocence, watching for suicide attempts, and marveling at the irony of his situation—a man who had fled Nazi Germany interned as an enemy alien and ordered to guard the life of the only Nazi spy in Hawaii. But he looked shocked when I asked if he harbored any lingering bitterness. "But I *hoped* to be interned!" he said. "It was important to me that America win the war, and if I hadn't been picked up I would have lost confidence in the authorities."

He was among 112 Germans and Italians, aliens and naturalized citizens, interned the day after Pearl Harbor and three days before the United States and their countries were formally at war. This number represented 100 percent of the population of these communities in Hawaii, while the Japanese detainees made up less than 1 percent of their community. Former intelligence officer Don Woodrum says this happened because "there were so few [Europeans] we didn't have to be discriminating and could grab them all. So we took all the German chefs from the hotels, Little Joe Pacific the Italian shoe repairman, a man claiming to be a Finnish count, and all the other European alcoholics and eccentrics."

The more you examine the detentions of aliens on Hawaii, the more curious they become. Consider, for example, that Robert Shivers, John Burns, and Kendall Fielder, the very men responsible for choosing which Japanese should be detained, were among twenty-two non-Japanese honored in 1985 by a committee of prominent Japanese-Americans for contributing "to the success and well-being of the Japanese immigrants to Hawaii and their descendants." In the foreword to a booklet published on the hundredth anniversary of Japanese immigration to Hawaii, Governor George Ariyoshi praised them as "outstanding individuals whose dedication to humanitarian interests had significant impact on the economic and social well-being of Hawaii's Asian immigrants . . . [and] who promoted fair treatment of persons regardless of their race, color or creed."

One reason for these astonishing testimonials is that the first post–Pearl Harbor detentions on Hawaii were also the last. In March 1942, when a Japanese invasion was still feared, and when every Japanese resident on the West Coast was being rounded up and interned, 99 percent of Hawaii's 160,000 Japanese remained free, largely because of the efforts of Robert Shivers, John Burns, Colonel Kendall Fielder, and General Delos Emmons. Of course, there were economic and practical considerations mitigating against detention, and it was argued that Hawaii's Japanese were too numerous and too necessary to the economy and war effort. But that did not keep President Roosevelt's cabinet from sending a directive to General Emmons on December 19, instructing him to intern Hawaii's forty thousand Japanese aliens on the island of Molokai. Nor did it prevent the Joint Chiefs of Staff from recommending he follow California's example by evacuating all Japanese residents to mainland internment camps. Emmons ignored these directives at considerable risk to his career, stalling until he could persuade Washington to change its mind, and until the American victory at Midway made them less compelling.

Emmons was a recent arrival in Hawaii who had initially mistrusted the Japanese. He defended them now because Shivers, Fielder, and Bicknell had persuaded him most of Hawaii's Japanese, as Fielder put it, "were just as American as you are, or I." Fielder and others gave Shivers credit for convincing them, and Sue Isonaga remembers Fielder saying, "I came from the mainland not knowing anything about the local Japanese, but Bob Shivers pushed and shoved me in the right direction." In a 1943 letter to Charles Hemenway, president of the Hawaiian Trust Company and trustee of the University of Hawaii, Shivers described how, based on an order issued by General Short on December 7, "not a single person could be interned or released from internment without my approval up to the time I left Honolulu." This order, he continued, "pretty well placed control in my hands, which enabled me to carry out the ideas and plans which I knew were yours as well as mine. . . . Fortified with this fact [the absence of Japanese sabotage], we were able to stand up for what we thought was right against the opposition of, as you know, some high-placed officials."

What explains Shivers's brave, stubborn defense of the Japanese, one his Southern background made all the more remarkable? (Ted Tsukiyama remembers meeting him just before leaving for Army training in Mississippi. "I still can't understand him," he told me. "He was all for us [the Japanese] but then he said, 'When you get to the South, don't have anything to do with the damn niggers.' ") He did have frequent contact with informal "advisory" groups of prominent Japanese-Americans, and his affection for Sue Isonaga was undoubtedly important. She remembers him saying, "I just can't see mass internment. Why, look at Sue, she's just as American as you and I are. I'm not putting them in camps and ruining their lives." And nine months after arriving in Hawaii he had sought out Masaji Marumoto, a prominent young Japanese-American attorney, and told him he had been "bombarded with all kinds of anti-Japanese information" and now wanted to know the "Japanese side of the story." Marumoto introduced him to Japanese community leaders who began meeting for breakfast every Sunday morning at his home. Meanwhile, Shivers and Marumoto also met weekly to discuss ways of encouraging the loyalty of the Japanese community. Their wives became friendly, and soon the two families were close. After Shivers left Honolulu, he wrote Marumoto, "We miss you . . . more than I thought we would at the time we left. You know, Masaji, how much I value your friendship and the association our families had together. . . ."

Before the war, Marumoto had been the first Oriental admitted to the Harvard Law School and the first Oriental to argue a case before the United States Supreme Court. Afterward, he continued his record of being the "first Japanese," becoming the first Oriental president of the Hawaii Bar Association and the first Oriental judge of Hawaii's supreme court. His memory was beginning to fail when I met him, but although he was vague about some events on December 7, he still recalled in detail how he and Shivers had met and worked together, and how his had been the "honor" of being Shivers's first Japanese friend.

Sue Isonaga continues honoring Shivers as a courageous friend of the Japanese. She moved in with him and his wife during the war, keeping Mrs. Shivers company when he was called to Washington. When she was married in 1949, he gave her away, and after he died in 1950, she exchanged frequent visits with his widow. She has named her oldest son Robert, and her daughter May after Mrs. Shivers's sister. Her brother has a child named Corinne, Mrs. Shivers's first name. She showed me her children's photographs, proudly pointing out that her son had married a half haole, half Japanese woman, one daughter had married a Chinese, and the other, a haole. And did I know, she said, that Robert Shivers once said that "the sooner we're all intermarried the better it will be"?

Mementos of the Shiverses fill her home. She keeps Mrs. Shivers's vases filled with flowers, and displays their silver tea service behind a glass case. There is a large photograph of them inscribed "To our own Sue, with love," showing a kindly looking Southern couple, a woman with the sweet expression of a Sunday-school teacher and a dark-haired man with a direct, honest face. It was not until she talked of her visits to Shivers's grave, where she took flowers on Father's Day, his birthday, the anniversary of his death, Memorial Day, Christmas, Valentine's Day and, "of course, whenever I'm out that way," that I realized that long after whatever distant blood relations he may have left on the mainland have forgotten him, she and her children, and their children, and their children's children, will probably, in dutiful Japanese fashion, be honoring his grave.

Hawaii's peculiar culture and racial atmosphere was also a factor in the generous treatment of its Japanese. Although there were discrimination and prejudice, they lacked the brutal edge—the violence and hatred—of mainland racism. Newcomers among the military and defense workers distrusted the Japanese, but kamaainas had Japanese friends and understood the difference between the nisei and the more passive, or pro-Japanese, issei. Listen, for example, to a speech given in February 1942 by Lester Hicks, president of the Hawaiian Electric Company, terming any proposal to intern the Japanese "fantastic" and declaring that they had "woven themselves into our community fabric . . . in such intimate fashion as to be an integral part of us." Or to General Briant Wells (Ret.) denouncing Navy Secretary Knox's charge of Japanese fifth column activity as "slanderous" and telling the Roberts Committee, "Our whole country is made up of people from all races and one race is just as good as another citizen as far as rights are concerned. By rounding them [the Japanese] up and putting them in a corner, you can make them disloyal." Or, finally, to Shivers himself, denouncing Admiral Kimmel's accusations of fifth column activity, saying, "In spite of what Admiral Kimmel or anyone else may have said about the fifth column activity in Hawaii, I want to emphasize that there was no such activity in Hawaii before, during or after the attack on Pearl Harbor. Consequently there was no confusion in Hawaii as a result of fifth column activities. . . . I speak with authority when I say that the confusion in Hawaii was in the minds of the confused."

The generous treatment of the Japanese on Hawaii makes their suffering on the mainland even more senseless and shame-

ful and is a reminder that not every Japanese internee was an
innocent victim of racism. In the panicky days after the attack,
the internment of small numbers in Hawaii was understandable, and sometimes, as Nancy Sato believes, merited. If in
many cases it was an injustice, it was a forgivable one. Since all
West Coast Japanese were interned, they could have no lingering doubts or questions about why they were chosen. But some
Hawaiian detainees still feel stigmatized by their selective internment, if only in their own minds, and are still haunted by
the question of "why me?"

Seiyei Wakukawa is a brittle man in his eighties who lives
in a ground-floor apartment in a Nuuanu Valley neighborhood
little changed since the war, surrounded by a cocoon of books
that cover tables and fill floor-to-ceiling shelves. His internment
remains the great mystery of his life. He argues it was an obvious injustice, because during the summer of 1941 he had
toured Japanese schools and churches, encouraging loyalty to
America. Furthermore, his University of Hawaii Ph.D. thesis on
the social and liberation movements in Japan and its colonies
had been "very antifascist," containing "strong criticism of
Japanese territorial aggression on the Asian mainland."

"Until this day I cannot imagine the basis for their conclusion I was dangerous to the nation," he said, shaking his
head. "I still can't figure it; it still puzzles me." Had he been
interned because of that portrait of Karl Marx? Because he was
rude to his interrogators? Because after his arrest an agent
searching his office reported to his superiors, "This guy is a very
smart fellow—he didn't leave a single thing to implicate himself"? Because the haole professors at the university who had
rejected his thesis because it was "rather too radical for the
time, too Marxist-oriented" had spread rumors he was a "parlor pink"? Or because his older brother had been a special
attaché at the Japanese embassy in Washington, depicted in a
Newsweek photograph burning official papers after the attack?

This brother had sent him a telegram on December 5, saying, "This is a goodbye. Take care of yourself." It was kept from him, he says, by pro-Japanese relatives in Honolulu who worried he might warn the Americans, but perhaps the authorities had intercepted it, and that explained his detention.

Perhaps he was betrayed by prominent Japanese on Robert Shivers's Moral Committee? "But if they were such one hundred percent Americans, why would they persecute someone as anti-Japanese as myself?" he wondered. "Perhaps they were suspicious because I was a radical. I still don't have much love for them. They have been highly praised here, but I believe they would have been just as loyal to the invading Japanese. Many cooperated with the government because it was convenient. Some were friends of mine from college days, and after the war, they did not suspect I still harbored grudges against them."

I thought any or all of his theories might explain his internment. After all, he was a Japanese alien who had traveled widely in Japan's occupied territories. He had probably been accused of disloyalty by Japanese leaders, and his brother, who was employed by the Japanese embassy in Washington, had telegraphed him a last-minute warning.

Reflecting again on the possible reasons for his internment had caused Wakukawa to become so distraught that, hoping to cheer him, I mentioned the Civil Liberties Act of 1988, granting twenty thousand dollars in government reparations to the sixty thousand surviving Americans of Japanese ancestry interned during the war. He said he had plans for his twenty thousand dollars. He would move to a larger apartment and publish his book about Japanese immigration. He agreed it would make a big difference to have at last a concrete, official acknowledgment of his unjust imprisonment.

Like the unsuccessful Pearl Harbor reconciliations, the internment compensation program, which is an attempt at reconciliation between Japanese-Americans and their fellow citizens, has stirred up some unwanted ghosts. Ike Sutton, the ensign who was strafed while pulling sailors from Pearl Harbor, settled in Hawaii and became a businessman and politician who was several times elected to the state legislature. He was Republican candidate for lieutenant governor in 1990, and even though he needed the votes of Japanese-Americans to win, during a televised interview he could not restrain himself from attacking the reparations program. "That strafing made me so goddam mad," he told me, "that I made the mistake of saying, 'Well, why not give forty thousand dollars then to the Japanese boys who strafed me?' Needless to say, I did not win any points for that."

Pearl Harbor survivors and Bataan death march survivors have also protested that the legislation rewards the "enemy" and that Japan never paid reparations to American POWs for their years in horrifying camps. Pearl Harbor Survivor Jesse Forster of Maryland complained in a letter to the *Gram,* "I can't remember ever reading that Japan has compensated the families of all POWs that had to endure such torture and hardship. . . ." In August 1990, the Survivors campaigned against a measure passed the year before by the California legislature requiring schoolchildren to be taught there was no military basis for the internment, and that it resulted from "race prejudice." They persuaded a legislator to introduce a resolution stating the camps had not been "concentration camps" but "relocation centers," and that the program was prompted by military necessity.

Such attacks infuriate Japanese-Americans. Attorney Earl Nishimura has been prominent in the Hawaiian campaign for reparations. When I mentioned that some Pearl Harbor Survivors objected to the twenty-thousand-dollar payments he pounded his desk in anger, saying, "We fought two wars— against the enemy and against skeptics. It gave us a chance to show our loyalty and we did pretty well. Listen—we were as good Americans as anyone!"

Ted Tsukiyama thought that arguing Japan should pay reparations to American POWs if Japanese internees received compensation was "outrageous!" "We had no compunction about fighting the Japanese," he said. "But now they want to lump us together with those damned Japs. How can they *still* do this to us?"

The Fukuda sisters are as obsessed as Wakukawa with solving the mystery of their internment—in their case, why they were among forty Japanese families chosen to accompany male detainees to the mainland. Their father was one of 242 Japanese consular agents on Hawaii. It was an honorary post, carrying no diplomatic immunity; nevertheless, U.S. authorities offered him a choice between internment in America or repatriation to Japan. He was one of the few Japanese alien residents of Hawaii to decide on repatriation. His daughters say he thought he would be unable to earn a living in Hawaii, since his language school had been closed and the teaching of Japanese was forbidden. He was moved to the mainland and held with other aliens and diplomatic personnel awaiting repatriation. A first group left for Japan in March 1942 on the Swedish liner *Gripsholm*. He was scheduled for the second sailing.

Back in Hawaii, the Fukuda sisters and their mother were among several hundred families requesting repatriation with the men. It had been a difficult decision, and I sensed they would have preferred to stay behind, although their desire to honor their father's memory made them reluctant to admit it. "We were brought up to obey our parents. We had no preparation for working outside the home, and we thought our decision would help him in being released to Japan," said one.

"We were living miserable financial lives," said another. "Yet, we were sad to leave our friends and school life."

They were among forty Hawaiian families the State Department chose for repatriation. They traveled by ship to San Francisco, then by train to New York to join their father on the *Gripsholm*. But its sailing was canceled, and, along with other Japanese and German diplomatic families, they were incarcerated in a resort in North Carolina. They said, "For two months we enjoyed more luxury than we had at home, maids to clean our rooms, and a full menu." In 1943, they moved to a repatriation camp in Crystal City, Louisiana, and were reunited with their father. They stayed there for the duration, attending a special high school and, because of the Geneva Convention, enjoying rations and clothing equivalent to those of American enlisted personnel.

When the war ended, their father was offered the opportunity of returning to Hawaii. But still believing he could not make a living there, he insisted on repatriation. In December 1945 the family arrived in Japan, a country the sisters had never seen. "We weren't looking forward to Japan. We would have preferred Hawaii but wanted to remain a family," one said.

"We imagined how cold it must be, and we worried there were snakes," said another.

Japan was a disaster. It was cold and they had to barter their warm clothes for food. Their father took them to Hiroshima to see his birthplace, but the bomb had obliterated all traces of it. Three weeks after arriving he died. They tried to return to Hawaii but found by choosing repatriation they had lost their citizenship. When regulations were eased in 1952, they regained it and returned to Hawaii. They worked as Japanese-language teachers, then joined the public school system, finding that because of their experiences they were years behind other teachers their age, missing any chance for a thirty-year pension. "We taught with people ten years younger than us," Fumiko said. "Now people our age are really enjoying these years because they have better pensions, while I'm living on only a one-third pension." Although they gave pained smiles, speaking softly, and even apologetically, as they voiced their gentle complaints, it was clear they held Pearl Harbor, the war, and their internment (but not their father) responsible for leaving them in this flimsy tract house, located up a hot valley behind Kahala, and all the while "wondering," as Yukiko said, "what would have happened to us if we had not been interned."

Since they believed their lives had been determined by this event, it became their retirement hobby. "We're just kind of curious to see how things were decided," Fumiko said.

"And to find out how we and the other forty families were selected for repatriation."

They have become experts in this narrow historical field, and yellowing documents and books clutter their sitting room. Since retiring, they have made three trips to the National Archives in Washington, D.C., finding the official files about the Hawaiian repatriatees and a list containing their father's name. "We even saw our own files," one said, "'and until then we hadn't known we had the status of POWs." They discovered that twelve people from the forty families chosen to join detainees on the mainland had refused to go. They found photocopies of the official reports of their transcontinental journey, detailing their complaints, clothing, and menus. (One said, "After the expatriate party boarded the *Army Queen* [a ferry to Oakland], the Red Cross, under the supervision of Mrs. T. Bacigalupi, served the expatriates all the fresh milk and several kinds of sandwiches they required.")

On their last Washington visit they found the solution to the mystery of their selection in letters exchanged between Secretary of War Stimson and Secretary of State Hull. Stimson had written Hull that General Emmons was opposed to repatriating Japanese currently held in camps in Hawaii for fear that upon returning to Japan, they would divulge information about the

Islands' defenses. But Hull overruled his objections, saying it was essential forty Japanese families from Hawaii be chosen. Japan held American internees taken on Guam, Wake Island, and the Philippines (who were probably not being served all the milk and sandwiches they required), and the State Department believed their repatriation and humane treatment might depend on equivalent treatment for Japanese from Hawaii.

The letter explaining the sisters' fate had been written by an Assistant Secretary of State to Navy Secretary Knox. It said, "Realizing the difficult situation in Hawaii, the department has left to the discretion of the War Department the selection of thirty or forty Japanese [families] who are considered less dangerous or who, for special reasons, it is considered desirable to remove from the Hawaiian area." The Fukudas liked to believe the description "less dangerous" applied to them. It represented a vindication of their loyalty and proof they were unjustly penalized by their smaller pensions.

If you thought the Fukudas regarded their years in that Louisiana internment camp as grim ones, you would be mistaken. Instead, they were nostalgic for Crystal City Federal High School. They proudly showed me their yearbooks with all the traditional pictures of football teams and cheerleaders, and the smudged signatures of their German, Japanese, and Italian classmates. For many years the Hawaiian alumni had celebrated Crystal City reunions at Mrs. Ishiko Mori's Wylie Street home, and the Fukuda sisters would soon be attending a gala forty-fifth reunion in San Diego. A brochure promised trips to Disneyland, picnics, and a gold tournament. Camp Crystal T-shirts and a souvenir book were being readied, and, as with the Pearl Harbor Survivors Association, sons and daughters were being urged to attend. The Fukudas were going for free, using the frequent-flier miles they had accumulated traveling to Washington to research their imprisonment.

23

"A Deep, Powerful Thirst for Revenge"

ONCE THE PANIC RECEDED, SOME FELT AN ODD EXHILARATION. Mary Ellen Lawrence remembers "people seemed relieved for the chance to show heroism," "singing on the evacuation buses," and "a certain pride in being able to measure up to the wartime heroism of the Brits." The attack made Kathy Cooper think of the newsreels she had seen of bombing raids on London. Miss Mary Hall, a Punauhou schoolteacher, remarked in her diary that "more men lay dead and wounded on Oahu than had fallen in any of the heaviest attacks on London." Soon, many Anglophile haoles were grandiloquently referring to this single two-hour raid as "the Blitz."

After the panic and exhilaration, and after 0950, when the last Japanese planes had finally returned to their carriers, almost everyone was gripped by an intense anger that, in some cases, lasted a lifetime. A chief petty officer who pulled bodies from the harbor "like fish" became so furious he said, "If I could have gotten my hands on any one of those Japanese, I would have crushed him like an insect."

A crewman on a minelayer was mad "because the Japanese envoys had been down on the dock only a week or so before and there was the ambassador in Washington talking peace." A gunner's mate on the *Oklahoma* described "a deep, powerful thirst for revenge on the part of every enlisted man," adding he "wouldn't have given any Japanese a second of mercy after Pearl Harbor." Pat Morgan said, "We couldn't call anybody up and say, 'What shall we do to help?' We were all consumed with an urge to do something violent." Kathy Cooper had "an utter feeling of horror, helplessness, and anger, consuming anger. If a Japanese pilot had walked into the house, I would have tried to kill him." Matilda Faufata, whose daughter was killed by shell fragments, heard her husband swear, "Dammit, some Jap is going to pay for this." She later wrote that she "had a hard time restraining him from carrying out this threat. Knowing him like I do, he would have killed the first person of Japanese ancestry whether he be friend or foe." The gravediggers at the Oahu cemetery were so furious they called a work stoppage, refusing to bury the dead until they could be reassured enemy corpses would be segregated from the American ones. And Admiral Halsey vowed the Japanese language "will be spoken only in hell" and exhorted his men, "Kill Japs, kill Japs, kill more Japs."

Anger was intensified by people seeing, or believing they saw, the faces of Japanese pilots, their mustaches, and even "the slant of their eyes." Pilots were described as waving, smiling, and laughing, taunting sailors before killing them. Marines at Ewa Field said a tail gunner stopped firing long enough to thumb his nose. Another let go of the handles of his gun, clasped his hands high above his head, and shook them in that greeting with which American prizefighters salute their fans. Then he grabbed his gun and shot some more. Since attacking planes flew slow and low, particularly during early torpedo runs, it is likely some did see the pilots. But so many reports surfaced of Japanese gloating and waving that I suspect them of being manufactured, perhaps from an urge to personalize the attack and increase the anger that followed.

One source of anger was the "treachery" of attacking on a Sunday morning, without a declaration of war and while Japanese envoys were holding peace talks in Washington. Within days, respondents to a mainland poll had chosen "treacherous," "sly," and "cruel" as words best describing the Japanese people. Authorities in Norfolk, Virginia, had jailed every Japanese resident, and the Tennessee Department of Conservation had requisitioned six million licenses for "hunting Japanese." (The purchasing department turned down the request, noting it was "open season on 'Japs'—no license required.") On Hawaii, however, despite some verbal threats and random assaults, there was more tolerance and less racial hatred. By the end of the war, Mrs. Faufata would be writing, "My husband is still plugging along at Pearl Harbor . . . to 'beat them Japs.' We both mean the ones on the other side of the big pond called the 'Pacific,' and not the loyal ones here in Hawaii among whom we have many friends."

But even in Hawaii, anger over Pearl Harbor has proved to be a resilient emotion, leaving several generations thin-skinned toward the Japanese. Like Hiroshima, Pearl Harbor has become a backdrop to Japanese-American interactions, the curtain against which political and economic transactions are projected. Since Pearl Harbor was uniquely shocking and humiliating, it is only logical that American attitudes toward Japan should be uniquely sensitive, and that today's economic disputes should be haunted by Pearl Harbor ghosts. And so Japan's trade policies are likened to a form of "treachery," a U.S. senator describes the export of Japanese cars to America as "an economic Pearl Harbor," and advertisements for American automobiles feature references to Emperor Hirohito, exaggerated Japanese accents, and ridicule of the Japanese physique.

An Alabama country club rejects the application for membership of a Mr. Hiroshi Isogai, manager of the Honda All-Lock Manufacturing Company, "amid lingering ill feelings about World War II," and when the decision is reversed, members admit their first vote was motivated by "resentment dating back to Japan's 1941 attack on Pearl Harbor."

Because Rhode Island continues celebrating a holiday known as V-J Day or Victory Day, the Japan Society of Rhode Island mounts a campaign, backed by Japanese business interests, to change its name to Rhode Island Veterans Day. It is defeated by the Rhode Island American Legion, whose commander, a Mr. Cliff Wilson, says, "If they were offended when we called it V-J Day, we were pretty offended when they bombed Pearl Harbor. Why should we have to pacify them?"

American investor T. Boone Pickens runs full-page newspaper advertisements in September 1990 headlined "AMERICA YOU LOST THE ECONOMIC WAR," and beginning, "That taunt was hurled recently at Boone Pickens and fifty American shareholders in Japan, along with 'Yankee Go Home!' and 'Remember Pearl Harbor!' " Pickens argues his investment company is unable to gain a single seat on the board of a Japanese company controlled by Toyota, despite owning 26 percent of its stock, for the same reasons America is "losing the economic war with Japan." It is "not because Japanese workers are smarter or more industrious than Americans . . . [but] because corporate Japan takes advantage of our open markets, but plays by an entirely different set of rules—rules that mock American principles of free and fair trade." Here it is again, the assertion that a Japanese victory is the fruit of Japanese treachery, of attacking while peace negotiations continue in Washington, or according to Pickens, of refusing "to play on a level playing field."

Try imagining a state celebrating V-E day as a state holiday, or for that matter, German business interests lobbying to change its name. Or a German executive denied membership in a club because of resentment over the Battle of the Bulge. Or a campaign for American cars taking digs at Volkswagen and Mercedes by superimposing its advertisements over newsreel footage of the liberation of Buchenwald. And because the Germans are Caucasians, declared war on the United States before fighting, and never humiliated America, of course you cannot.

Opinion polls now reflect an increased dislike and distrust of the Japanese, corresponding to a rise in Japanese investment in America and the purchase of symbolic American assets such as Rockefeller Center, Pebble Beach, and Columbia Pictures. In 1988, 63 percent of Americans believed Japanese investment in the United States should "be discouraged," and 44 percent said Japan was "America's least trustworthy ally" (29 percent chose West Germany, and 18 percent France). Although the higher level of resentment and anger may be new, its existence is not. "There is anger left," a kamaaina who had lived through Pearl Harbor told me, "and it comes to the fore when the Japanese are overwhelming." This residual resentment is strong in Hawaii, which in addition to having the largest population of Pearl Harbor eyewitnesses of any state has felt the impact of Japan's economic success and foreign investment more than anywhere else.

If I mentioned Pearl Harbor to a resident of Hawaii I usually heard something like "They couldn't invade us, so now they're buying us." "What they couldn't do with their bombs they're doing with their yen." Or, if the speaker had a certain perspective, "We have turned their yen into bombs." (Cy Gillette told me, "It's our damn fault. . . . This is the difference now, we're doing Pearl Harbor to ourselves.") And always it was "they" or "them," telltale words signifying the enemy in any society under assault. "They" were the million and a half Japanese tourists a year, or the Japanese investors who owned most choice industries and commercial properties, or the Japanese speculators who were buying land and houses of every description.

In public, I read and heard testimonials to the Japanese

contribution to Hawaii's prosperity. In private, I heard something different. A real estate agent who had fattened herself on
Japanese commissions described them as "arrogant sons of
bitches." The widow of a Pearl Harbor–era Army officer said,
"I sometimes have trouble getting to my husband's grave at
Punchbowl because Japanese tourists are in the way." A
woman who had converted her family's ranch into a private
amusement park where Japanese tourists paid handsomely to
ride horses and go-carts complained, "We used to ranch cattle,
but now we ranch Japanese."

Sometimes grievances were aired in public. "Are we, the
people of Hawaii, going to end up as the busboys, drivers,
cooks and maids for the Japanese?" asked a correspondent to
the *Honolulu Advertiser*. Wallace Fujiyama, now a successful
Honolulu lawyer, told me, "Some of these Japanese speculators are raping this state. They're very snobbish and cliquish.
People here bend over backward for the Japanese, but no one
had ever really looked at whether this is good for our community." Maryann Langevin informed the *Honolulu Star-
Bulletin*, "Many of my friends and relatives have said they
will not return again and told me some of the distressing
things that happened to them. One woman who lost her husband on the *Arizona* had finally been able to make the trip
here. While she was visiting the memorial a Japanese tourist
kicked the monument, used foul language and said, 'The way
the Americans repeat the story of Pearl Harbor is not accurate.' She was crushed." For weeks after this letter appeared,
I heard different versions of the story—that a Japanese tourist
had spat on the monument, and that he was a returning Zero
pilot—all cribbed from Mrs. Langevin's letter, but embellished by their raconteurs.

Japanese tourists in Hawaii resemble an earlier generation
of Americans in Europe: incurious, clannish, fond of traveling
in large groups, trying hard to please but considered impolite,

and resented because of their numbers and money. Like Americans in Europe, they complain about seeing too many of their fellow countrymen, and a recent poll reported many disappointed because Hawaii's Japanese influence made it too much like home. They move about in buses, minivans, and white limousines with smoked-glass windows. They like shooting automatic weapons in firing ranges, and riding off-road vehicles, parasailers, and jet skis. They have turned areas of Waikiki into something of an enclave, with signs in Japanese, and blond surfers in Japanese sandwich boards passing out Japanese fliers.

When Hawaiians praise Japanese visitors, it is usually for keeping to their group tours and their Waikiki hotels, and you often hear condescending comments such as "They're good tourists because they stay in a small area . . . they're easy to manage." Or they are praised for spending money at a fabulous rate, three or four times that of an average mainland tourist, with spokesmen for the tourism power structure often mentioning this as reason enough for offering them "a sincere aloha."

Since the 1950s, Japanese investors have been buying Hawaiian enterprises and commercial real estate, and by 1990 they owned fast food chains, construction companies, dry cleaners, car dealerships, and office buildings, the largest bakery, golf courses, more than three quarters of the state's luxury hotel rooms, more than half the rooms in Waikiki, 51 percent of downtown office space, and a controlling interest in Honolulu's largest shopping mall, the Ala Moana Center. Like most islands, Hawaii has always been starved for capital, and at first Japanese investment was welcomed, particularly because it coincided with the decline of Hawaii's sugar and pineapple industries. But as it accelerated, attitudes have changed. By 1989 the cumulative Japanese real estate investment had grown to $13.5 billion, making it second in this category only to California's $17.9 billion. Almost a fourth of the Hawaii invest-

ment was made in 1988 alone, and at the beginning of 1989, the
First Bank of Hawaii made the startling and controversial assertion that in 1987, Japanese spending and investments had accounted for 45 percent of Hawaii's economic activity. "Hardly
a hotel is built, or a major commercial development begun," the
bank said, "without some participation by Japanese investors."
Jokes about Hawaii becoming the next Japanese prefecture became suddenly less amusing. If the Japanese accounted for 45
percent of economic activity, it was easy to imagine them reaching 51 percent.

But it has been Japanese speculation in residential real
estate that has upset Hawaii the most. The Japanese first bought
in Waikiki and the expensive beachfront communities east of
Diamond Head—Kahala, Portlock, Black Point, and Hawaii
Kai—and by 1987 it was estimated that 40 percent of all residential properties sold in Waikiki and 27 percent of those sold
in Kahala were purchased by Japanese nationals. In March
1988, a Japanese investor paid $21 million for a single house in
Kahala, a record for Hawaii surpassed a month later when Mr.
Genshiro Kawamoto bought the Henry Kaiser estate in Portlock for $42 million.

The Japanese bought Hawaiian houses as speculations,
reselling them in Tokyo weeks later to a second tier of buyers
who had never seen them. They bought them as vacation
homes, occupying them for only a few weeks a year, as retirement homes, or as long-term investments, sometimes leasing
them back to the original seller. After acquiring Oahu's best
waterfront properties, they moved inland into middle-class
neighborhoods, picking up ranch houses in Hawaii Kai and
windward Kailua. They bought because the yen was strong and
the dollar weak, and even Hawaii real estate sold for a tenth of
its Japanese equivalent. They bought because regulations in
Japan made speculation difficult, because they already owned
Hawaii's best resorts and beachfront hotels and these houses

were the only quality left, and because they had won a trade war, and these were simply the minor spoils.

The Japanese were resented because they bought too much too quickly, driving already high Oahu housing prices beyond the reach of most local families. (The price of an average single-family house had risen only 14 percent from 1984 to 1986, but in the next two years increased 49 percent to $314,000. And between 1989 and 1990, the price rose another 38 percent.) They were resented because Hawaiians knew they themselves were forbidden from making similar investments in Japan, and because islanders always resent outsiders gaining control of their scarcest resource, their land. As the Japanese bought, neighborhoods changed character and property taxes rose. When Hawaiians saw the houses of Japanese speculators standing empty and watched modest houses double in price, they saw places where their children might be living and raising families, instead of moving to the mainland.

As Hawaii becomes an economic colony of Japan, the Japanese are feeling the traditional resentment of the colonized for the colonizer. What makes this resentment unique and gives it an unmistakably bitter edge is that the victors of a war are being colonized by its losers, and the place being colonized is the one this enemy once attacked. It is believed in Japan, and by some Americans, that opposition to Japanese investment is motivated solely by racism, and they argue that for years British, Canadian, and Dutch investors in Hawaii have escaped censure because they are Caucasian. But if racism alone is responsible for this resentment, then why do investments by other Asian nations generally escape similar censure? And why are Japanese-Americans on Hawaii themselves such bitter critics of the foreign Japanese? Instead, anger at the Japanese, particularly in Hawaii, is directed less against their race than against their nationality.

Such animosity is sometimes admitted in Hawaii, although

usually in sentences beginning "I am not 'Japan-bashing,' but
. . ." It is said to be directed against "foreign speculators" of all
nationalities, although Hawaiians leave no doubt which nationality they fear most. The Sunday *Honolulu Star-Bulletin
and Advertiser* published a poll showing 80 percent approving
a law to prohibit "foreign purchase of homes for investment,"
and everyone knew which foreigners were the targets. Some
people were honest, or foolhardy, enough to acknowledge this.
A headline described Mayor Fasi saying, "Act Now or We'll Be
a Tokyo Suburb." Honolulu's finance director asserted, "Japan
could buy all of Oahu," since Japan had accumulated $52
billion because of trade imbalances with the United States,
while all of Oahu's real property was worth only $51 billion. It
was preposterous to imagine the Japanese clubbing together to
spend all their last billion on Oahu. But the point was, it was
possible, and this represented a Japanese victory more enduring
than Pearl Harbor.

At times, the shadows that Pearl Harbor cast over the new
Japanese presence in Hawaii were faint. A haole man informed
me every Japanese-owned golf course—proposed or under
construction—faced military property. Japanese developers
even planned a resort opposite the gates of the naval weapons
arsenal at Lualualei, and what did I think of that? A haole
woman gave me a written summary of the issues facing Hawaii,
including the observation "The Japanese people need *Lebensraum* now, even more than ever—not just to move but to play
golf etc. Couldn't do by military conquest, so do by purchase."
And the mayor of Maui threatened to withdraw his island's
"aloha" for Japanese tourists if the Japanese navy joined the
United States in using the uninhabited island of Kahoolawe as
a target range. Neither he nor the environmental or native
Hawaiian groups that opposed these exercises spelled it out,
but their language made it clear that for the Japanese to shell a

Hawaiian island was an outrage of a greater magnitude than for the Australians or British, who in previous years had been persuaded to skip this phase of joint maneuvers without threats of withheld aloha.

At other times, the Pearl Harbor shadows were dark and unmistakable. A Mr. Del Oleson wrote to the *Honolulu Advertiser:* "We were called upon, both men and women, to defend these islands and hundreds of others, from an aggressor who had three goals in mind. To conquer, to control and to own. . . . Yet it was only a delay, not a victory. There are people among us who, because of greed, have placed 'For Sale' signs on land we saved for future generations."

A real estate agent working with Genshiro Kawamoto spoke about him in the embarrassed voice of a traitor. "Yesterday I had seven closings with Kawamoto," she said. "All day I've been clicking my heels and saying 'Sieg Heil.' " (There was a pattern here: The Japanese needing *Lebensraum,* the sudden increase in Japanese investment in Hawaii needing a "blitzkrieg," and saying "Sieg Heil" to Japanese investors.) Another Japanese company was buying six houses from her, and she was dealing with their representative, a Mr. Yamamoto. "Hey, wasn't that the admiral's name?" she said. "You know, I was thinking of that."

At the university, I discussed Japanese real estate purchases with an elegant Japanese-American academic in her fifties who spoke English with a faint British accent. She blamed the Japanese for her daughter's moving to Boston because real estate was so expensive in Honolulu. She had been thirteen in 1941, and remembered her father describing pulling bodies from the harbor. "And now," she said, "even Pearl Harbor is infested with Japanese." She lowered her voice, saying, "I'm sorry, but I guess I'm just prejudiced against them."

A leaflet published by Na'opio Aloha'aina, an organization of Waianae coast residents opposed to the new Japanese

West Beach resort development, contained several references to 1941. The Waianae coast is Oahu's last relatively inexpensive neighborhood. Its homes are wood and cinder-block bungalows, its towns clumps of fast-food franchises, convenience stores, and churches. Its land is arid, backed by stark red mountains, and it has large communities of native Hawaiians, Filipinos, and other "locals," as the Honolulu newspapers call them in crime reports, in order to distinguish them from haoles, who, no matter how long they live in Hawaii, are never, in this context, known as "locals." The Waianae "locals" fill low-paying jobs, many in the Japanese-owned luxury hotels. They endure long commutes, having been priced out of more convenient neighborhoods. Pushed into the least lovely corner of Oahu, they are now in danger of losing even this.

The headline of the Aloha'aina protest leaflets asked, "How Will This Japan-Owned Resort Affect Us Waianae Coast Residents?" and answered that it would mean Waikiki prices, congestion, pollution, expensive real estate, water shortages, and the destruction of family farms that supplied 95 percent of Oahu's local produce. The leaflet condemned Japanese developers in terms evoking 1941, and a headline described them bringing "WINDS OF DANGER!"—an echo of *Winds of War.*" The leaflet contained crude racial stereotyping—"We called West Beach Estates to ask about future condo prices. The guy said, 'Soddy. We only sell $20 million parcels now. Sayonara' "—and it echoed 1941, by charging that West Beach would cause more traffic fatalities, saying, "In effect, Japan's big bucks tourism will increase injuries and death among our local people—another tragic FACT! Should we just sit back and wait for this new [as opposed to the 'old' Pearl Harbor] bloodshed?"

One page showed a cartoon with an enormous Rising Sun as its background. It had a single, slanted Oriental eye staring at two versions of Oahu. The one labeled "1987" was straddled by a huge Japanese yen Y, and crisscrossed with tour buses flying Japanese flags. A real estate sign reading "Up for Grabs!" was planted near Diamond Head. Antlike people, excursion boats, and a sign saying "Jet Skis No Fishing" jammed Waikiki. Two Japanese jumbo jets flew overhead, dropping skyscraper hotels that fell like bombs. The other version of Oahu said "1941," and here planes with Japanese markings dropped bombs on warships moored in Pearl Harbor.

On April Fool's Day, 1988, a popular morning radio program on KQMQ pretended Japanese investors had bought the station overnight. During the half hour I listened, I heard the same racial clichés I had been collecting from books and articles published around 1941. Then the Japanese had been nearsighted, bucktoothed, rice-eating midgets who spoke poor English and could not shoot straight. Now there were jokes about "little men," and the new owners being so small the microphones had to be lowered several feet. Someone banged a gong and spoke fractured English, pronouncing all his *r*'s as *l*'s. A new game was announced, "Banzai Bumper Stickers," with first prize a sack of rice. It was said station employees had been ordered to do hours of calisthenics, and Japanese disk jockeys insisted on endlessly playing their favorite song, "The Bunny Hop." An announcer, promising to explain Japanese investment in Hawaii, began, "It all started on December 7. . . ."

Some listeners believed it. Japanese-American callers seemed the most upset. "How sorry I am for you guys at the station," said one Japanese-American woman, "and I pray every day that they don't buy in my neighborhood."

Imagine the uproar if the radio host in Chicago pretended his station had been purchased by Africans, then made jokes about the staff being told to carry spears and the cafeteria offering boiled missionary and watermelon. Yet the Japanese-Americans of Hawaii saw themselves as so much American and so little Japanese that instead of protesting the crude racial stereotypes, they seemed more outraged than anyone at the idea of another Hawaiian property fallen to Japanese investors.

Behind the nervous jokes about Japan's buying Hawaii was the belief that for Japan to own so much of the state had somehow rewritten history, challenging the picture of World War II as a morality play in which Japanese treachery was rewarded with suffering and defeat. And if, as many Japanese do, you considered that war as simply a lengthy battle in a century-long competition between America and Japan for control of the Pacific and Asia, then Japan's economic victory in the eighties became as significant as the American military victory of the forties, and one promising more lasting consequences.

The Zeros of the 1980s were the stretch limousines of the Japanese speculators, made sinister by their smoked windows and black-uniformed chauffeurs. They reportedly cruised Kahala, Kailua, and Hawaii Kai, stopping for passengers to photograph a house or approach its occupants with an unsolicited offer. Other Japanese flew over desirable neighborhoods in helicopters, selecting targets from the air. Everyone had a story of friends or neighbors opening their door to face a Japanese with a checkbook, and the offers often came unexpectedly, and at unlikely times, late at night or early in the morning.

Dorothy Bicknell told me about the neighbor of her piano tuner, shown $250,000 in a suitcase by a Japanese gentleman hoping the sight of so much cash would persuade him to sell his house. Dorothy Anthony said Japanese nationals had bought six apartments in her condominium in the last months, in one instance offering $700,000 to a neighbor who had paid $300,000 the year before. Who could resist taking such a profit?

The Admiral Yamamoto of the speculators was Genshiro Kawamoto, ranked among the six richest men in Japan and credited with unlimited resources of cash and cunning. He purchased seventy-eight Oahu homes in four months, closing on twenty-five windward houses in a single day, afterward telling a reporter for the *Boston Globe* that Hawaiian houses were poorly constructed and "lousy, candy houses." He refused to inspect homes unless owners provided a new pair of slippers at the door, and recommended Honolulu change its zoning laws so they more closely resembled those of Japan.

It was said he was behind legislation to prohibit foreigners from buying more real estate, so that his houses would become more valuable. It was feared he would buy radio and television stations "to tell us how to think." Talk-show hosts invited listeners to guess where the "Kawamotomobile," a stretch limousine of legendary proportions, would be seen next, and callers were divided between fearing it and those hoping it would roll to a stop in their driveways.

The obsession with Japanese investment led newspapers, television stations, and magazines to run frequent, sometimes contradictory polls. In one 1990 poll, Hawaiians were asked to reveal whether their feelings toward Japan were "friendly" or "unfriendly." Not surprisingly, the majority said "friendly," but even 36 percent seems rather a lot admitting to being either "not sure" or "unfriendly." A more telling poll found two thirds in agreement with the statement "The sale of land in Hawaii to Japanese investors is the biggest contributor to the high cost of living here." Another poll revealed that only 31 percent of all Hawaiians "trusted the political motives of the Japanese nationals," only 16 percent did not believe Japan wanted to "replace or challenge America as an economic power," and almost half believed "Hawaii is on the verge of becoming a colony of Japan."

I lived in Kailua, a middle-class suburb on the windward coast that is forty miles from downtown Honolulu on a spectacular highway tunneling through the Koolaus. During the seventies and early eighties, Japanese nationals had acquired beachfront properties here without alarming its residents, but in the spring of 1988, they began buying ranch houses on small inland lots. They paid asking prices for houses already listed, making cash offers for others they increased until the seller succumbed.

The first community meeting held on Oahu to discuss what newspapers were describing as "the Japanese Invasion" attracted over a hundred people to the auditorium of Kailua's Maunawili Elementary School. Despite claims that all foreign investment would be discussed, posters listing the names of every Japanese-owned enterprise in Hawaii covered the walls. The atmosphere reminded me of a meeting of campus activists in the sixties. The room was hot, lit by fluorescent bulbs and television lights, and someone shouted, "A people's movement started tonight." Posters described terrifying facts about Japanese investment, such as Hiroshi Kato, economic adviser to the former Japanese Prime Minister Yasushiro Nakasone, saying, "Japan would be glad to purchase some of America's assets. Hawaii, for example!"

The Kailua Neighborhood Board sat at a table facing the audience. We were told that colonies of native Hawaiians were living in forlorn ghettos in West Coast cities, pining for Hawaii but unable to return because of housing costs, that food prices would rise as farmers lost their land to Japanese golf courses, and that Japanese hotel owners were making expensive renovations and would soon raise room rates, pricing mainland tourists out of the market. We listened to fantastic rumors, one being that Japanese investors wanted to create "silver cities" for low-income retirees and would transform Hawaii into a sort of Japanese Miami Beach.

There was panic, and I heard, "If something isn't done soon—now!—it will be too late." "The land will be lost forever in a 'Tokyo loop.' " "It says to our kids: 'Get out of Hawaii!' "

There was anger, directed against Kawamoto for suggesting Hawaii change its zoning laws to accommodate his development programs. A white-haired Japanese-American woman was the most indignant of all, demanding, "How *dare* any foreigner tell us to reduce our lot sizes!"

There was fear Japan would "take over," and fear Hawaii was being abandoned by the mainland, left to suffer this new Japanese onslaught alone.

Mayor Frank Fasi made an appearance, asking for support for a law he was proposing to the state legislature prohibiting the sale of residential, agricultural, or preservation land to anyone not a United States citizen. (It was introduced too late for consideration in 1988, and failed to pass in 1989.) Soon afterward, he sent a letter to property owners warning, "Many of you may be facing increases in your property assessments of 30 percent or more this year due to the impact of overseas investors paying inflated prices for nearby residences."

There were five times as many "For Sale" signs in the expensive Waiailae-Kahala neighborhoods in March 1988 as the year before, yet not once was it suggested by Fasi, or anyone else, that the greed of the Hawaiian sellers should also be blamed, or that community pressure might be used to persuade friends and neighbors not to sell to Japanese speculators. (One reason so little property accumulates in foreign hands in Japan is the shame attaching itself to anyone participating in such a transfer.) Instead, one Kailua board member admitted, with a giggle, "Of course, if someone offered me five million for my house, well, I might sell it." And during a later press conference, Fasi said if someone offered him an outrageous sum for his Makiki home, "I'd be walking to the bank with a check, with mixed emotions."

Here was clear proof that behind the alarmist poster, rumors, and newspaper articles was the same complacency and selfishness that had originally fed the trade and budget deficits, making it possible for the Japanese to buy these Oahu homes. Just as Hawaii residents in 1941 considered a Japanese attack only a theoretical threat, few today really believe Hawaii could become a de facto Japanese possession.

Where before there had been overconfidence, now there was collaboration. Hawaii real estate agents (numerous in a state where one out of every forty-five people has a license) opened offices in Tokyo to sell houses by videocassette, and worried their state might "run out of inventory." None seemed to worry that once they sold a house to a Japanese speculator it might thereafter be resold in Japan, depriving Hawaiian agents of commissions. Instead, they mailed seductive letters, urging property owners, "Sell now!" My neighbor received one of these mailings at least every week. A typical notice, from a Mr. Grunder of Scully Rogers Ltd., announced in large green letters, "YOUR HOME INVE$TMENT: OPPORTUNITY KNOCK$ . . ." Under another headline, "JAPAN BUYER SEEKS WINDWARD HOMES," Mr. Grunder said, "If you have been thinking of selling your home, now may be the time. . . . Our format remains: all cash, no contingencies, closing within thirty days, option to rent back, no signs, no open houses." Cartoons showing the top-hatted banker from the Monopoly game hauling away a sack of cash decorated Mr. Grunder's communication. In encouraging Hawaiians to sell their houses to Japanese speculators, then stay on as tenants, he implied that a seller enjoyed a cash windfall, yet everything remained unchanged. But when a Hawaiian who already worked for a Japanese enterprise sold his home to a Japanese landlord, then stayed on as a tenant, Oahu took another step toward becoming a company town, although when the owners are foreign nationals and when what is owned is an entire island, the more common term for this entity is "colony."

A few days after the Kailua emergency meeting I happened to visit Bob Bekeart, one of Mr. Kawamoto's new neighbors. In

1941 he had been based at Pearl Harbor aboard the destroyer tender *Dobbin*. He had married a native Hawaiian wife and returned to Oahu after the war, living ever since in Portlock, a waterfront neighborhood near Koko Head that is now popular with Japanese buyers. As I arrived, a burglar alarm sounded in a neighboring house belonging to Kawamoto. Seconds later, a representative of Alert Alarm called, promising to send an agent and wanting to know if Bekeart had noticed anything suspicious. For fifteen minutes we shouted over the clanging alarm.

Ever since the Japanese had begun buying houses and leaving them empty, Bekeart said, these alarms had become a nuisance. They shorted and there was no one to turn them off, or they were tripped by the cat burglars who followed Japanese buyers. "I'm surrounded by absentee Japanese," he shouted. "But I won't move. They'll have to take me out of here feet first." When the alarm fell silent he said, "You know, I look after Kawamoto's house, and report when his burglar alarm goes off, but I can't even get an aloha from him or his yardman." He spoke more in sadness than bitterness, smiling as he complained gently about his Japanese neighbors, laughing, shaking his head in amazement to remember how he had underestimated the Japanese on December 7.

He had been off duty, spending the weekend with his wife at their home in Manoa, out of sight of Pearl Harbor. He remembered that after hearing about the attack on the radio, "I went to my room to get ready for war. I said to myself, 'We're going to get these guys and within two months we'll all be marching through Tokyo. It's winter now in Japan, so I should take my heavy raincoat and my Hart Schaffner & Marx warm, double-breasted suit and my brown Stetson.' So I wore the suit, carried my alligator raincoat over my arm, and put everything else into a ditty bag. I was dressing for Tokyo."

He has never again underrated the Japanese, and he believes they will soon own most of his neighborhood, "because

they have great allegiance to brand names," he said, "and Portlock has a reputation as a place for rich haoles, whereas it's
really a place that's making the haoles who leave it rich."

He gave me a tour, pointing out how it had changed in the
last five years. Portlock is a backwater, without traffic or commercial development, and hemmed in by Koko Head, Maunalua Bay, and the Kalanianaole Highway. The most desirable
houses are on the ocean side of Portlock Road, now lined with
the colorful "For Sale" signs of competing real estate agents.
Some of these face Maunalua Bay and have lawns running
down to a seawall and a view west across the water to Diamond Head; others sit just behind them, lacking ocean views
but enjoying access to the water. Bob Bekeart lived in one of
these, and once Mr. Kawamoto's burglar alarm had been si-
lenced, we walked through a gate and across an absentee Japanese owner's lawn to the seawall, from which we could admire
a shoreline containing at least $100 million worth of Japanese
real estate. "There's a three-million-dollar house over there,
and a fourteen-million one down there," Bekeart said, swinging
his arms like a weather vane. "That one went for nine hundred
and ninety-five thousand, and that one belonged to Dolly Par-
ton, but even she sold out."

Sailboats and sampans had once filled this bay. Its waters
were clear, its beaches white and inviting. But in the fifties and
sixties, dredging for the nearby Hawaii Kai development had
turned the sand gray, lining the bottom with soft sludge. Every
day, a concession towed out a floating platform and a flotilla of
jet skis filled it with their insect buzzing. The customers were
mostly tourists from Japan, and several years back one of
Bekeart's daughter's school friends had been run over and killed
by a jet ski while swimming here.

Until recently, these lawns had run together seamlessly,
and neighborhood children played across them. The new owners were erecting walls and fences. There had been a strong

community association and frequent block parties, but participation had dropped off. "We still have a newcomers party," Bekeart said. "But every year fewer people bother to attend. Instead of a place to live, we have become a place to make an investment."

Evidence of this could be seen in the high walls, spotlights, and reflecting glass windows, or heard in the hammering carpenters, malfunctioning burglar alarms, and grinding engines of backhoes and bulldozers. The new owners demolished typically Hawaiian houses with low roofs and deep lanais, or "improved" them into palaces with half-moon windows, circular stairways, and chandeliers. Despite the beach and trade winds, most were now equipped with swimming pools and air conditioning.

We passed a Mediterranean villa busy with workmen. "That used to be a Japanese teahouse," he said. "It was a very pure building, more lovely than a temple." A haole couple in love with Japan had shipped it in pieces from there during the thirties, and its last haole occupants had taken to sitting on futons and wearing kimonos. He said a Japanese speculator, "brainwashed" by *Architectural Digest,* had gutted it and was "preparing it for investors."

We walked toward Koko Head and Mr. Kawamoto's $42 million estate. "That one should sell for three million soon," Bekeart said, pointing to another waterfront house. "Look, they've turned that one into a Moroccan bordello, don't you agree? . . . And that one was owned by a friend who gave great Fourth of July parties. He was tending bar at his party last year when a Japanese man drove up and offered him a million. He said no and a few days later the offer became one point two million. He couldn't resist. He sold, and forty-eight hours later, that Japanese had flipped it to another buyer for one point three million. My friend moved to a condo. He regrets it now, but he can't afford to move back."

Before the war, native Hawaiian families had lived in Port-lock. They were fishermen and squatters lacking legal title, but following a long tradition. The outlines of their fish ponds remained visible, and Bekeart said Hawaiians sometimes set up temporary encampments here. It is easy, and true, to say Ha-waii is the last place haoles should complain about foreigners taking over their land, and easy to see some rough justice in haoles like Bekeart being displaced in turn by the Japanese, and with considerably more compensation than they offered the Hawaiians they chased off this shoreline forty years earlier. Nevertheless, I could not help feeling sorry for Bekeart and his neighbors. They had lived here most of their adult lives, raising children and investing themselves in this once easygoing, slightly bohemian place that would never be that way again.

The day after I visited Portlock, I heard an argument for unlimited foreign investment during a Rotary Club luncheon at the Royal Hawaiian Hotel. The speaker was an investment adviser who held the comforting position that Japanese invest-ment was a racket in which Americans were the winners and Japanese the suckers. The trade deficit simply meant we pur-chased Japanese cars and appliances with dollars the Japanese invested in fixed assets here. We took their cars, and they bought companies and real estate they could not, after all, move to Japan. The geographic location of an asset meant everything, its ownership nothing. It was a large-scale applica-tion of the idea that if you sold your house to the Japanese and continued living in it, meanwhile spending your windfall, noth-ing important had happened. As delusions go, it ranked with Bob Bekeart's packing a suit to wear in Tokyo while outside his window Japanese planes destroyed the American fleet.

Both delusions were animated by a reckless underestima-tion of the Japanese, by imagining, for example, that they could account for almost half of Hawaii's economic activity, own its best commercial and residential properties, and not also put their stamp on the place—lobbying the legislature, seeking changes in zoning laws, and converting agricultural land to more profitable uses, such as golf courses. Instead, it seems to me inevitable that the Japanese will eventually impose their standards on Hawaii for what is too crowded, developed, or expensive. And since by Japanese standards even Oahu is still cheap, uncrowded, and undeveloped, it can only become much less so.

24

"No Can Eat Golf Balls!"

FOR SIX WEEKS AFTER THE ATTACK, NISEI SOLDIERS GUARDED telephone lines, utilities, and reservoirs. There were minor incidents between them and mainland soldiers, and some derogatory comments, such as by the visiting Army officer who asked Hawaii Territorial Guard commander Wilhelm Andersen, within hearing of his men, how he could dare sleep in a place "where these Japs can slit your throat." Yet the niseis were proud of being trusted to bear arms and to defend Oahu from a possible Japanese invasion. But on January 19, Richard Ishimoto, Ted Tsukiyama, and other niseis of a guard unit camped at the Koko Head rifle range were driven back to Schofield Barracks to be discharged. "It was the saddest thing that ever happened to me," Ishimoto remembers. "By taking away our rifles they were saying we could not be trusted."

Ted Tsukiyama remembers, "Our officers gave us a farewell speech and cried. We had Chinese, Hawaiian, and black American officers, and none of them imagined this would happen. [The black officer was Nolle Smith, who according to Tsukiyama was "born and raised here, and never thought of as black."] For me, being discharged because of my race was devastating, more traumatic than learning the Japanese had bombed Pearl Harbor. We could accept the fact by then that Japan was our treacherous enemy. But to have our own country, in its most extreme time of need and danger, repudiate us, that was something more than we could take. To this day, I have difficulty in grasping words in the English language that can adequately and sufficiently describe our feelings. . . . The very bottom had dropped out of our existence."

Ralph Yempuku was dismissed from the Army at the same time. He blamed the new troops from the mainland, who looked at the niseis and saw the enemy in American uniforms. He had overhead one mainland soldier, upon finding nisei troops guarding the waterfront, saying, "Jesus, we're too late. The Japs are here already."

At Pearl Harbor Navy Yard, military policemen rounded up all Japanese workers on December 10 and marched them to the gate. "They made us march double-time," Spud Ishimoto (no relation to Richard Ishimoto) remembers, "even the ladies from the laundry, and you know how hard it is for the ladies to double-time like that. At the main gate they took away our badges, threw them in a wastebasket, and said, 'We don't want to see you Japs around here anymore.' But you figure you can't get mad at them. They're not in their right mind. They don't know what to think of us. They're just hot, hot, hot. They look at my face and see the people who killed their buddies and think, 'Goddam him to hell.' "

The Marine guard at the Pearl Harbor gate pushed Wymo Takaki back into the road with his rifle, saying, "Fucking Jap! You're not going to work here." After tempers had cooled, Takaki found work as a machinist at Wheeler Field, and although the soldiers were kind to him, he says, "I hated hearing the mail calls. When they would read names, and their buddies would shout back, 'killed, killed, he's in the hospital.' Then I felt guilty because these people had been killed because of my ancestors, and because the attack was a surprise."

Instead of feeling bitter at these rude dismissals, niseis like Takaki, Yempuku, and Ishimoto launched a campaign to prove their patriotism that bordered on the fanatical. They purged their lives of anything "Japanesy," making public displays of burning kimonos and language textbooks, destroying so many Japanese documents, photographs, and phonograph records that the Office of War Information later had trouble finding enough for its research and propaganda. They blacked out the Japanese flags in graduation and wedding photographs and pulled Japanese signs off shrines and stores. They stopped speaking Japanese in public and withdrew from local elections, fearing their victory might cause a backlash. In 1942, 250 Japanese even changed their names to Chinese, Hawaiian, Portuguese, and haole ones; the Haraguchis became the Kanekoas, the Jujitas the Ah Hees, and the Nakamuras the McFarlanes.

Young niseis became the authority figures in their families, setting down rules for their parents such as "Don't talk in Japanese," "Don't talk on the telephone, because you don't speak English," and "Don't bow like a Japanese." Niseis took out newspaper advertisements protesting their loyalty. One in the *Honolulu Star Bulletin* said, "You dished it out with a head start by treachery—now we're going to see how you can take it. We're ganging up on you, Tojo, in a way you and your Nazi friends don't understand. . . . Get it Tojo? It isn't the Jap way, the Nazi way, nor the Fascist way. It's the FREE AMERICAN WAY." Every patriotic activity became a test of loyalty the Japanese were determined to win. They wrapped more bandages, dug more public bomb shelters, and bought so many war bonds that in 1942 Hawaii had a per capita purchase rate two to four time the national average.

Japanese students formed a "kiawe corps" to clear kiawe trees from beaches and prevent invading Japanese soldiers from using them as shelter. Japanese community leaders formed the "Emergency Service Committee," whose announced purpose was "to strengthen loyalty to America, demonstrate loyalty with America. . . ." It exhorted Japanese residents with slangy slogans such as "We must take our bumps, keep our chin up. Don't brood or gripe." It arranged for anti-Japanese sayings to be baked into rice cakes, and soon, at tea parties across Honolulu, elderly Japanese were reading, "The chrysanthemum does not prosper in Hawaii" and "The sun rises but always sets."

It was stirring, touching, and sometimes too much. Japanese launched a special drive to buy a bomber to attack Tokyo. In 1943, seventeen hundred Japanese contributed $10,340 to a fund for buying bombs to "drop on Tokyo." While presenting the check to the commander of the Hawaiian Department, one of its organizers declared, "We're real Americans and we're going to act and fight like Americans. We hope that this money will be used for bombs which will give Tojo and his cutthroats bloody hell."

When Masao Akiyama, a nisei who had studied in Japan, refused induction into the Army in 1944, admitting he could not be "100 percent American" because his "mind" was with Japan, the Japanese community disowned him. Dr. Ernest Murai, chairman of the Emergency Service Committee, said, "His action is contemptible and an insult to the rest of us. . . . It is a dirty slap in the face. . . . We doubt that there are many others like Akiyama waiting to be discovered. But if there are . . . it will be the job of all of us to smoke them out."

Seiko Ogai submitted a patriotic essay titled "Am I Haole?" to a competition sponsored by the regional director of the Office of War Information in Honolulu. It related the experiences of a brother then serving in the Army in Europe, describing him as "about as American as a bottle of soda water" and telling how, as a boy, he had been proud of "his wallet with pictures of Caucasian and Hawaiian girls, not an Oriental face in the group." Ogai had written a covering letter addressed "Dear Judges," declaring, "I do not especially want any of the prizes, but I did want . . . to let others know that a Jap is not necessarily a Jap." His essay won first prize.

Despite their humiliating dismissal from the Territorial Guard, the niseis campaigned to be allowed to serve in the armed forces. Within a month of being stripped of their weapons, Yempuku, Tsukiyama, and other former ROTC and Territorial Guard soldiers had formed an all-nisei labor battalion they called the Varsity Victory Volunteers. It worked for eleven months at Schofield Barracks quarrying rock and constructing roads and military installations.

Many nisei personnel in the 298th and 299th Infantry Regiments, which had been federalized before the attack, were permitted to remain in the Army, as were nisei serving in an engineering construction battalion. In June 1942, Japanese personnel from these units were sent to the mainland for training and consolidated into the 100th Infantry Battalion, which fought with distinction in the early days of the Italian campaign, taking high casualties, earning numerous battle citations, and earning the nickname "Purple Heart Battalion."

The exemplary record of the 100th, combined with lobbying efforts in Hawaii, persuaded the War Department to raise an all-nisei unit to fight in Europe. In January 1943 a call for fifteen hundred volunteers was answered by 9,507 Hawaiian niseis. About 2,500 of these were combined with a smaller number of mainland Japanese to form the all-Japanese 442d Regimental Combat Team, which absorbed survivors of the 100th Battalion on arrival in Italy. It fought until the end of the war in the Italian, French, and German campaigns, coining the slogan "Go for Broke!" and becoming the most decorated unit in United States military history.

The 442d RCT was also the most written-about and

praised military unit of the war. In fewer than three years, the "Go for Broke" myth of the nisei soldier as superhuman fighter and superpatriot replaced the myth of the treacherous Japanese-American fifth-columnist. Particular attention was given to the exploits of the 442d in Hawaii, where the unit increased the standing and self-esteem of the Japanese community. Compare, for example, the expulsion of the Japanese from the Territorial Guard in 1942 with the official 1944 *Army Pocket Guide to Hawaii,* which was provided every serviceman upon arrival in the Islands and advised, "In 1941 there were 157,990 people of Japanese descent here. That means that 34 out of every 100 civilians were Japanese. Now get this straight. Most of them went to American schools. They learned to pledge allegiance to the same flag you salute. They like American soft drinks. And one of their favorite radio comedians is Bob Hope. They're Americans."

The sacrifices of the nisei soldiers discredited earlier attacks on Japanese loyalty and made anti-Japanese racism unseemly. They gave the Japanese community a strong claim on Hawaii's future prosperity at a time when martial law and immigration from the mainland had weakened the power of the haole oligarchy. A direct line can be drawn from the war record of the 442d RCT to the postwar defeat of the Republican Party in Hawaii, the rise of labor unions, statehood in 1959, and the considerable economic and political successes of the niseis and their children.

The Japanese did not fight only in Europe. Many of the niseis I met were in the Pacific war, which they were credited with having "shortened by two years" by the Army's chief intelligence officer. Nisei intelligence agents served from the Battle of Guadalcanal until the Japanese surrender, interviewing prisoners, infiltrating the enemy's lines, and translating radio communications. They worked alone, scattered among battalions, and without the camaraderie and reinforcement of an all-Japanese unit. Like the Indian scouts employed by the cavalry in the West, they ran unique risks. To prevent them from being mistaken for the enemy, many were assigned American "bodyguards." To reduce their military appearance, they sometimes wore civilian shirts over their uniforms. They worried that if captured they would be tortured and executed as traitors, and that they might find themselves interrogating or shooting relatives serving in the Japanese army.

Ralph Yempuku did everything possible to prove his patriotism, though it put him on the opposite side from his four brothers serving with the Japanese forces. After being denied induction into the 442d RCT, because of an injured knee, he begged to take the six-week Ranger training course at Schofield as a civilian. After passing, he was sent to Fort Benning, Georgia, where he was one of three nisei volunteering for intelligence work with the OSS (Office of Strategic Services), making it a virtual certainty he would fight the Japanese.

He parachuted behind enemy lines in Burma and organized hill tribes into partisan bands that ambushed Japanese convoys. He often thought, "What will I do if my brother is in that convoy? What if my brother is one of the prisoners I have to interrogate?" He finally told himself, "If one of my brothers should be caught in an ambush, he would be caught in an ambush, that's all." Later, he and his brother Donald crossed paths at the surrender ceremony in Hong Kong, proving the possibility of the tragic coincidence feared by many niseis.

He supported the decision to drop the atomic bomb, although his parents lived near Hiroshima and could have been killed. After the war, serving with the occupation Counterintelligence Corps, he went there to search for them. His first visit convinced him his parents had not survived. But he returned, forcing himself to walk into the ruined city and learning that Atata-shima, where they lived, was on an island distant from the city center. There he finally found them. They had believed all the Japanese in Hawaii had been slaughtered after Pearl Harbor, and were equally astounded to see him alive.

Richard Ishimoto served as an interpreter in New Guinea, where he was followed everywhere, even into the latrine, by a counterintelligence officer who was part of a War Department program checking on nisei loyalty. "What still bitches me the most," he says, "is that haole officers never promoted me, never credited me for the Japanese who surrendered, even though I had written the leaflets persuading them to do it. I really wanted to become an officer. It was my dream."

Ted Tsukiyama, who became an interpreter for the Tenth Air Force in Burma, remained so angry over Pearl Harbor he still "wanted to kick the first Japanese I met in the balls." He persuaded another nisei interpreter to let him into a prison stockade. "I wanted revenge," he said, "but they were not the arrogant supermen I had imagined, just meek and downtrodden, beaten dogs. The desire I had to kick them disappeared. I thought the war must have been someone else's making, because those guys sure didn't look as if they'd done it."

Wymo Takaki says he "wanted to enlist in the worst way," because he believed Pearl Harbor was really "a lucky accident for the niseis. In the past, we were accused of being disloyal, and finally we were given this golden opportunity to prove our patriotism." He failed the physical for the 442d RCT, and his Japanese was so poor he flunked the test for nisei interpreters. He persuaded the recruiting officer to take him by saying, "I was strafed in Pearl Harbor and I'm still angry. It's my battle." He arrived in Japan after the surrender, in time to fight one of the first intelligence battles of the Cold War. He was ordered to interview Japanese POWs returning from Soviet prison camps in Siberia, searching for ones recruited as "sleeper" intelligence agents by the NKVD. He made a career of Army intelligence, serving seven years in Japan, marrying a Japanese woman, returning to Japan as an undercover operative in civilian clothes, and volunteering to fight in Korea first as a frogman, then as a parachutist—anything to see combat and demonstrate his patriotism.

He volunteered for Vietnam after being shocked by the stories of draft evaders fleeing to Canada, and because "for me, my country always comes first." He was sent undercover, sometimes posing as an agricultural specialist or a Chinese-American or Japanese businessman. His friends in the Japanese community proved excellent sources of information because the Vietcong held the Japanese in such high regard. After World War Two, three hundred Japanese soldiers had stayed in North Vietnam, unable to bear the humiliation of returning home. They fought for the Vietminh against the French, suffering heavy casualties and earning the respect of Ho Chi Minh. A residue of pro-Japanese feeling among the Vietcong made it easy for Japanese to travel through Vietcong territory, and Takaki remembers many of them having flag stands on their cars, "and whenever there was danger you could see all these Japanese businessmen and technical advisers racing around with their jeeps flying Japanese flags. Here were American GIs dying, and these guys were being protected by that flag. Oh, I was displeased with that."

He had cultivated a former Japanese soldier who had become a prosperous South Vietnamese businessman with close ties to the Vietcong. The Tet offensive caught him in the rural town of Vung Tao, forcing him to hitch a ride back to Saigon with this man. Intense firing stopped them just outside Saigon. The businessman ordered his chauffeur to put a Japanese flag on a pipe attached to the car's bumper. Takaki heard gunfire and mortars, and saw the Japanese flag, framed by explosions. "I was under fire again, like at Pearl Harbor, and seeing the Japanese flag," he says. "I started screaming, 'Hey! I don't want to be protected by this flag! I was at Pearl Harbor, I can't forgive the Japanese. Let me out!'" He tried to jump from the car, but the businessman restrained him until the flashback was over. But he still feels guilty about permitting himself to be saved by this "enemy flag."

When I arrived in Hawaii I assumed that Takaki's generation of niseis would have forgiven Japan for Pearl Harbor. I imagined them as a bridge between Hawaii and Japan, cultural intermediaries and, like other hyphenated Americans, sympathetic to their country of ancestry. I first began to doubt this at a meeting of the executive committee of the MISLS (Military Intelligence Service Language School) veterans association. This is an organization of Hawaiian niseis who, prior to serving in the Pacific, had attended language school together on the mainland, a necessity since none of them knew Japanese well enough to become interpreters immediately.

The MISLS veterans reminisced about the "good old days up on the CBI [China-Burma-India] border," traded playful punches to each other's stomachs, and joked over golf scores. They popped open beers and apologized to me for a "light agenda" consisting mostly of opening their junk mail. The main event was a brief speech by a member of a Japanese-American group that hoped to build a Japanese cultural center in Honolulu. He wanted the veterans to make individual donations to it and consider pledging a more substantial gift from their endowment. This sounded like a rather good final destination for the money, and I was surprised most of them seemed hostile to the idea. After some rough questioning, the cultural center man finally conceded many of the center's visitors would be Japanese tourists, and there were no plans to charge admission. This news was received coolly. Clearly, they were viewing the decision as "Should we donate the endowment of a World War Two veterans' association to construct what will essentially be a free tourist attraction for citizens of the former enemy nation?"

*   *   *

No Hawaiian ethnic group is more touchy about Japanese tourists, real estate speculators, and the growing influence of Japan on island affairs than the Pearl Harbor generation of niseis.

Seiyei Wakukawa agreed with Mayor Fasi that Japanese "land rollers" should be controlled. Sue Isonaga said, "We feel it's an invasion, and that they're ruining things for the local people. It's just gone too far." Ted Tsukiyama was "uncomfortable among the Japanese from Japan" and felt "foreign" among them. The wife of an AJA war veteran who taught Japanese exchange students at the university complained they were "loud, rude, and come from rich families that throw their money around." Even the Fukuda sisters did not mind a little "Japan-bashing," saying, "We need legislation. It's terrible that foreigners can buy up our property."

Earl Nishimura told me, "Every acre of our land is precious"—it should be "preserved for our grandchildren, not for Japanese golf courses." He was angry at the Japanese for being so ungrateful. "They have forgotten how good we were as occupiers," he said. "We never asked for reparations, and just imagine what might have happened had they been occupied by the Soviet Union."

Edwin Kawahara wanted me to know his wartime Japanese language courses had not made him pro-Japanese. "I enjoy my Japanese," he said, "but as any other American would enjoy speaking another language and understanding another country's culture." He had visited Japan, considering it "a nice place to visit but I wouldn't want to live there. We are considered foreigners, and they are not nice to us." His profession did not help. He is an insurance agent, "and they are rather low on the totem pole there, so whenever Japanese people come here and do business with me they make me feel inferior."

Attorney Wallace Fujiyama, who was accompanying his father's baseball team over the Pali Highway on December 7, sometimes represents Japanese investors. He thinks most of the larger Japanese corporations have acted responsibly, but accuses the recent wave of speculators of flaunting their money, failing to hire local residents, breaking their word, and being rude to the Hawaiian Japanese. "We are still just a bunch of farmers to them," he says, "and they look down on us as uncouth." The more he spoke about boorish Japanese investors, the angrier he became. "We get some bad ones," he said. "Guys who've owned some noodle shops or used-car dealerships. They're not accepted in Japan so they come to make a big name for themselves here, although they don't know the language or customs, and are without social graces."

It can be difficult listening to the Japanese of Hawaii damn Japanese nationals without letting on you find it somewhat surprising or ironic. But by doing so, you imply they should react to Japan differently from other Americans, precisely the misconception they struggled against during the war. In 1941, it was feared Japanese-Americans in the Hawaii Territorial Guard could not be trusted to fight Japanese invaders. Now it is sometimes assumed they might be less opposed to the colonization of Hawaii by foreign Japanese. Perhaps I made an offhand comment in this regard, or perhaps it was an expression on my face that prompted Mr. Fujiyama to crank up his Japan-bashing and say, "We don't need Johnny-come-latelies with cash to run everything here. The postwar Japanese businessman has picked up some bad Western habits. As far as I'm concerned we should get a big bulldozer and bulldoze them into the ocean!"

Behind his anger was fear the foreign Japanese would encourage a new round of anti-Japanese prejudice. "These Japanese don't understand what they're doing to me and other niseis," he said. "They don't understand the sacrifices we made during the war. We worked hard to have our place in the sun and nobody says to me now, 'Hey, boy, cut my grass,' 'Park my car.' But now they're rocking the boat for all of us."

Tadeo Fuchikami, the RCA messenger entrusted with the last warning from Washington, lives in a weathered bungalow in the same Kalihi neighborhood through which he rode delivering telegrams on December 7. No one had asked him about Pearl Harbor in two decades, and he seemed happy to give me a few hours. His last moment of fame had come in 1966, when he was hired as a technical consultant for *Tora! Tora! Tora!* and taught the young nisei playing him how to ride an antique motorcycle. Now, in his retirement, he can indulge his passion for golf. He was honest about his love for this sport, too honest really, considering his wife was bustling around the kitchen and could hear him announce, "Golf is the thing that gives my life meaning. It keeps me alive . . . it's my life now."

When not playing golf, he makes sculptures out of coat hangers and golf balls he finds in the weeds bordering Honolulu's public courses. His sitting room is filled with wire stick men with golf-ball bellies that double as coaster racks, and cats with golf-ball bodies and pink plastic hair whose wire arms hold notepads and digital clocks. They are much in demand, he says, and his friends take them to hospitals to cheer the sick. In concept they are middle-class American, but in execution—in their delicate legs, tiny clocks, and clothespin noses—they are unmistakably Japanese.

In 1941, Fuchikami had been a skilled plumber, not a messenger boy, but an appendix operation kept him from practicing his trade for several months and he passed time delivering telegrams. He insisted if only General Marshall's last warning had been marked "Urgent," he would have rushed it to Fort Shafter on a special run. Had it even been marked "Priority," he would have gone there first. Instead, there was nothing distinguishing it from happy-birthday or anniversary cables, so he followed his usual route. It was not until several days later, when FBI agents accused him of having intentionally delayed its delivery, that he suspected it was important, and not until the early fifties that he learned its contents. "Hey, when I first heard about that, I felt really bad," he said, putting his hands behind his head and rocking backward in a leather recliner built for American men three times his size. "I wished I could have had the message sooner. Then I would have warned people, and I might have been a national hero. For a while, I thought that Day of Infamy might have been my fault. Then I realized that I was just one of the sands of time."

I had no doubt the national hero Mr. Fuchikami wished to have been was an American one, celebrated for delivering a message that sent hundreds of Japanese to their deaths. Nor did I doubt that when he saw Japanese tourists, he saw foreigners, and when he saw families of blond Californians, he saw fellow Americans. If I shut my eyes and listened, I heard an American; if I opened them, I saw a Japanese. When Mr. Fuchikami finally shot out of that leather lounger like a missile, and with a cruel smile on his face said, "I'm all for the USA whipping their asses," I was sure he really did want the USA to whip some Japanese asses. But I still could not help thinking, "But Mr. Fuchikami, *you're* Japanese!"

The Japanese asses he wanted whipped did not belong to the Pearl Harbor pilots, but the to Japanese businessmen who were buying Japanese's golf courses. In Japan, membership to a top-rated country club can cost as much as $3.5 million. Golf club memberships are negotiable instruments, and there is a market in them. There is also considerable opposition to new course construction by the Japanese public and environmental groups, who charge that chemicals used on greens are dangerous pollutants and that courses make the landscape "less Japanese." Six Japanese prefectures have recently instituted regulations banning or restricting new golf course development.

This explains why Japanese will happily pay $150,000 for

an "international" membership card to the Honolulu Country Club, and why two Japanese businessmen tried buying their way into the prestigious Waialae Country Club by pledging $1 million in donations to local charities. (Their applications were rejected anyway.) It is also why Japanese interests have come to own nineteen of the thirty-six nonpublic courses on Oahu (and have sharply increased their greens fees), why there are thirteen new courses under construction or near completion in Hawaii, and why forty more are proposed (if they are approved, 80 percent of Hawaii's improved recreational land will be tied up in golf courses, most of them Japanese-owned). All of which is more proof of an evolving colonial relationship between Hawaii and Japan. Colonialists often use a colony as a place to indulge in activities that are dangerous, expensive, or forbidden in the metropole, and so Japanese tourists shoot assault rifles in Oahu firing ranges, drive Japanese-made jet skis, whose use is severely restricted in Japan, and play golf on courses that bring Hawaii environmental problems and certainly make its landscape "less Hawaiian."

Local golfers in Oahu now complain of waiting while Japanese tourists are placed ahead of them on Japanese-owned courses, and they see the sudden increases in monthly club dues as a conspiracy to force them to resign, so their memberships can be sold in Japan for ten times the price. Many golf course protestors are Japanese-Americans, and in one celebrated case, a Japanese-American doctor on the board of governors of the Honolulu Country Club was removed following a public confrontation with the club's new Japanese owner.

Tenant farmers have protested their eviction from agricultural land bought by Japanese golf course speculators. The most celebrated recent case involved farmers Ryoie and Nancy Higa, whose supporters coined the slogan "You can eat vegetables but you no can eat golf balls"—soon shortened to "No can eat golf balls!" The Higas received an eviction notice from their new Tokyo-based Japanese landlord, Sanjiro Nakade, dated December 7, 1987, a circumstance the Waianae Farmers Ag-Water and Land Use Concerns Committee described as an "anniversary present from Japan." Their reply to Nakade said, "Sanjiro Nakade—In Hawaii, we eat vegetables, not golf balls. . . . You are trying to do with money what Imperial Japan failed [to do] with bombs in 1941. Be forewarned: Whoever spreads seeds of misery reaps bitter fruit."

Mr. Fuchikami could not afford a country club membership, but the Japanese golf invasion still affected him. "I used to treat myself to the private courses, and I enjoyed playing Makaha East," he said. "But now the Japs have raised the greens fee for outsiders to almost a hundred dollars, we poor retirees have no hope to play there—maybe once a year if you're lucky and someone treats you." The Japanese had further ruined his hobby by buying up so many private courses that mainland tourists now crowded municipal courses. This was why, he believed, " 'Japs' money is . . . bad for golfers," and why he was all for "the USA whipping their asses again."

The Japanese occupation of Oahu's golf courses was particularly galling for Fuchikami, since he had served with the American occupation forces in Japan, where he learned golf from his commanding officer. He remembered the Japanese civilians as a pitiful lot. "They were hard up, man, and for many people in the streets I was the first American soldier they had ever seen," he said. "They were always curious about our jeeps. They just loved them and now they copy them. Boy! Now the shoe sure is on the other foot." He shook his head and looked close to tears. "I just can't understand how this has happened."

On his face was an expression I had seen on other niseis of his generation, a look of betrayal. These men had chosen the United States, remaining loyal despite the racist rumors, conflicts with their parents, and humiliations visited upon them following Pearl Harbor. Now, in their retirement, they had to watch as the enemy who caused them such embarrassment and suffering, and whom they had helped to defeat at great personal sacrifice, bought all the golf courses and best houses, evicted them from farms, and perhaps touched off a second wave of anti-Japanese prejudice.

To answer Fuchikami's question about how this had happened you only had to look at his own living room, and its wall of Japanese electronics. He had an elaborate stereo system with miniature speakers hidden around the room, pumping out the slushy French love songs he liked. He had two videocassette recorders and two large-screen televisions with earphones so he and his wife could watch different programs. As my eyes hopped from Sony to Hitachi to Sanyo, he gave a sheepish grin and, proving he really was "100 percent American," gave the excuse all of us use to explain such purchases. "You know, I would really *like* to 'Buy American,' " he said. "But the quality . . ."

At first I considered Fuchikami an eccentric, touched by his love of golf. Even the Pearl Harbor Survivors were not suggesting "another good smack" for the Japanese. But then I met Ralph Yempuku. Since leaving the wartime OSS he has become a successful impresario, depending on Japan for much of his business, promoting foreign circus acts and sumo wrestling there and booking shows into Honolulu's Blaisdell Arena, where I met him in a windowless office papered with posters of his blubbery sumo stars.

I had already read that on the twenty-fifth anniversary of Pearl Harbor, he had not changed his mind about the atomic bomb, telling the *Honolulu Star-Bulletin,* "The blast was destructive but it had to be done. . . . I feel it was the only way to end the war." In 1966, he had said that the sacrifices made by niseis had been worthwhile, including the risk he took of killing his own brothers. "Today, our children don't face any of that business of not feeling one hundred percent trusted as the nisei felt before the war and especially in the early part of the war," he had said. "That is why I felt the nisei boys who died didn't die in vain. They made a helluva lot possible for coming generations."

Now he was not so sure. He told me, "I think that the majority of all the people like me who served in the war felt that we have been, well, not 'cheated'—that is too harsh a word—but as far as this thing with the Japanese has been concerned that we have been sold down the river by our government." The "thing" with the Japanese was their purchase of Hawaiian real estate, and if Yempuku felt "betrayed," it was because he had chosen the United States, and now the Japanese were "buying it out from under me," he said.

"I jump over all those years from Pearl Harbor to today," he said, "and I find myself getting the same feelings about the Japanese who are coming over here to Hawaii, taking over the hotels and putting their money into everything."

He leaned across his desk and lowered his voice. "Most of my friends are local Hawaiians. I go out with them every day, and they are beginning to talk about the Japanese. They say, 'Hey, what the hell are these Japanese up to? They're buying here and there, making golf clubs, this and that. You know? Taking our land away.' And one of them, maybe it was a slip of the tongue, said, 'Hey! What the hell are *you* Japanese doing?' I don't think he really meant it, but it made me uncomfortable, made me ashamed again of being Japanese. It gave me a shiver, you know?"

Just remembering this comment made him angry. "Between you and me," he said, "you cannot trust a Japanese farther than you can spit. They proved this between 1931 and 1941, they proved it during the war, and they're proving it now. They will talk nice to you and they will bring gifts—this is their custom, you know, the first time they give you a Seiko watch, allow you to think, 'Hey! This guy must be all right.' And then, before you know it, you've got this knife in the back. This is what happened at Pearl Harbor and it's happening again."

He had the usual complaints about the Japanese, the same ones I heard from other Hawaiians. They were causing taxes to rise, and inflating housing costs. Soon his children and grand-children might have to live on the mainland. There was no reciprocity. As an American he could not buy land in Tokyo, and one of his sumo stars had been prevented from managing his own stable of wrestlers because he was not Japanese.

He mistook the expression on my face for skepticism, slammed his hand down hard, and said, "Thurston, don't you ever lose sight of the fact the Japanese of today are the same kind of Japs that were in Japan in 1941. Just because they bow and bring you gifts you [and by "you" he had to mean "You dumb mainland haoles"] think: 'Well, the Japs have changed from the arrogant militarists who ran Japan and started these wars and bombed Pearl Harbor.' No! This is the same mistake our government is making. I say this: *They are the same Jap-anese*. Give them time, another fifteen years, and they will do the same thing they did in 1941. Our government is doing nothing about this, and my grandchildren will suffer for it."

It had not been skepticism he had seen, but amazement at these echoes of 1941. Again Hawaiians believed themselves menaced by Japan, and again the Japanese of Hawaii were making strident speeches and extravagant gestures, second to none in their denunciation of the enemy. His denunciation of Japanese duplicity—"Just because they bow and bring gifts"— reminded me of the essay by the Army wife in the Hawaii War Records Depository that described polite Japanese smiles as "masks of deceit."

The worry expressed by Ralph Yempuku and Wallace Fu-jiyama that foreign Japanese investment will trigger a resurgence of post–Pearl Harbor–style racism seems excessive. The exploits of the 442d RCT, the state's large number of interracial marriages, and the simple fact that minorities like the Japanese are the majority all make them less vulnerable than mainland Japanese-Americans. Nevertheless, this war generation is nervous. A recent newspaper article described Japan-bashing as stirring up "uneasy memories of what happened during World War II," and Albert Misayo, a former aide to Hawaii's first Japanese governor, George Ariyoshi, has expressed a "small fear" that "newcomers to Hawaii," not understanding Hawaii's tradition of racial tolerance or the dynamics of its different groups, will "lump us all together." This happened to him in 1989, when a visiting admiral believed him to be a Japanese national. The fact that the AJAs of Hawaii so fear being mistaken for foreign Japanese gives you a truer idea of how unpopular such Japanese are than all the polls inviting people to admit to "unfriendly" feelings.

For thirty-five years, Richard Ishimoto has lived in Black Point, a thumb of land pushing into the Pacific from the back side of Diamond Head. It was once a laid-back neighborhood of breezy ranch houses, but is now the most expensive and desirable neighborhood on Oahu. For statistical purposes it is usually included with the larger Kahala neighborhood to its east, where in the first three months of 1990, fifty-four homes changed hands at an average price of $900,000. According to Ishimoto, the Black Point average is much higher, in the $2 million to $3 million range. The neighborhood now has two kinds of houses—the new concrete villas of the absentee foreign Japanese and the simple wooden bungalows of the locals. It is only a matter of time, perhaps less than a decade, before the remainder of these are purchased by Japanese investors for astronomical sums, torn down, and replaced.

Ishimoto says his house will be the last to go. He lives one lot back from the ocean in a typical island bungalow with tanks of tropical fish, linoleum floors, and a breezy parlor opening onto a screened porch. Until two years before, he had a sweeping view of a beach so secluded and lovely it was often used as a backdrop for movies and television programs such as *Hawaii Five-O*. Look in the same direction now and you see the concrete wall and locked and shuttered windows of a new $5 million beachfront house bought six months ago by a Japanese family who have yet to use it. If they are like his other absentee neighbors, they will show up twice a year and stay a week or two each time. Theirs is one of six villas jammed together on a lot that once contained houses like Ishimoto's. "Before, I had neighbors, breezes, and a view of the ocean," he says. "Now I have higher taxes." Because of this development and ones like it, the value of his house has increased by $240,000 in two years, and his property taxes have risen accordingly. He had hoped to leave the house to his son, but taxes will force his son to sell it. In the meantime, to afford the increased property taxes, Ishimoto has had to take a second job, as caretaker and general handyman for his new Japanese neighbors.

He sees the irony in this, and it does not please him. He shook the keys to his neighbors' houses in my face, saying, "We're supposed to be the victors, the conquerors, and I do their yard work."

He took me on a tour. He unlocked first a gate, then an automatic door that slid back across the driveway. Inside, six concrete bunkers attached to central air conditioning units were grouped around an aggressively watered lawn. "Take a look!" he said. "Do these look like houses? No! They're battleships."

Except for a Filipino maid cleaning patio furniture, the grounds were deserted. "You see any activity?" he asked. "None!" Shades were drawn and the one-way windows had a brown tint. Spotlights and floodlights were built into roofs and walls. They clicked on every evening at sunset, flooding the lawn, beach, and ocean with light and terrifying the fish.

"This used to be a paradise for fishing," he said. "I caught squid to eat at New Year, twenty-five lobster at a time. Oh, I had the knack."

We walked to the beach and he swept his arm north toward the Black Point lighthouse. "Before this was a carpet of green. Now it's brown—brown grass, brown algae. There's no crab, no fish, nothing, it's like a ghost town because rich people flush their fertilizers and swimming-pool chlorine into the ocean. I got rid of my fishing nets at a swap meet."

We looked down the coast to the other Japanese beachfront mansions, lined up like luxury cabin cruisers at a marina. He could recite the price of each one, and when it had been built, replacing a Hawaiian "tear-down." "They don't give a damn for us," he said, speaking with the bitterness of a man who once fought them at such risk. "See how they've blocked everyone's view? They only think about themselves. Let's face it. They won the economic war, and now we're working for them."

PART FOUR

1990

25

"Now We're an American City"

"THE DAY I ARRIVED IN HAWAII WAS THE DAY I VOWED NEVER to leave," Dorothy Bicknell said. "I came in 1936, aboard the *Lurline,* and the moment I saw people climbing aboard from the pilot boat, carrying armfuls of flower leis, with their overpowering fragrance, I knew I wanted to stay forever."

Eva Marie Judd said, "As soon as I stepped off the boat, I told myself, 'This is it!' I was attracted by the racial mixture and physical beauty."

Dorothy Anthony had come with her husband, just days after their wedding and his graduation from Harvard Law School, "because it seemed like a madcap, exotic idea to live here." She was taken by the open trolley cars that traveled out to Waikiki, and "the little Chinese ladies in black pearls, dripping jade, driving these big cars at a time when it was unusual to see a woman behind the wheel on the mainland."

"It was the most glamorous place," Mary Ellen Lawrence remembered. "I think it was the colonial atmosphere, and the way it smelled, with flowers everywhere, Chinatown being so exotic, and then driving to Wheeler through miles of empty pineapple fields. I was just struck dumb by Hawaii."

I did not solicit these similar statements with questions about their first memories of Hawaii. They came out in conversation because there was a connection in their minds between prewar Honolulu and Pearl Harbor, between the romantic city that bewitched them and the event setting in motion the forces that destroyed it.

Prewar Hawaii has been variously described as "a polite tyranny," a place of "benevolent paternalism," or a "tough little oligarchy." It was ruled by the descendants of the nineteenth-century New England missionaries who had come to control its political, economic, and social life through their positions in the "Big Five"—former sugar trading houses, or "factors," which occupied five granite buildings a shadow's reach from one another in downtown Honolulu. By 1941, the Big Five enjoyed a monopoly on Hawaii's agriculture, transportation, trade, and communications, and the haole oligarchy had secured its grip on Hawaii through interlocking directorates. Consider, for example, Castle & Cooke, the Big Five company whose Matson Lines controlled 98 percent of the shipping between Hawaii and the mainland in 1941. In that year, a Castle was president of the Honolulu Gas Company, a Cooke was president of the Hawaiian Electric Company, and another Castle headed the Honolulu Rapid Transit Company.

The December 7 declaration of martial law finished Big Five control of Hawaii at a stroke, accomplishing in a day what might otherwise have taken years of economic and social evolution and ending the colonial system as surely as the Japanese occupation had the British, Dutch, and American regimes in Southeast Asia. This shift in power was symbolized on the morning after the attack when the Corps of Engineers requisitioned Punahou School for its headquarters, making office space by throwing students' chairs and textbooks out of the windows of the institution that had educated generations of Hawaii's elite, and most of the Big Five's directors.

The military government of Hawaii immediately assumed all legislative, judicial, and executive power. It seized control of all land and maritime transportation, fixed prices, set wages, awarded defense contracts (often to mainland firms), censored the press, abolished civilian courts, and regulated everything from bowling alleys, rent, and garbage collection to prostitution, gasoline sales, firearms, and water chlorination. It facilitated the entry of war workers and mainland capital, which for the Big Five meant labor organizers and business competitors. Although Army rule was profoundly undemocratic, it presided over changes that made the resumption of the prewar oligarchy impossible. The Hawaii it returned to civilian rule in October 1944 was far more populous, wealthy, and cosmopolitan than the one it took over on December 7, 1941.

After the war, a generation of niseis, native Hawaiians, and Filipinos returned from the armed forces unwilling to tolerate a resumption of Big Five paternalism. They and the new mainland immigrants joined the Democratic Party and organized labor unions. Racial barriers in employment ended, mainland firms entered Hawaiian economic life, and the Asian population, led by the Japanese, gained increasing economic and political power. But although Hawaii was undergoing these profound changes throughout the 1950s, Honolulu looked much as it had in 1941. There were no skyscrapers, no suburban developments at Hawaii Kai or Pearlridge, and no H-1 Freeway. But the social changes prepared the way for the physical transformation that began in 1959, with statehood and the start of passenger jet service to the mainland triggering construction and tourist booms that continue today. These have brought to Oahu 7.5 million square feet of downtown office space and a skyscraper resort at Waikiki. Even without Pearl Harbor and martial law, the Big Five monopoly position would eventually have eroded, jet aircraft would have revolutionized the tourist industry, and agricultural production would have declined. But the changes would have been less dramatic, more evolutionary than revolutionary, and less of a shock to Hawaii's unique culture and environment, and to residents with memories as long as Dorothy Bicknell, Eva Marie Judd, Dorothy Anthony, and Mary Ellen Lawrence.

Dorothy Bicknell is confined to a wheelchair and has not traveled from her windward home to Honolulu in several years, which is fine with her. By not seeing it now, she said, "I never see what's missing. The last time I went to Waikiki, well, I might as well have been in Florida."

Eva Marie Judd lives three miles from the coast, in the same Maunalani Heights home from which she witnessed the attack. From her windows, Waikiki resembles a concrete dam, blocking views of the ocean. On December 7, she saw shells splashing in the Pacific; now she sees the smog that gathers over the city whenever it is locked in a so-called kona weather pattern, with rain-bearing winds from the south and southwest. "Once the war was over, everything changed," she said. "Now Waikiki turns me off, and I only go once or twice a year, when I absolutely must."

Mary Ellen and Wells Lawrence live in a condominium high rise within sight of the church where they were married and the school where he taught mathematics for twenty-five years. Their Makiki Heights neighborhood is a densely populated, unplanned jumble of cottages and condominiums that have progressively stolen one another's mountain and ocean views. They agree they would not now choose to settle in Honolulu for its atmosphere and natural beauty. "In the past twenty-five years, it has become like any other city," she said, "with all the traffic jams and chicanery. And we never had these sweltering summers before. I think the big buildings are blocking the flow of the trade winds."

"So many trees have disappeared," he said, "the weather is definitely changing, becoming hotter. There is less shade, less green, and more asphalt. I can see why tourists would still love the place, but for residents it's gotten much worse for everyday living."

"Sometimes we go to the Royal [Hawaiian Hotel] to remind ourselves what it was like," she said. "It's still pretty nice, but not the romantic and glamorous place it was."

Dorothy Anthony lives a block from the Lawrences in a condominium building with the marble walls, concrete waterfalls, security systems, and other "amenities" now expected of hotels, cruise liners, and office "plazas." The building's distinguishing feature is that the Manoa Stream, once celebrated by travel writers for its beauty and wild tropical flowers, runs through a concrete sluice bordering the lobby. From her seventh-floor apartment, she pointed to roofs climbing the bulldozer-flattened slopes of the nearby Koolaus and to Punahou School across the street, its once-spacious grounds crowded with new buildings and said, "I don't like what Honolulu has become." She is a mile from Waikiki, but has not gone there for years. "If I was arriving now," she said, "other than the beautiful skies and ocean, I don't think I'd be as taken with Honolulu. Now we're an American city, hardly different from those on the mainland."

Complaints like these are motivated by more than nostalgia for Hawaii's prewar colonial system. Instead, these people fear the loss of exactly what had attracted them in the first place and continues drawing visitors and immigrants, Oahu's exceptional natural beauty. Every kamaaina I met of the Pearl Harbor generation voiced similar sentiments. Cy Gillette thought Honolulu had become "pretty horrendous." Elwood Craddock said it was a "horrible place. I stay away as much as I can. Last time we went, we sweated, it stank, and I came home with a sore throat." Don Woodrum thought Waikiki was an "isolation ward for tourists" and did "everything possible to avoid going there." Sue Isonaga said she never went downtown

or to Waikiki any more "for pleasure," and every year there
seemed to be fewer neighborhoods in which she felt safe. This
is a paradox common to postwar American cities, that even as
they grow in size and population, neighborhoods considered
safe and pleasant shrink in size and number.

I tried keeping these complaints in perspective by reminding myself that before Pearl Harbor, Hawaii had been a
stratified colonial society, while now it was a prosperous multiracial one that, while not perfect, is as tolerant as any in the
world. Before, Asians had been unable to rise to positions of
power in the Big Five companies and were denied employment even as bus drivers and telephone workers. Since 1975,
Hawaiian Asian-Americans have achieved a higher social and
economic status than Caucasians. Before, Honolulu had been
a pleasant yet stagnant backwater; now it has fine libraries,
an opera, theaters, and a respectable university. Despite all
the development, much of Oahu is still fabulously beautiful.
Its north-shore beaches are gorgeous and wild, its windward
coast has small farming settlements overshadowed by curtains
of soaring green cliffs. The Koolaus' upper slopes remain untouched, a dragon's back of spiky peaks cut by narrow valleys and treacherous cliffs. Downtown Honolulu is still as
distinctive and interesting a small American city as you can
find. Surviving between its office plazas is a memorable
hodgepodge of architecture—a rococo Victorian palace,
the heavy granite temples of the Big Five, and fine examples
of the tile-roof-and-stucco "territorial architecture" of the
twenties. It is still a place of palm shadows, flowering hedges,
and the sharp Pacific light you find in San Francisco on a
good day.

I reminded myself of all this, and yet, I still felt that almost
everything added to Oahu since Pearl Harbor detracted from
its beauty, and everything that pleased the eye predated it.
Before Pearl Harbor, Honolulu had been a smaller, less just

city. Now it was almost three times the size, and more equitable, but what had been added was a monotony of fast-food restaurants, package-tour hotels, shopping strips, and condominium villages. Before, there had been more than met the eye, now there was less. The Royal Hawaiian Hotel remained lovely and gracious, but most of its famous gardens had become a multilevel shopping center. The Waikiki Theater had preserved its fine art-deco facade, but its remarkable auditorium had been chopped into a triplex. The military bases had kept their generous homes and gardens, but just outside their gates were developments with no room for the gardens and backyards that made living in Hawaii worthwhile. Hawaii, I realized, had not just changed slightly since Pearl Harbor, but had become the perfect opposite of its prewar self, the purest and most extreme example of the physical and social changes the war visited upon mainland cities.

Before Pearl Harbor, Honolulu was a languid, low-pressure city where people worked half a day and took the morning off to welcome an ocean liner. Now its cost of living is so high that it has the highest percentage of two-income families and the highest percentage of people holding two jobs of any state in the nation, and it is not unusual to find a husband and wife with three or four jobs between them. This causes the endless, weirdly timed traffic jams and, since its residents' hectic work schedule leaves little time for cooking, is also responsible for the greatest per capita number of fast-food franchises in the nation. When I moved to Hawaii I was assigned the recently disconnected telephone number of "Perfect Tan." I asked its many callers why they needed a tanning parlor in Hawaii, and the most common answer was that the caller was too busy earning the money necessary to live here to spend time at the beach.

Before, Waikiki was described as resembling a coconut plantation. There are still palm trees there, and elsewhere on

Oahu, but they are not as numerous, not as large, and have fewer nuts. Trees still shading beaches and streets are repeatedly neutered, their nuts removed when green to prevent them falling on pedestrians or cars and bringing lawsuits. Now so few productive trees are left that the owner of a bakery complained of having to make traditional Hawaiian coconut cakes with coconut imported from Thailand. Waikiki lost many of its trees during the construction booms of the sixties and seventies. Some were replaced, but by saplings that have yet to mature. Elsewhere, residents have been selling their mature backyard trees to Ko Olina, a 640-acre Japanese-owned resort under construction on the formerly barren southwest coast. I sometimes saw trucks loaded with palms, their roots and trunks secured in the back, their fronds dragging on the highway. Residents of Nanakuli protested this loss over the radio, with one man complaining he saw fewer palm trees every time he returned from work. "Wake up, Nanakuli!" he shouted. "Stop selling your heritage to the Japanese!"

Before Pearl Harbor, Hawaiians had been so unconcerned with crime they had permanently lost their house keys, and in 1939, Maui's chief of police boasted his entire county (which includes the islands of Maui, Molokai, and Lanai) was crime-free. Now the only "House Without a Key" on Oahu is probably the bar of that name in the Halekulani Hotel. Honolulu's crime rates, particularly for murder and violent offenses, are low when compared to those of mainland cities, but most Hawaiians compare them to the city they remember, and on that basis Honolulu is suffering a major crime wave. Guidebooks warn female tourists against jogging alone on cane roads, louvered windows are seldom used in new construction because they are difficult to secure against thieves, and new homes come with elaborate security systems. Car trunks are jimmied open so often (mine was hit twice) that locals never lock valuables in them. Residential areas are papered with "No Trespassing"

signs warning of dogs and alarms and promising vigorous prosecution.

Mr. Preis, the architect, had insisted on meeting me at
Burger King because he feared his guard dog might attack me.
Sue Isonaga said, "Before we felt so safe, and I had no fear
living here alone when my husband was called for the Korean
War. Now I never leave my door unlocked, even if I'm only in
the yard." In 1988, Wymo Takaki decided to take his son on a
hike to show him the remote cave he had stocked with provisions against a Japanese invasion, but friends dissuaded him,
saying it was in an area controlled by violent marijuana culti-
vators. Mrs. Marumoto had told me, "We used to pretend we
were tourists and walk through Waikiki, but we can't anymore." The security system in her building was so complicated,
involving codes, several buzzers, and no names on apartment
doors, that she finally had to come downstairs to fetch me.

Public manners in Hawaii are excellent. Rarely did I hear
a voice raised in anger or a horn honked in impatience, and I
was the recipient of numerous acts of kindness difficult to imagine on the mainland. Yet, residents believe the true "aloha
spirit" has suffered since Pearl Harbor. "It was genuine when I
arrived, but now it's merely a veneer," Eva Marie Judd said.
She described it as being "kindliness, thoughtfulness, and everyone being very polite." Jack London once wrestled with
defining it, and came up with "the positive affirmation of one's
own heart giving." A Hawaii State Commission on Environmental Planning held hearings on aloha and concluded that
although difficult to define, it is "identified with empathy, tolerance, graciousness, friendliness, understanding, and giving."
Whatever its precise definition, it is agreed to have roots in the
Polynesian culture of native Hawaiians, which places a high
value on friendliness, cooperation, and sharing.

"Aloha" is marketed as a Hawaiian attraction by the same
visitor industry that, by encouraging mass tourism, promoting

homogeneity, and undermining agriculture, is also destroying it. In 1941, 35,000 tourists a year came to Hawaii; today the figure is almost seven million. No wonder I sometimes encountered "aloha fatigue," and people forcing their aloha. I read about a Kauai resident admitting, "Many times I want to escape to a secluded spot to relax with my family and to fish. Almost always I am approached by visitors. I feel like saying, 'Go away and leave me alone, I see enough of you.' But the better side of me takes over and I find myself giving a smile and answering questions about 'our paradise.' " And it would be difficult to imagine a better example of what aloha is not than this comment, made by the director of the Kauai Chamber of Commerce, while speaking of his efforts to lure "world class" tourists to his islands: "We don't want families who come here for the hundred-and-forty-five-dollar round trip and ask for the El Cheapo rent-a-car and three coupons to Dairy Queen, we prefer the upscale tourist. . . . [They] are a different breed of people. They are most pleasing to deal with."

Before Pearl Harbor, the tourist industry promoted the harmless myth of the grass-skirted hula girl standing in front of a grass hut playing a ukulele. In fact, grass skirts were a late-nineteenth-century import from Micronesia and were never worn by native Hawaiians. The ukulele, although adopted by Hawaiian musicians as their own, was brought by Portuguese plantation laborers. The last Hawaiian to live in a grass hut was an eccentric curiosity even in the 1930s, and probably the most photographed hula girl of all time was a woman in the Kodak Hula Show named Tootsie Notley.

The newest Hawaii myth is that the islands are some vast Indiana Jones type of adventure playground, in which every "adventure" requires some form of exotic, and expensive, motorized transport. Already, this myth has convinced visitors that Hawaii must be seen from a helicopter, all-terrain vehicle, motorized rubber raft, or a parachute attached to a speedboat, but never on foot, perhaps because it is difficult to charge for walking. Already, there are reports of a smog of motorboat exhausts hovering in the spectacular sea arches of Kauai's Na Pali coast, of jeeps altering the terrain of remote valleys and beaches, and of environmental problems caused by the washing and fueling of the sightseeing craft that board nine hundred passengers a day at the mouth of the Hanalei River. I hiked into the countryside of Kauai and Maui only to have sightseeing helicopters pass overhead at the average rate of one every five minutes, ruining what really was an "Eden of paradise and pleasure," and making me feel as pursued as a Vietnamese peasant in 1968.

The tourist industry has portrayed the Islands as enjoying universally abundant sunshine and dry weather, as well as lush, tropical foliage. In fact, every Hawaiian island but Lanai has both sunshine and a rain forest, but not in the same place. They have a dry south-and-west-facing leeward coast with plenty of sunshine, but, not surprisingly, this is accompanied by the barren Greek-island terrain that comes with under twenty-five inches of rain a year. The forests and waterfalls are found on the east-and-north-facing windward coasts, accompanied by rainfall and clouds.

Before Pearl Harbor, the most common tools employed to make the real Hawaii conform to the visitor industry's mythical one were the pencils, etching knives, India-ink cakes, and split razor blades of the photographic retouching studio. Between the wars, men like Norman D. Hill, "Hawaii's Doctor of Photography," added fleecy clouds to drab skies, set lights blazing from black hotel windows, erased electric lines and telephone poles, filled every night sky with a harvest moon, highlighted palm fronds, enhanced rainbows, and created the image, in the language of one 1925 tourist brochure, of "an Eden of peace and pleasure . . . love and laziness . . . and plumbing that is American."

After Pearl Harbor, the most common tool for making Hawaii conform to the fantasy was the bulldozer. Developers reshaped, watered, and planted miles of leeward coastlines, transforming them into Brobdingnagian resorts that squat like toads on lily pads of bogus tropical landscaping, and changing a wild and distinctive Hawaiian landscape into a manicured California country club. Here, at last, watered by recessed sprinklers, guarded by gatehouses, and tricked out with transplanted shrubbery and concrete waterfalls, a visitor could enjoy both a dry climate and the foliage of a wet one, and the visitor industry's mythical Hawaii became a reality, of sorts.

The environmental damage caused by such resorts is considerable, although the sugar plantations many of them replaced had already caused significant damage. Surfaces are graded, soil and vegetation cover stripped, and land paved for parking lots and walkways. The golf courses, gardens, and lawns require tremendous quantities of water, which seeps back into the water table and ocean, carrying pollutants from waste treatment plants and putting greens and damaging reefs, fishing grounds, and whatever shoreline and tide pools have escaped being blasted and rearranged. Coastal roads are moved inland, and ocean views blocked. Beach access, once easy and unlimited, becomes more difficult, and locals begin feeling unwelcome on beaches their families have enjoyed for generations.

The largest, most outrageous fantasy resorts in Hawaii, the Westin Kauai and the Hyatt Regency Waikaloa on the Big Island, are the creation of Honolulu developer Christopher Hemmeter. Either can be amusing or depressing, depending on your mood, but neither has much to do with Hawaii. They float in their settings like space stations, full of whirring gadgets, but unconnected. The pre–Pearl Harbor visitor industry fantasy was at least somewhat Hawaiian, but Hemmeter's fantasy is a jumble of Reagan-era excesses and already has the atmosphere of a dated World's Fair.

His $360 million Waikaloa has 1,241 rooms, a museum walkway of art from Asia and the Pacific, two air-conditioned monorails, and a dozen motorboats, modeled on Venetian water taxis, which travel on underwater fixed rails along artificial canals. Since the site lacks a natural beach, there are man-made ones bordering artificial swimming lagoons. One lagoon is stocked with bottlenose dolphins, imported from the Atlantic Ocean and available to swim with guests paying fifty-five dollars the half hour, although the longevity of this amusement has been placed in doubt by the sudden and, to their handlers, inexplicable death of two of the animals.

The Westin Kauai has more fake canals and Venetian launches, carriages pulled by the world's largest collection of Clydesdales, and six wildlife islands filled with such non-Hawaiian creatures as kangaroos, wallabies, zebras, flamingos, and swans. There is a reflecting pond surrounded by a concrete colonnade displaying more foreign art, and "marble" pillars that are concrete encased in fiberglass. Most everything is made of concrete, brass, and expensive wood, and little reflects Hawaii's brilliant tropical colors. The fountains, pillars, and urns give the resort the feel of a temple, devoted to the worship of money, while the putting greens, perfect gardens, and slow-moving black carriages are reminiscent of a cemetery.

The most authentically Hawaiian feature of such resorts is the way they reflect the social structure of a 1930s plantation, where overseers were Caucasians from the mainland or Europe. If you think that is stretching things, consider the following guidebook description of one hotel: "European efficiency at the executive level and island good humor at the service level are keynotes here."

The message of these resorts is that not only does the real Hawaii lack the natural beauty and exotica to entertain a visitor, but even the traditional mythical Hawaii of the prewar years falls short and would disappoint a generation raised on

Fantasy Island. But it would appear Hemmeter knows what visitors want. One airline magazine describes the Waikaloa as "the dawning of a new age, as tourists who once compared notes on going around the island now wait for boats and trams while sharing strategy on the fastest way to travel across the hotel." Meanwhile, the Waikaloa's manager is reported to have boasted, "What we didn't understand is that when people get here, they don't want to go anywhere else."

"These Disneyland hotels are totally divorced from Hawaii," said intelligence officer Don Woodrum, who has since become an advertising and public relations executive specializing in campaigns to promote Hawaii and its products. "They're theme parks that could be anywhere," he said. "This is a radical change for us. Before the war, visitors came to enjoy our unique culture and atmosphere and they all wanted hotels that would let them mingle with Hawaiians. Now, as Hawaii has lost what made it unique, people just come for the weather and stay a whole week without ever hardly venturing outside the walls of these compounds. I call them 'concentration camp holidays.' "

In 1941, despite complaints about crowded sidewalks and defense workers from the mainland, Oahu was still an uncrowded, spacious island, with much of its population of 300,000 concentrated in the city. Houses were surrounded by generous gardens. You could drive for miles through cane and pineapple fields without seeing a house, or walk along rural beaches and see only a few fishermen. The lower slopes of the Koolaus were good for hiking and gathering wild orchids, and the windward coast, reached over a twisty mountain highway, was a place of agricultural villages and weekend beach houses.

Today, Oahu feels crowded. Its population has tripled to almost 900,000. Tunnels running through the Koolaus have transformed the windward villages of Kailua and Kaneohe into sprawling commuter suburbs. Housing developments have claimed all but the Koolaus' most inaccessible slopes and valleys. Cane and pineapple fields shrink each year, and some forecast that within two decades Oahu will lose its remaining agriculture and accessible open spaces, becoming an urban island like Singapore or Hong Kong.

You can see evidence of Oahu's crowding in the frequent yard sales thrown by military families who have arrived with too much furniture for their cramped off-base housing, in the all-day traffic jams and the lines of cars waiting to pull into downtown parking garages, in the uninterrupted flow of weekend motorists filling narrow windward- and north-shore highways, in the patrols set up by police at scenic lookouts in Oahu to prevent overcrowding by local teenagers seeking an open place to gather, and in the traffic cones lifeguards set along the beach at Waikiki to clear a corridor to the water through carpets of sunbathers.

Zoning laws have been modified to allow the residents to build second "ohana" or "family" houses, with the result that many older houses have lost their gardens, and lots now carry twice as many houses as in 1941. Few homes have garage space for the two or three cars most Honolulu families need to commute to several jobs, and cars end up parked on front lawns and filling every inch of driveway.

Every day, flotillas of catamarans, parasailers, and powerboats fill the ocean off Honolulu. Every evening, dinner cruises compete for the best sunset views, blocking one another's view of the setting sun with their sails and jockeying for position like yachts before a race. Lovely Hanauma Bay has become so popular that the city now prohibits tour vans from parking more than fifteen minutes on the overlook. Its waters are so crowded that by midday it suffers from a kind of snorkeler gridlock, and commercial dive companies have been forbidden from dropping off their patrons here. Its beach is so littered with the frozen peas snorkelers feed to the fish that the city has just announced that soon "feeding the fish will be controlled."

Waikiki has become more densely populated than New York or Tokyo. Every day, 120,000 people pack themselves into its square mile, so many that if they visited the beach at once, there would be trampling deaths along the lines of a South American soccer riot. It has a Las Vegas feel to it now, of architecture in the service of money, and of every square foot put to work generating profit. Hotel lobbies and corridors are lined with boutiques, while restaurants are relegated to less valuable upper and lower floors. Older hotels have had their gardens replaced by high-rise annexes, and by the kind of fluorescent-lit windowless shopping arcades that Montrealers patronize in winter.

The greatest current and future cause of Hawaii's crowding is the rapid growth of its tourist population, currently over six million, but projected to rise to nine million by the turn of the century, and to almost eleven and a half by the year 2010. Tourism is labor-intensive, and growth in the visitor population means permanent residents immigrating from Asia or the mainland, and more roads, schools, and housing in a state where there are already not enough to fill current needs, yet too many relative to environmental constraints.

Already, most Hawaiian islands enjoy essentially full employment, and labor shortages threaten remaining sugar plantations and newer agricultural enterprises. Already, crowds at Maui's Haleakala Crater are so dense that people stand two or three deep at the overlook, and at the best whale-watching areas cars wait in line for someone to leave. Already, blossoms are imported from California to satisfy the demand for airport welcome leis, and local surfers complain of California "surf Nazis" crowding the best beaches and hogging the best waves to impress surfing-magazine photographers. Already, there is a tourist on Kauai for every three residents, and an average of five hundred rental cars a day drive down the twisting scenic road to Hana, a Maui village facing the task of accommodating an invasion of day-trippers while conserving the natural beauty and rural life-style that attracts them. Already, two competing convention-center complexes of hotels, offices, and condominiums are planned for Waikiki and have been granted exemptions from height and density regulations. The one being built by Daiichi Real Estate of Tokyo will boast the three tallest structures in Hawaii, which are described by Daiichi's Honolulu representative as being "a prestige thing" for Daiichi chairman Yukio Sato. And already, destination resorts are planned or under construction on the best remaining unspoiled beaches on the Big Island (Hawaii), Kauai, and Maui. The planned Kau Riviera Resort will add three thousand rooms, a four-hundred-slip marina, 930 resort homes, and ten thousand residents within twenty years to the Big Island's undeveloped Kau region, where the entire population is now only 4,700. The resort will consume the traditional native Hawaiian fishing village of Milolii, which has become bitterly divided over it. "This is the last Hawaiian fishing village in the whole world," the opponents point out, "so we will have no place to go after this is ruined."

26

Postscript: Wymo Takaki Revisits Japan

WYMO TAKAKI LEARNED AT THE MILITARY LANGUAGE SCHOOL at Fort Savage, Minnesota, that the writing on the life jacket of the airman who had ditched in Pearl Harbor was the man's name, Asahi. "When someone shoves the kanji [Japanese script] letters in your face and is choking you and calling you 'a dirty Jap spy,' you don't forget them," he said.

In 1987, he had radical cancer surgery and lay in Tripler Army Hospital reviewing the unfinished business of his life. He had read about the anguish of families of Vietnam War servicemen who were missing in action. Remembering the Japanese airman, he promised himself that if he lived, he would find Asahi's relatives in Japan and tell them how he had died. Shortly afterward he and his wife flew to Japan. She is a Japanese national whom he met when she was a translator working for American military intelligence during the occupation. On a list of the Japanese killed at Pearl Harbor, they found Nagaaki Asahi, a teenage noncommissioned officer who had served as a gunner on a bomber based on the carrier *Kaga*. They called an association of former World War Two pilots only to be told no record was kept of the enlisted men because, as the association's secretary put it, "those youngsters . . . they were supposed to die." ("You see," Wymo told me, "even to this day some of these guys are bastards!")

After almost two months, they located Asahi's relatives in a village on the southernmost island of Kagushima. His parents had died without fulfilling a lifelong dream of visiting Pearl Harbor. But his other relatives welcomed the Takakis. There were tears, countless retellings of December 7 memories, and a visit to the local school, where a romantic oil portrait of Asahi hung in a place of honor in the principal's office.

Takaki says he now holds no bitterness toward Japan, and I think this visit is responsible. He began to feel more "mellow," he says, after the Japanese businessman in Vietnam held him in the car during his Pearl Harbor flashback, probably saving his life. But the visit with Asahi's relatives and the opportunity to recount the story that had haunted him for years completed the reconciliation.

He had succeeded in putting his Pearl Harbor ghosts to rest because he had not hurried things, his plan was modest and sensitive, and he had no other agenda. He had not appeared at Asahi's village shortly after the war in his United States Army uniform. He had not come with a film crew and retinue of journalists, nor used the visit to promote a career or religion, nor attempted something as grandiose, and controversial, as Robert Hudson's Pearl Harbor cruise for Sakamaki and Fujita.

These details, the mechanics of reconciliation, are important because the underlying gulf remains. Japan and United States still view December 7 differently. For Americans, it is the century's most important historical marker, a day that more than any other determined the shape of the next fifty years. For Japan, it is a splendid feat of arms, but only a single battle in a war that began eight years before with the attack on Manchuria and was part of a century-old struggle for domination of Asia and the Pacific.

Before the attack, American animosity toward Japan was largely motivated by racism, and expressed in those terms. Afterward came a bitter loathing, intensified by Japanese treachery and the shock and humiliation of a defeat made more painful by the overconfidence preceding it. This poisonous hatred of Japan has eased, but not evaporated. What was pure racism in 1941 has become a more complex distrust of the Japanese nation, grounded in Pearl Harbor and amplified by Japan's economic success and its investors' obsession with acquiring American "trophies."

In 1941, Pearl Harbor was a symbol of American naval power in the Pacific. It was a trophy, just as houses in Black Point are the trophies of Oahu real estate, and just as Columbia Pictures, MCA, Rockefeller Center, and Pebble Beach are symbolic American trophies. By going for these trophies, Japanese investors have summoned up Pearl Harbor ghosts, again shocking and humiliating Americans, and perpetuating the resentments that undermine reconciliation.

With the passing of the war and postwar generations, Pearl Harbor animosity will fade, the shadow December 7 throws over life in Hawaii will diminish, and the only strong Pearl Harbor legacy remaining will be a sense of vulnerability. During the Cold War, the insecurity of living under the threat of a Soviet sneak attack was the reason to remember Pearl Harbor. Asked in 1970 why he had made *Tora! Tora! Tora!*—then the second most expensive film in history—Darryl F. Zanuck said that "the basic reason for producing the film" had been "to arouse the American public to the necessity for preparedness in this acute missile age where a sneak attack could occur at any moment."

With the Cold War over, the insecurities have become economic and ecological. Pearl Harbor is now a reminder that a disaster experts and leaders believe impossible can still happen. There is good basis for this insecurity, because beneath the smooth skin of computers, interstate highways, and prosperous suburbs are the same character flaws that made Pearl Harbor possible.

The more I come to understand the role that these flaws—racism, overconfidence, and an obsession with internal security—had played in Pearl Harbor, the harder it became to blame only Japan, and the more I had to agree with former Hawaii Governor Lawrence Judd when he said, "Reduced to its essentials the situation was this: the military which was supposed to protect Hawaii against enemy attack failed to do so." I could no longer consider Pearl Harbor simply the result of "bad luck" and Japanese treachery. Japanese militarism may have motivated the attack, and Japanese skill and bravery made it successful, but it was these American flaws that transformed it into a catastrophe.

NOTES

Abbreviations

PHA = Hearings before the Joint Committee on the Investigation of the Pearl Harbor Attack, U.S. Congress

HA = *Honolulu Advertiser*

HSB = *Honolulu Star-Bulletin*

HWRD = Hawaiian War Records Depository

Preface

AT THE FOUR PADDLE CONDOMINIUM

page

11   Hudson material: interview with Hudson and his book, *Sunrise Sunset*.

15   Telephone calls with Darcy. Correspondence with Aiken.

17   Fate of midget submarine: Stewart, December 1974.

18   Environmental hazards of December 7 ordnance from *Marine Pollution Bulletin* 19(2): 68–71.

21   Return of Bando reported in *HSB*, December 8, 1981.

21   "Goodwill visit" from interview with Nancy Haynes.

21   Victory societies: Allen, p. 364; *HA*, October 29, 1946, and August 21, 1948; Stephan, pp. 172–74.

22   *Tora! Tora! Tora!* complaints: *HA*, September 25, 1970.

22   Midget sub protest: Hudson interview; *HA*, September 21, 1988.

22   Atom bomb pilots reunion: *New York Times*, August 27, 1990.

23   Flowers on grave of FBI agent: interview with Isonaga.

23   Military governor praised in *Kanasha,* published by Honolulu Japanese Junior Chamber of Commerce.

23   Comments from Japanese-Americans: interviews with Ralph Yempuku, Tadeo Fuchikami, and Wallace Fujiyama.

24   Backhoe story: *Pearl Harbor–Gram*, January 1988.

26   "I am the proud son . . . ": Pearl Harbor–Gram, January 1988.

Chapter 1

THE GREAT WHITE SHIP LEAVES HONOLULU

29   Descriptions of Boat Day and *Lurline* departure: five articles by
      Alf Pratte in *HSB,* beginning December 4, 1966; *HSB* and *Adver-
      tiser* editions of December 4, 1941, and December 6, 1941; nu-
      merous articles in *Paradise of the Pacific,* 1938–1942; interviews
      with Peter Van Dorn, Mary Hughes, Bob Stroh, Walter Miller,
      Mrs. P. R. Sellers, Mrs. Claude Aleck, and Colonel Tetley.

35   Radar on Oahu from Tetley interview.

37   Description of last peacetime crossing: interview with Dillingham.

37   Davidson story: *HA,* December 4, 1941.

39   Operation Aloha: *Paradise of the Pacific,* September 1948.

41   The 1939 guidebook is Gessler.

Chapter 2

VICE-CONSUL MORIMURA SEES THE SIGHTS

43   Background on Yoshikawa's spying activities: Yoshikawa article
      in *Naval Institute Proceedings;* Shearer article in *Parade,* articles
      in *HA,* December 7, 1969, and December 3, 1981; article in *HSB,*
      December 7, 1960; Farago, particularly chapters 18 and 19; in-
      terview with Woodrum; post-attack Investigative Reports of the
      14th Naval District found in the appendix of the 1945 investiga-
      tion conducted by Major Henry C. Clausen, reproduced in PHA,
      part 35.

45   The best explanation of the importance of the Bomb Plot message
      is in Layton, pp. 162–68. See also Farago, chapter 18.

46   Voyage of the *Taiyo Maru:* Farago, pp. 245–47, *HSB* and *HA,*
      November 1–6, 1941; Layton, pp. 174–75.

47   Yoshikawa's cables: Farago, pp. 291–312.

48   RCA office gives cables to counterintelligence: described in Lay-
      ton, pp. 277–80.

48   Layton's conclusion about Yoshikawa's cables: Layton, p. 278.

49   The "Lights" cable: Layton, pp. 277–84; Farago, pp. 300–2;
      Prange, *Dawn,* pp. 450–51. Layton has the most reliable, detailed
      explanation of how information that could have averted Pearl
      Harbor had already been received in Washington the day before,

and of why this information was not properly evaluated. He stresses the misuse of radio intelligence as the root cause of the disaster, while Prange believes it was the "gap between knowledge of possible danger and belief in its existence." The argument is over which was a more important cause of the debacle. I think it is virtually impossible now to "prove" that one or the other was more responsible; both were culpable, and both "root causes."

51   Prange points out the serious consequences of the failure to close the Honolulu consulate in *Dawn,* pp. 149–52.

51   Hughes's comments about Yoshikawa: *HA,* December 7, 1981.

52   Woodrum comment from interview.

52   Mayfield comment made to Roberts Commission, PHA, part 23, p. 650.

53   Shivers comment made to Roberts Commission, PHA, part 23, p. 857.

53   Kimball comment made to Roberts Commission, PHA, part 23, p. 923.

54   Army Intelligence report from a January 5, 1942, memorandum written by Second Lieutenant Clifford M. Andrew, available in HWRD.

54   Bicknell report from his unpublished manuscript.

Chapter 3
GEORGE AKITA DELIVERS A SPEECH

56   Speech contest: *HSB,* December 5 and 6, 1941.

57   Excerpt from Akita's diary furnished by Akita to the author.

58   Discussion of intergenerational strains among Japanese community in Hawaii: Lind; Fuchs; Hazama and Komeiji; Saiki; Stephan; Ogawa; interview with Larry and Minnie Nakatsuka; series of articles by Nakatsuka under the pseudonym "Mr. Sato" published throughout summer 1940 in *HSB.*

60   Difficulties placed in way of "Americanization" found in Bicknell manuscript.

61   "Not very pretty to look at" comment made to the Army Pearl Harbor Board by General Wells, PHA, part 28, p. 1422.

61   Sources for efforts by AJAs to prove loyalty are same as for pp. 58–60.

Chapter 4

FROM WALTER DILLINGHAM'S WINDOW

64   Interview with Dillingham.

66   Background material on Honolulu in 1941: Hoehling; Sheehan; Porteus; Allen; *Paradise of the Pacific; HSB; HA;* author interviews.

69   *Fortune* article: "Sugar-Coated Fort," August 1940.

72   Morgan article in *HSB,* July 11, 1941.

73   Kurusu's stop in Honolulu: *HSB* and *HA,* November 13, 1941.

74   Litvinov's stop: *HSB* and *HA,* December 5, 1941.

75   Visit from Thai royal family and dispute over the hula: unpublished autobiography of author Catherine Mellen, shown to the author by Richard Van Dyke.

Chapter 5

OMENS ARE SEEN

79   Football game reported in copies of the December 7, 1941, *Advertiser,* printed before its presses broke.

80   Omens in the Honolulu sky: Mellen, p. 168.

82   Good's comment is in Prange, *Dec. 7,* p. 27; Chapman's is on p. 38; Layton's reaction to the national anthem on p. 47.

82   Short's "What a good target": Lord, p. 6.

82   Mellen "considered it sinister": Mellen, pp. 168–69.

83   Poindexter's suspicions about Japanese rice purchases are from his testimony to the Roberts Commission, PHA, part 23, p. 821.

83   Testimony of Honolulu police chief to Roberts Commission is in PHA, part 23, pp. 795–96.

84   Story about the luau at Wahiawa is in Ollila, p. 104.

85   Search of Hawaii Importing reported in Hazema and Komeiji, pp. 129–30.

85   *Murder by the Yard* quotation: Yates, p. vii.

Chapter 6

THE SUBMARINERS' WIVES THROW A PARTY

88   Kathy Cooper material from interview.

88   Moseley comment: Prange, *Dec. 7*, p. 104.

90   Same sources as pages 58–60; also author's interviews in Honolulu, and Porteus.

Chapter 7

ALERTED FOR SABOTAGE

93   Bicknell statement from his unpublished manuscript in HWRD.

93   Fielder statement made to Roberts Commission, PHA, part 22, p. 179.

94   Dillingham statement: PHA, part 28, p. 1443.

94   Message from War Department: PHA, part 14, p. 1407. Prange, *Dawn*, p. 403.

94   Marshall misses his opportunity to intervene: PHA, part 3, p. 1421.

94   Stimson's statement in Prange, *Verdict*, p. 210.

95   Short's comment to Roberts commission: PHA, Part 22, p. 102.

95   Martin believes there will be no Japanese strike: PHA, part 28, p. 962; Prange, *Verdict*, p. 253.

95   Martin's report: Prange, *Dawn*, p. 94.

96   The "war warning": PHA, part 14, p. 1406.

97   Shoemaker's alert: Prange, *Dec. 7*, p. 15.

98   Martin's alert: Prange, *Dec. 7*, p. 23.

98   Dybdal account from interview.

98   Camp Malakole antiaircraft preparations: interviews with Myron Haynes.

99   Farthing calls a meeting: Prange, *Dec. 7*, p. 24.

99   Ahola's account from interview.

102   Blake Clark statement from Clark, p. 44.

Chapter 8

"THE SUPREME OVERCONFIDENCE OF A GREAT ATHLETE"

111   Belief in sabotage of *Advertiser* presses: Catherine Mellen autobiography.

113   Mass comment from *HA*, September 4, 1941.

113   May comment from *HA*, December 2, 1941.

113   Knox speech reported in *HSB* and *HA*, and in Ketchum, pp. 724–26.

113   *New York Times Magazine* article: Hanson W. Baldwin, "Our Gibraltar in the Pacific," February 16, 1941.

114   *Collier's* article by Walter Davenport, June 14, 1941, p. 11.

115   Wakukawa comment from interview.

116   The kamaaina woman whose father joked about a Japanese raid was Patricia Morgan (now Swenson), from interview.

116   The Marine bugler was Richard Fiske, from interview.

116   *Paradise of the Pacific* article appeared in January 1936.

116   Sutton comment about "great athlete" from interview.

116   Kinzler comment from interview.

117   Woodrum comment from interview.

117   Clarey comment from interview.

117   Cooper comment from interview.

117   McMorris comment from Prange, *Dawn,* p. 401.

117   Kimmel comment to Harsch from Stillwell, p. 264.

118   Layton quotation from Layton, p. 244.

118   Pye comment from Layton, p. 274.

118   Layton says an attack "far from our minds": Layton, p. 275.

118   Bicknell's summary from his manuscript in HWRD.

Chapter 9

MRS. MORI TALKS TO TOKYO

120   Flynn records Mori call: from interview.

121   Text of Mori call reproduced in report of Roberts Commission in PHA, part 24, p. 2023.

122   Bicknell learns of Japanese consulate burning its papers: Prange, *Dec. 7*, p. 22; Bicknell manuscript in HWRD.

122   Bicknell worries about Mori call and meets with Short and Fielder: Bicknell manuscript in HWRD; Congressional investigation of 1945, PHA, part 10, p. 5089–122; Lord, pp. 5–6; Prange, *Dec. 7*, pp. 40–41.

123   Bicknell mumbles about flowers on December 7: interview with Dorothy Bicknell.

123   Woodrum's reaction to Mori call: from interview.

124   Article about Mrs. Mori: *HSB*, December 5, 1957.

125   Bicknell's interpretation of call: see reference for pages 135–37.

126   Interview with Mr. and Mrs. Breitinstein.

Chapter 10

ENSIGN YOSHIKAWA'S LAST CABLE

130   Yoshikawa's last evening and further life: Yoshikawa article in *Naval Institute Proceedings;* Shearer article in *Parade;* articles in *HA*, December 7, 1969, and December 3, 1981; article in *HSB*, December 7, 1960; Farago, particularly chapters 18 and 19; interview with Woodrum; post-attack Investigative Reports of the 14th Naval District, which can be found in the appendix of the 1945 investigation conducted by Major Henry C. Clausen, reproduced in PHA, part 35.

130   Nissan spying story: *New York Times*, December 9, 1989.

Chapter 11

A WHITE RIVER FLOWS DOWN HOTEL STREET

135   Background for Honolulu on the eve of war: author's interviews; Porteus; Hoehling; Allen; Sheehan; Lord; *Paradise of the Pacific; HA*, December 7, 1941.

135   "Battle of the Bands" reported in *HSB*, April 2, 1942.

136   Bicknell remembers Kita's parties: Prange, *Dec. 7*, p. 45.

137   Dorothy Anthony comment from interview.

137   Description of party at Royal Hawaiian cottage: interview with Ruth Flynn.

140   Kinzler comment from interview.

142   Temperance League investigates Hotel Street: testimony to Roberts Commission, PHA, part 23, pp. 835–52.

142   Prohibitionist tract quotation: Gilbert, pp. 11–12.

143   Honolulu Chief of Police Gabrielson testified to the Roberts Committee that December 6 had been an ordinary Saturday night: PHA, part 23, pp. 794–96.

143   Material on defense workers: Sheehan; *HSB; HA.*

144   Labor Day parade: *HA,* September 2, 1941.

145   "Lights twinkling in their periscopes from Sakamaki.

145   Photograph of Japanese pilots doing hula: Hudson, p. 3.

Chapter 12

HAWAII TAKES A DEEP BREATH

149   Midget submarines head for Pearl Harbor: Sakamaki; Stewart; Jackson; *HSB* series written by Burl Burlinghame and beginning December 6, 1988.

149   Description of Pearl Harbor on night of December 6: Farago, p. 361.

150   *Ward* fires on a midget submarine: same references as p. 169; also Prange, *Dec. 7,* pp. 91–92, 100–3, *Dawn,* pp. 495–98, *Verdict,* pp. 461–62; Lord, pp. 38–42.

151   First Shot Naval Vets: *HA,* December 7, 1978.

151   Opana radar station story: Lord, pp. 44–49; Prange, *Dec. 7,* pp. 95–99.

152   Missed chances in Washington: Layton, pp. 302–6; Prange, *Dawn,* pp. 493–95.

153   Fuchikami collects telegram: interview with Fuchikami.

155   "Prep" flag is raised: Lord, pp. 66–67.

156   Amateur army pilots shot down: interview with Myron Haynes.

156   Cornelia Fort story: Clark, pp. 113–16.

157   Vitousek story: interview with Roy Vitousek; Swenson manuscript; Lord, pp. 86–87; *HA,* December 7, 1966.

Chapter 13

THE MANEUVERS ARE REALISTIC

159   Craddock story from interview with Craddock.

161   Short thought the Navy was having practice: PHA, part 22, p. 57.

161   Bicknell describes incredulity of other officers: Bicknell manuscript.

161   Yee Kam York: testimony to Roberts Commission, PHA, part 23, p. 926.

162   World War One veteran thinks it's a hoax: letter of Richard Wrenshall to HWRD.

162   Ethelyn Meyhre: *HA,* December 7, 1966.

162   A woman near the university: Grace Tower Warren, who described her experiences in an essay, "War in Paradise," submitted to the HWRD.

162   Dorothy Anthony's reaction from interview.

163   Joseph C. Harsh from his article "A War Correspondent's Odyssey," found in Stillwell, p. 264.

163   Pye from testimony to Roberts Commission, PHA, vol. 22, p. 533.

163   Shivers persuades Hoover: *HSB,* December 8, 1981.

163   Ruth Flynn from interview.

163   Dillingham from interview.

163   Izuma and Johnson's experiences: article by Dr. Harold Johnson, "Reminiscences of December Seventh II," published in *Hawaii Medical Journal,* December 1966, pp. 143–44.

164   Smythe and Oyama stories: *HA,* December 7, 1976.

164   Judd story from interview.

164   Kimmel sees the attack: Prage, *Dec. 7,* p. 119.

165   Hudson's reaction from interview.

165   Dickinson reaction from "I Fly for Vengeance," *Saturday Evening Post,* October 19, 1943.

165   Fiske story from interview.

166   Dybdal story and Pearl Harbor cruise from interview.

Chapter 14

"THE WARM AIR OF AN UNENDING SUMMER LAND"

171   Japanese pilots' memories of the attack: Prange, *Dec. 7*, pp. 113–16; Fuchida, "I Led the Attack . . ."

171   The number of Japanese pilots is a matter of some controversy. This figure from *HSB* article published on the twenty-fifth anniversary. David Aiken (see Chapter 1, p. 15) is making an extensive study of this subject, and his figures, when they are published, will probably be the most reliable.

172   Genda visit described in *HA*, March 4, 1969.

172   Comment by Yoshio Shiga from *HSB*, December 8, 1981.

172   Return of Bando to Pearl Harbor from *HSB*, December 8, 1981.

172   Hudson described the return of the six pilots in an interview.

174   Fuchida's conversion and frequent visits to Hawaii: Fuchida's book; *HSB*, December 8, 1966.

176   Fuchida attends the dinner party: interviews with Smyser and Dorothy Bicknell; *HSB*, December 8, 1966.

176   Fuchida's 1966 visit: *HSB*, December 8, 1966.

177   Don Stratton refuses to pose: *HSB*, December 7, 1981.

177   Film is confiscated: *HA*, December 9, 1966.

177   Fuchida visits Pearl Harbor with Akaka: interview with Akaka; *HSB*, December 7, 1981.

177   Fuchida's comment "joy in my heart" reported in *HSB* during his 1952 visit to Honolulu.

178   Fuchida's comment about Vietnam War reported in his 1978 obituary published in *HA*.

Chapter 15

"A VOICE FROM THE BOTTOM OF THE SEA"

179   Midgets on December 7 from Stewart, "Those Mysterious Subs"; Jackson.

179   Sakamaki's experiences: Sakamaki; Saiki, chapter 12; interview with Sakamaki by Buck Buchwach, *HA*, December 7, 1969.

181   Sakamaki's 1981 visit to Oahu reported by De Yarmin in interview.

182   Story of the raising of Midget "D": Jackson; Stewart; *HSB*, July 6 and 16, 1960; *HA*, July 21, 1960 ("Clues Indicate Crew Escaped Midget Sub"), February 3, 1975, and December 7, 1985.

182   Article in *Naval Institute Proceedings* is Stewart.

183   Okino Sasaki story: *Our Navy*, December 1967.

Chapter 16

THE *ARIZONA* OPENS LIKE A FLOWER

188   Description of deaths on Arizona: Fleet Reserve Association booklet, p. 45; *HSB*, May 7, 1984; Prange, *Dec. 7*, pp. 144–45.

189   Casualties are described in Cloward article and *HSB*, December 7, 1982.

189   Description of explosion and casualties on *Arizona:* Lord, pp. 98–99; Prange, *Dec. 7*, p. 146.

192   Tucker Gratz decides to build *Arizona* Memorial: interview with Gratz; Slackman, *Remembering Pearl Harbor*, p. 44.

192   Efforts to memorialize *Arizona* explosion: Slackman, *Remembering Pearl Harbor*, pp. 44–47.

193   Interview with Kokunu.

198   Pearl Harbor as a place for honeymoon: Stephan, p. 174.

199   Infamy Flight: interviews with Pearl Harbor Survivors; *Pearl Harbor–Gram*, April 1988. *HA*, November 18, 1987.

199   Infamy Flight advertisement in *This Week in Oahu* magazine, March 1988.

200   Krumpholz advertisement: *HA*, December 7, 1975.

201   Preis material from interview and Slackman, *Remembering Pearl Harbor*, pp. 72–74.

204   Congressional reaction to memorial and fund-raising: in Slackman, *Remembering Pearl Harbor*, pp. 58–71.

205   Copies of anniversary speeches kept in *Arizona* Memorial visitor center archives, and reported on December 8 following the anniversary in Honolulu newspapers.

205   Aurand: *HSB*, December 7, 1986.

205   Kidd: copy of speech in *Arizona* Memorial visitor center archives.

206   Flood comments: Prange, *Dec. 7*, p. 198.

Chapter 17

THE "LITTLE YELLOW BASTARDS" DESTROY THE ARMY AIR FORCE

207   Ahola memories from interview and from article in *HA,* December 7, 1986.

212   Description of Hickam Field in early days from articles in Hickam Field historical archives.

213   Kinzler remembers attack on Schofield: from interview.

214   The book of Pearl Harbor photographs: Cohen, p. 98.

214   James Jones's account of the attack on Schofield: *From Here to Eternity,* pp. 822–47.

215   Garcia material from interview.

215   *From Here to Eternity* photograph: Cohen, p. 99.

217   Jones returns in 1973: Jones, *Viet Journal,* p. 249.

218   Picture caption: Cohen, p. 101.

218   Gillette's experiences at Kaneohe: from interview.

219   Attack on Kaneohe: Gillette interview; *HSB,* December 7, 1979; Lord, pp. 116–17, 153–54; Prange, *Dec. 7,* pp. 282–86.

219   Fortieth-anniversary ceremonies at Kaneohe, return of Finn, Kikuyo Iida, and Nemish protest: material in files of Kaneohe MCAS public affairs office files; *HA,* December 6, 1981; *HSB,* December 7, 1981.

221   Gillette comments from interview.

Chapter 18

"ONCE A JAPANESE, ALWAYS A JAPANESE"

223   Thompson material from her article in HWRD.

225   Kay material from "Summary of Verbal Report Submitted to Colonel Bicknell and Lieutenant Dyson, U. S. Army," found in HWRD.

226   Kita thinks the planes are "French,": *HA,* January 4, 1948.

227   Description of *Women's Voice* article in Prange, *Dawn,* p. 843.

228   Layton quotation from Layton, p. 298.

229   Kimmel hit by bullet: Prange, *Dawn,* p. 516.

229   Kimmel says he was a scapegoat: AP interview published in *HA,* December 8, 1966.

230   Rumors about Japanese residents of Hawaii: Porteus, pp. 160–63;
       Allen, pp. 47–56; Lind, pp. 38–61; *HSB*, December 8–12, 1941;
       HA, December 8–12, 1941.

231   Two heroic Japanese teenagers: Clark, p. 184.

233   Story of dead Japanese in truck: ". . . A Hell of a Christmas," in
       Stillwell, p. 224.

233   Knox makes his report: Prange, *Dawn*, pp. 586, 589.

234   Stimson announcement: *HSB*, May 14, 1942.

236   Notes made by Hite of Poindexter's conversation in his diary in
       HWRD; see also Anthony, pp. 5–10.

237   See Anthony, pp. 34–59, for discussion of military government in
       Hawaii; Allen, pp. 166–83.

238   Affidavits swearing to loyalty of Hawaii's Japanese residents: a file
       in HWRD.

239   Story about kimono-clad Japanese: Allen, p. 56.

Chapter 19

"A DEEP SHOCK WAVE" IS FELT

249   "Shock wave" comment: Patricia Swenson, in her unpublished
       manuscript.

249   Peggy Ryan memories: "A Navy Bride Learns to Cope," in Still-
       well, p. 232.

250   Harsch memories: "A War Correspondent's Odyssey," in Still-
       well, p. 264.

250   Experiences of Mary Ellen and Wells Lawrence: from interview.

251   Clarey experiences and flashback: from interview.

252   Sutton experiences: from interview.

252   Hickam Field private: *Newsweek*, December 12, 1966.

253   Fiske experiences: from interview.

257   Details about the Pearl Harbor Survivors Association from issues
       of its quarterly, *Pearl Harbor–Gram*, 1987–1989.

260   Survivors give medals to Kimmel and Short relatives: *HSB*, De-
       cember 5, 1986.

Chapter 20
"HOW COULD THEY DO THIS TO ME?"

262   Maid who wished she could change her face: Reported by Grace
        Tower Warren in "War In Paradise," in HWRD.

262   Cooper maid never returns: from interview with Cooper.

262   Mackay describes Sumi: from Mackay article.

263   William Diem account in HWRD.

263   Oyama's sister: *HA,* December 7, 1976.

263   Tsukiyama from interview.

264   Yempuku from interview and Knaefler article.

265   Inouye from Hazama and Komeiji, p. 125.

265   "Spud" Ishimoto from interview.

266   Akita from his diary.

266   Sato from interview.

266   Fujiyama from interview.

266   Isonaga from interview.

267   Tsubota from interview.

267   Richard Ishimoto from interview.

267   Kawahara from interview.

267   Stevenson from interview.

269   Nakatsuka material: interview with Nakatsuka; Lord, pp. 170–
        71; *HSB,* December 7, 1941 (third extra edition); Prange, *Dec. 7,*
        pp. 344–45.

271   Wakukawa from interview.

271   Fuchikami from interview.

272   Takaki from interview.

Chapter 21
THE UNITED STATES NAVY SHELLS HONOLULU

276   Pearl Harbor heroics: Editors of the Army Times, *Pearl Harbor
        and Hawaii: A Military History,* pp. 39–77.

276   Harsch: Harsch article in Stillwell, p. 264.

277   Cooper from interview.

277   Panic and shelling of Honolulu: Allen, pp. 5–8; Lord, p. 158; *Revolt in Paradise,* pp. 56–60; Prange, *Dec. 7,* pp. 331–36, *Dawn,* pp. 561–72; *HSB,* December 7, 1976; *HA,* and *HSB,* December 7–10, 1941.

278   The death of Matilda Faufata is described in a poignant letter sent to the HWRD by her mother.

278   Craddock from interview.

278   Petrie comments published in *Western City* magazine, January 1942.

279   Herbert Coryell in HWRD.

279   The shells belonged to the U.S. Navy: PHA, part 28, p. 1059; Lord, p. 220.

280   Morgan from interview and Morgan manuscript.

280   Woodrum from interview.

281   Poindexter is nervous: Warren paper in HWRD.

282   Warden is beaten to death: Peggy Hughes Ryan article in Stillwell, p. 233.

283   Morgan arms herself: from Morgan manuscript.

Chapter 22

THE A LIST JAPANESE PACK THEIR BAGS

284   Fukuda material from interview.

284   Internment of Japanese on Hawaii: Hazama and Komeiji, pp. 123–32; Fuchs, p. 303; Allen, pp. 134–38.

285   See Stephan, pp. 23–40, for an excellent discussion of the conflicting loyalties of the Japanese.

286   Nakatsuka from interview with Larry and Minni Nakatsuka.

286   Sato from interview with Nancy Sato (now Haynes).

286   Wakukawa from interview.

288   Preis from interview.

289   Woodrum from interview.

290   Most Japanese on Hawaii not interned, and praise for Shivers *et al:* booklet published by Honolulu Japanese Junior Chamber of Commerce (*Kanasha*); also article by Smyser in *HSB,* December 7, 1979.

290   Isonaga from interview.

291   Tsukiyama from interview.

291   Marumoto's friendship with Shivers: Marumoto interview and article in *East-West Photo Journal.*

292   Isonaga from interview.

293   Wells: PHA, part 23, p. 804.

294   Wakukawa from interview.

296   Sutton from interview.

296   Nishimura from interview.

297   Tsukiyama from interview.

297   Fukuda sisters from interview.

Chapter 23

"A DEEP, POWERFUL THIRST FOR REVENGE"

301   Lawrence from interview.

301   Cooper from interview.

301   Mary Hall's diary in HWRD.

301   Anger of military men: Prange, *Dec. 7,* p. 337.

302   Morgan from interview.

302   Cooper from interview.

302   Faufata from letter in HWRD.

302   Halsey vows revenge: Dower, p. 36. See Dower, pp. 36–41, for a discussion of the anger resulting from Pearl Harbor.

302   Japanese pilot thumbs his nose: Dickinson article.

303   Mainland poll: Cantril, p. 501.

303   Tennessee hunting licenses: Melosi, p. 5.

303   "Hunting Japanese": *Time,* December 22, 1941.

303   Faufata from letter in HWRD.

303   Economic disputes haunted by Pearl Harbor: *New York Times,* July 11, 1990.

304   Pickens advertisement: *New York Times,* September 6, 1990.

305   Opinion polls: *Fortune,* February 26, 1990.

307   Statistics about Japanese investment in Hawaii: *Hawaii Business,* January and April 1990; *Forbes,* February 22, 1988; *HA,* April 17, 1990; *HA,* April 27, 1988; *HSB,* April 9, 1989; numerous

articles in *HSB*, and *HA*, February–May 1988 and April 1990.

314   Bicknell and Anthony from interviews.

315   Polls of attitudes toward Japanese investment were made in March 1990 and published in a series of articles in *HSB*, April 23–28, 1990.

318   Bekeart from interview.

Chapter 24

"NO CAN EAT GOLF BALLS!"

324   Ishimoto from interview.

324   Tsukiyama from interview and *HSB*, December 7, 1978.

325   Yempuku from interview.

325   Ishimoto from interview.

325   Takaki from interview.

326   Japanese prove their loyalty: Allen, pp. 81–84, pp. 350–51; Ogawa, pp. 313–27; Hazama and Komeiji, pp. 130–50.

327   Murai comment reported in *HA*, July 9, 1944.

327   Ogai essay in HWRD.

328   Japanese units in World War II: Allen, pp. 266–73; Ogawa, pp. 313–27, 349–63; Hazama and Komeiji, pp. 150–76.

330   Yempuku from interview.

331   Kawahara, Ishimoto, and Tsukiyama from interviews.

331   Takaki from interview.

334   Wakukawa, Isonaga, Tsukiyama, Fukudas, Nishimura, and Kawahara interviews.

334   Fujiyama from interview.

336   Fuchikami from interview.

337   Golf: *Hawaii Business*, January 1990; *HSB*, March 20, 1988; *HA*, March 21, 1988; *New York Times*, April 16, 1990.

340   Yempuku: from interview and *HSB*, "Divided Families" series by Tomi Knaefler, appearing the week of the twenty-fifth anniversary of the attack.

343   Japanese of Hawaii worry about resurgence of racism: *HSB*, April 23–28, 1990.

344   Ishimoto from interview.

Chapter 25
"NOW WE'RE AN AMERICAN CITY"

349   Bicknell, Judd, Anthony, and Lawrence from interviews.

350   Martial law: Anthony, pp. 34–59.

352   Bicknell, Judd, and Lawrence from interviews.

353   Anthony from interview.

353   Gillette, Craddock, Woodrum, and Isonaga from interviews.

357   Preis, Isonaga, Takaki, Marumoto, and Judd from interviews.

360   Westin Kauai and Waikaloa: *HA*, April 13, 1988; Horton, "Waikaloa Wonderland."

361   "European efficiency...": *Birnbaum's Hawaii 1989* (Boston: Houghton Mifflin, 1988), p. 165.

361   Description of Waikaloa and boast of its manager: Horton, p. 48.

362   Woodrum from interview.

365   Kau Riviera Resort: *HA*, March 11, 1989; *West Hawaii Today*, March 3, 1989.

Chapter 26
POSTSCRIPT: WYMO TAKAKI REVISITS JAPAN

366   Takaki from interview.

SELECTED BIBLIOGRAPHY

This is a listing of the works consulted in the writing of this book, not an all-inclusive Pearl Harbor bibliography. The best one-volume histories of World War Two in the Pacific have been published in the last ten years—John Costello's *The Pacific War* and Ronald H. Spector's *Eagle Against the Sun*. Anyone wishing to learn more about the role racial hatred played in the war should read John W. Dower's excellent *War Without Mercy*. If there can be such a thing as a "last word" on Pearl Harbor it is probably shared by Real Admiral Edwin T. Layton's memoir, *And I Was There*, which lays out the failures to make use of radio intelligence before Pearl Harbor, and Gordon Prange's *At Dawn We Slept*, which is without question the most inclusive book written on the subject. The best revisionist history is John Toland's controversial *Infamy*, but no one should read it without also reading Prange or Layton. The best reconstructions of December 7 are Walter Lord's *Day of Infamy* and Prange's *Dec. 7, 1941*.

The best single work on twentieth-century Hawaii is Lawrence Fuch's *Hawaii Pono*. Ed Sheehan's *Days of '41* is a fine poetic description of Honolulu in the year before the attack. *Hawaii Under the Rising Sun* by John J. Stephan contains a thoughtful and realistic assessment of Japanese loyalty in Hawaii.

The files in the Hawaii War Records Depository at the University of Hawaii contain letters, excerpts from diaries, and essays that make up a fascinating record of civilian attitudes and reactions to the attack.

BOOKS

Allen, Gwenfread. *Hawaii's War Years*. Honolulu: University of Hawaii Press, 1950.

Anthony, J. Garner. *Hawaii Under Army Rule*. Stanford, California: Stanford University Press, 1955.

Barnes, Harry Elmer. *Perpetual War for Perpetual Peace*. Caldwell, Idaho: Caxton Printers, 1953.

Beekman, Allan. *The Niihau Incident*. Honolulu: Heritage Press of Pacific, 1982.

Biggers, Earl Derr. *The House Without a Key*. New York: Grosset & Dunlap, 1925.

Brown, DeSoto. *Hawaii Goes to War: Life in Hawaii from Pearl Harbor to Peace*. Honolulu: Editions Limited, 1989.

———, ed. *Hawaii Recalls: Selling Romance to America. Nostalgic Images of the Hawaiian Islands: 1910–1950*. Honolulu: Editions Limited, 1982.

Cantril, Hadley, ed. *Public Opinion 1935–1946*. Princeton, N.J.: Princeton University Press, 1951.

Clark, Blake. *Remember Pearl Harbor!* Rev. ed. Honolulu: Mutual Publishing, 1987.

Cohen, Stan. *East Wind Rain: A Pictorial History of the Pearl Harbor Attack*. Missoula, Mont.: Pictorial Histories Publishing Company, 1981.

Cooper, George, and Gavan Daws. *Land and Power in Hawaii: The Democratic Years*. Honolulu: Benchmark Books, 1985.

Correspondents of *Time, Life,* and *Fortune*. *December 7: The First Thirty Hours*. New York: Knopf, 1942.

Costello, John. *The Pacific War 1941–1945*. New York: Rawson, Wade, 1981.

Culliney, John L. *Islands in a Far Sea: Nature and Man in Hawaii*. San Francisco: Sierra Club Books, 1988.

Daws, Gavan. *Shoal of Time: A History of the Hawaiian Islands*. Honolulu: University of Hawaii Press, 1968.

Dower, John W. *War Without Mercy: Race and Power in the Pacific War*. New York: Pantheon, 1986.

Editors of the Army Times Publishing Company. *Pearl Harbor and Hawaii: A Military History*. New York: Walker, 1971.

Farago, Ladislas. *The Broken Seal*. New York: Random House, 1967.

Farrell, Bryan. *Hawaii: The Legend That Sells*. Honolulu: University of Hawaii Press, 1982.

Fleet Reserve Association, *U.S.S. Arizona: Ship's Data*. Booklet. Honolulu: Fleet Reserve Association, 1978.

Fuchida, Mitsuo. *From "Pearl Harbor to Golgotha."* San Jose, Calif.: Sky Pilots of America International, undated [probably mid-1950s].

Fuchs, Lawrence H. *Hawaii Pono: A Social History*. New York: Harcourt Brace, 1961.

Fussell, Paul. *Wartime: Understanding and Behavior in the Second World War*. New York: Oxford University Press, 1989.

Gessler, Clifford. *Tropic Landfall: The Port of Honolulu*. Garden City, NY: Doubleday, 1942.

Gilbert, Dan. *What Really Happened at Pearl Harbor?* Grand Rapids, Mich.: Zondervan, 1942.

Harrington, Joseph D. *Yankee Samurai: The Secret Role of Nisei in America's Pacific Victory*. Detroit, Mich.: Pettigrew Enterprises, 1979.

Hazama, Dorothy Ochiai, and Jane Okamoto Komeiji. *Okage Sama De: The Japanese in Hawai'i*. Honolulu: Bess Press, 1986.

Hibbard, Don, and David Franzen. *The View from Diamond Head: Royal Residence to Urban Resort*. Honolulu: Editions Limited, 1986.

Hickam Air Force Base, Public Affairs Division. *Hickam: The First Fifty Years*. Honolulu: Public Affairs Division, Hickam AFB, 1985.

Hoehling, A. A. *The Week Before Pearl Harbor*. New York: Norton, 1963.

Honolulu Japanese Junior Chamber of Commerce, Kanasha Program Committee. *Kanasha: In Appreciation*. Honolulu: Honolulu Junior Chamber of Commerce, 1985.

Hudson, Robert Stephen. *Sunrise Sunset: December 7, 1941, Pearl Harbor*. Honolulu: Hudson Historical Enterprise, 1986.

Jackson, Charles L. *On to Pearl Harbor and Beyond*. Dixon, Calif.: Pacific Ship & Shore, 1982.

Jardine, John, with Edward Rohrbough, and Bob Krauss, ed. *Detective Jardine: Crimes in Honolulu*. Honolulu: University of Hawaii Press, 1984.

Jones, James. *From Here to Eternity*. New York: Scribners, 1951.

———. *Viet Journal*. New York: Delacorte, 1974.

Kahn, David. *The Code Breakers*. New York: Macmillan, 1967.

Ketchum, Richard M. *The Borrowed Years 1938–1941: America on the Way to War*. New York: Random House, 1989.

Kimmel, Husband E. *Admiral Kimmel's Story*. Chicago: Regnery, 1955.

Layton, Rear Admiral Edwin T., USN (Ret.). *"And I Was There": Pearl Harbor and Midway—Breaking the Secrets*. New York: Morrow, 1985.

Lenihan, Daniel J., ed. *Submerged Cultural Resources Study: USS "Arizona" Memorial and Pearl Harbor National Historic Landmark*. Santa Fe, N.M.: Submerged Cultural Resources Unit, Southwest Cultural Resources Center, Southwest Region, National Park Service, U.S. Department of the Interior, 1989.

Lind, Andrew. *Hawaii's Japanese*. Princeton, N.J.: Princeton University Press, 1946.

Lord, Walter. *Day of Infamy*. New York: Henry Holt, 1957.

MacDonald, Alexander. *Revolt in Paradise*. New York: S. Daye, 1944.

Matson Navigation Company. *Ships in Grey: The Story of Matson in World War II*. San Francisco: Matson Lines, 1946.

Melosi, Martin V. *The Shadow of Pearl Harbor: Political Controversy over the Surprise Attack, 1941–1946*. College Station, Texas: Texas A & M University Press, 1977.

Millis, Walter. *This is Pearl! The United States and Japan—1941*. New York: Morrow, 1947.

Miyamoto, Kazuo. *Hawaii: End of the Rainbow*. Rutland, Vt.: Charles E. Tuttle, 1964.

Morgenstern, George Edward. *Pearl Harbor*. New York: Devin-Adair, 1947.

Ogawa, Dennis M. *Kodomo No Tame Ni: For the Sake of the Children: The Japanese American Experience in Hawaii*. Honolulu: University of Hawaii Press, 1978.

Ollila, John E. *"I Was at Pearl Harbor": The Life and Times of John E. Ollila*. Wichita, Kans.: Haag-Sumpton, 1984.

Porteus, Stanley D. *And Blow Not the Trumpet*. Palo Alto, Calif.: Pacific Books, 1947.

Prange, Gordon W. *At Dawn We Slept*. New York: McGraw-Hill, 1981.

———, with Donald M. Goldstein and Katherine V. Dillon. *Dec. 7, 1941: The Day the Japanese Attacked Pearl Harbor*. New York: McGraw-Hill, 1988.

———. *Pearl Harbor: The Verdict of History*. New York: McGraw-Hill, 1986.

Saiki, Patsy. *Ganbare!* Honolulu: Kisaku, 1983.

Sakamaki, Kazuo. *I Attacked Pearl Harbor*. New York: Association Press, 1949.

Sheehan, Ed. *Days of '41: Pearl Harbor Remembered*. Honolulu: Pearl Harbor—Honolulu Branch 46 Fleet Reserve Association Enterprises, 1976.

Shirota, Jon. *Lucky Come Hawaii*. Honolulu: Bess Press, 1988.

Slackman, Michael, ed. *Pearl Harbor in Perspective*. Honolulu: Arizona Memorial Museum Association, 1986.

———. *Remembering Pearl Harbor: The Story of the U.S.S. "Arizona" Memorial*. Honolulu: Arizona Memorial Museum Association, 1984.

Smyser, A. A. *Hawaii's Future in the Pacific: Disaster, Backwater or Future State?* Honolulu: East-West Center, 1988.

Spector, Ronald H. *Eagle Against the Sun: The American War with Japan*. New York: Free Press, 1984.

Stephan, John J. *Hawaii Under the Rising Sun: Japan's Plans for Conquest After Pearl Harbor*. Honolulu: University of Hawaii Press, 1984.

Stillwell, Paul, ed. *Air Raid: Pearl Harbor! Recollections of a Day of Infamy*. Annapolis, Md.: Naval Institute Press, 1981.

Toland, John. *Infamy: Pearl Harbor and Its Aftermath*. New York: Doubleday, 1982.

——. *The Rising Sun*. New York: Random House, 1970.

U.S. Congress. *Pearl Harbor Attack: Hearings Before the Joint Committee on the Pearl Harbor Attack*. 79th Congress, 1st Session. 39 vols. 1946.

Van Dyke, Robert E., ed., and Ronn Ronck, text. *Hawaiian Yesterdays: Historical Photographs by Ray Jerome Baker*. Honolulu: Mutual Publishing, 1982.

Weglyn, Michi. *Years of Infamy: The Untold Story of America's Concentration Camps*. New York: Morrow, 1976.

Wisniewski, Richard A., ed. *Hawaii: The Territorial Years, 1900–1959*. Honolulu: Pacific Basin Enterprises, 1984.

Wohlstetter, Roberta. *Pearl Harbor: Warning and Decision*. Stanford, Calif.: Stanford University Press, 1962.

Yardley, Maili. *Hawaii: Times and Tides*. Lawai, Kauai, Hawaii: The Woolsey Press, 1975.

Yates, Margaret. *Murder by the Yard*. New York: Harper, 1942.

Zacharias, Ellis M. *Secret Missions*. New York: Putnam, 1946.

NEWSPAPERS AND MAGAZINES

Baldwin, Hanson W. "Our Gibraltar in the Pacific." *New York Times Magazine*, February 16, 1941.

Boyd, Ellsworth. "A Voice from the Bottom of the Sea." *Our Navy*, December 1967.

Cloward, Ralph B., M.D. "A Neurosurgeon Remembers Pearl Harbor." *Surgical Neurology*, December 1976.

Davenport, Walter. "Impregnable Pearl Harbor." *Colliers*, June 14, 1941.

Dickinson, Lt. Clarence C. "I Fly for Vengeance." *Saturday Evening Post*, October 19, 1942.

East-West Photo Journal. "Masaji Marumoto: A Personal History. Part 1: The Formative Years." Winter 1980.

Forbes. "A Mixed Blessing." February 22, 1988.

Fortune. "Hawaii: Sugar-coated Fort." August 1940.

——. "Fear and Loathing of Japan." February 26, 1990.

Fox, Barry. "I Remember Pearl Harbor." *Harper's,* January 1943.

Fuchida, Mitsuo. "I Led the Air Attack on Pearl Harbor." Ed. by Roger Pineau. *United States Naval Institute Proceedings,* September 1952.

Hawaii Business. "The Billionaires Next Door," "The Japaning of Hawaii," "The Orient Express," and "A Teed-Off Public." January 1990.

———. "The Value of the Land" and "The New King in Town." April 1990.

Honolulu Magazine. Centennial Issue, 1888–1988: 100 Years of Paradise. Honolulu, November 1987.

Horton, Tom. "Waikaloa Wonderland." *Spirit of Aloha,* April 1989.

Knaefler, Tomi. "Divided Families." A series of articles running in *Honolulu Star-Bulletin* during December 1966.

Mackay, Margaret Mackprang. "Honolulu Flashes." *Asia,* April 1942.

Paradise of the Pacific. Honolulu, 1935–1945.

Pearl Harbor–Gram. Newsletter of the Pearl Harbor Survivors Association.

Shearer, Lloyd. "Takeo Yoshikawa: The Japanese Spy Who Fingered Pearl Harbor." *Parade,* December 7, 1969.

Stewart, Lieutenant Commander A. J. "Those Mysterious Subs." *U.S. Naval Institute Proceedings,* December 1974.

War Research Laboratory, University of Hawaii. Reports on race relations during war now found in Hawaiian War Records Depository.

Yoshikawa, Takeo. "Top Secret Assignment." *U.S. Naval Institute Proceedings,* December 1960.

UNPUBLISHED MANUSCRIPTS

Akita, George. Diary. Courtesy of George Akita.

Bicknell, George W. "Security Measures in Hawaii During World War II." On deposit in the Hawaii War Records Depository.

Martinez, Daniel A. "Japanese Naval Aircraft Crash Sites at Pearl Harbor, Dec. 7, 1941: A Resource Study." June 1986. Available at *Arizona* Memorial visitor center.

Mellen, Kathleen Dickenson. "The Hawaii That Was." Courtesy of Robert Van Dyke.

Swenson, J. Patricia (Morgan). "The Pearl Harbor Blitz: An Account of Events on or about December 7, 1941, in Honolulu as Seen and Experienced by a Honolulu Girl." 1961. Courtesy of Patricia Swenson.

Index

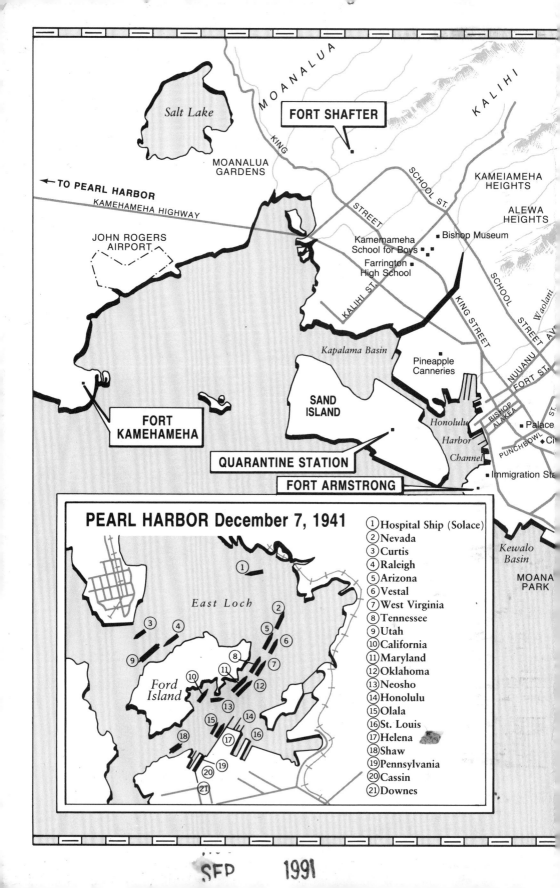

FORT SHAFTER

Salt Lake

MOANALUA GARDENS

← TO PEARL HARBOR
KAMEHAMEHA HIGHWAY

JOHN ROGERS AIRPORT

Kamemameha School for Boys

Farrington High School

Bishop Museum

KAMEIAMEHA HEIGHTS

ALEWA HEIGHTS

Kapalama Basin

SAND ISLAND

Pineapple Canneries

FORT KAMEHAMEHA

QUARANTINE STATION

FORT ARMSTRONG

Honolulu Harbor Channel

Palace

Immigration St

Kewalo Basin

MOANA PARK

PEARL HARBOR December 7, 1941

East Loch

Ford Island

① Hospital Ship (Solace)
② Nevada
③ Curtis
④ Raleigh
⑤ Arizona
⑥ Vestal
⑦ West Virginia
⑧ Tennessee
⑨ Utah
⑩ California
⑪ Maryland
⑫ Oklahoma
⑬ Neosho
⑭ Honolulu
⑮ Olala
⑯ St. Louis
⑰ Helena
⑱ Shaw
⑲ Pennsylvania
⑳ Cassin
㉑ Downes